"Sympathetic and even compassionate . . . honest . . . very well written. Brunhouse puts his finger squarely and honestly on each man's strengths and weaknesses, always giving the benefit of the doubt in terms of the times. A fine book, exhaustively researched and well presented."

—*Robert Wauchope,* Director of the Middle American Research Institute, Tulane University

---

ROBERT L. BRUNHOUSE is Professor of History at the University of South Alabama in Mobile. His most recent book is *Sylvanus G. Morley and the World of the Ancient Maya,* published in 1971 by the University of Oklahoma Press.

IN SEARCH OF THE MAYA

The First Archaeologists

Robert L. Brunhouse

BALLANTINE BOOKS • NEW YORK

Library of Congress Catalog Card Number: 73-75904

SBN 345-23892-3-165

This edition published by arrangement with
the University of New Mexico Press

First Printing: April, 1974

Cover illustration from Frederick Catherwood's
Views of Ancient Monuments in Central America, Chiapas & Yucatan, by courtesy of
Barre Publishers, Barre, Mass.

Printed in the United States of America

BALLANTINE BOOKS
A division of Random House, Inc.
201 East 50th Street, New York, N.Y. 10022

Acknowledgments

The following persons kindly gave of their time and patience on various details in the preparation of this book: Mrs. John Bayley, formerly of Drew University; John Blair of New Orleans; Betty Brandon, University of South Alabama; John Brew, Director, Peabody Museum, Harvard University; John Buchanan, Archivist, Metropolitan Museum, New York; I. Chaney, American Geographical Society; Ruth Currier, Librarian, Peabody Museum; Gordon Ekholm, American Museum of Natural History; Arthur Jones, Drew University; Marjorie LeDoux, Tulane University Library; Robert C. Miller, Senior Scientist, California Academy of Sciences; Walter Vesper, Drew University; Mrs. Doris Watt, History Department, University of South Alabama; Robert Wauchope, Director, Institute of Middle American Research, Tulane University. Michael Thomason, History Department, University of South Alabama, contributed his unusual skill in preparing photographs.

The resources of numerous libraries were drawn upon. Those to which I am grateful for unusual services include the libraries of the Peabody Museum, the American Philosophical Society, Princeton University, Drew University, and the University of South Alabama.

Quotations from Sylvanus G. Morley, *Inscriptions of Copán* (Washington, D.C.: Carnegie Institution, 1920) are used by courtesy of the Carnegie Institution of Washington. Passages from Justino Fernández, "El Diario de Waldeck," *Anales de investigaciones estéticas* 22 (1954), are used by permission of the *Anales de investigaciones estéticas* and the Universidad Nacional, Mexico.

Contents

List of Illustrations

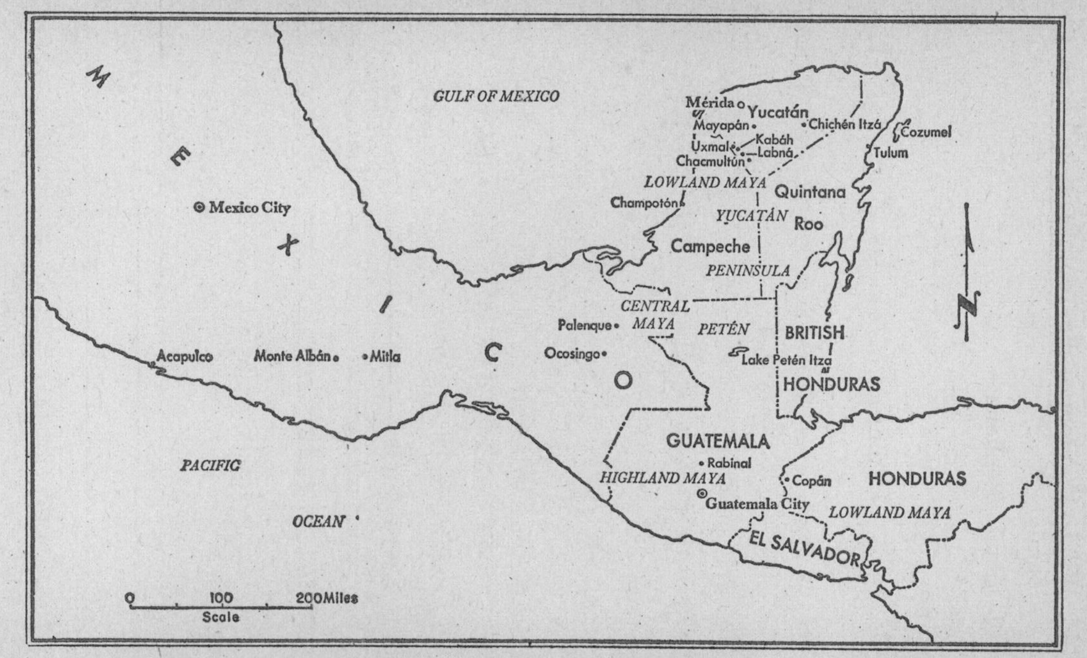

MEXICO
GULF OF MEXICO
Mérida
Yucatán
Mayapán
Chichén Itzá
Cozumel
Tulum
Uxmal
Kabáh
Labná
Chacmultún
LOWLAND MAYA
Quintana Roo
Champotón
YUCATÁN
Campeche
PENINSULA
Mexico City
CENTRAL MAYA
Palenque
PETÉN
BRITISH HONDURAS
Lake Petén Itzá
Acapulco
Monte Albán
Mitla
Ocosingo
GUATEMALA
Rabinal
HIGHLAND MAYA
Guatemala City
Copán
HONDURAS
LOWLAND MAYA
EL SALVADOR
PACIFIC OCEAN
0
100
200Miles
Scale
N

In Search of the Maya

1

Introduction

The men who opened up the field of Maya archaeology and cultivated it for many years were pioneers in a new area of investigation. They entered upon their work with a driving passion to probe the mystery of a civilization that lay buried and forgotten under rubble and vegetation. From the end of the eighteenth to the opening of the twentieth century, they wandered over the Maya area from southern Mexico to northern Honduras. Of all of the pre-hispanic remains of Middle America, those ruins were the most spectacular, intriguing, and provocative of speculation.

They garnered adventures in discovery rarely granted to later generations. As they penetrated the forest and underbrush with little expectation of what they might find, they discovered physical remains—sometimes entire sites like Palenque and Copán—which were strange and incomprehensible. John Lloyd Stephens, the most gifted in expressing his feelings, described the sense of adventure he felt when he first came upon Copán: "We could not see ten yards before us, and never knew what we should stumble upon next." As a native gradually removed vegetation from a figure, "I leaned over with breathless anxiety. . . . The beauty of the sculpture, the solemn stillness of the woods, disturbed only by the scrambling of the monkeys and the chattering of parrots, the desolation of the city, and the mystery that hung over it, all created an interest higher, if possible, than I had ever felt among the ruins of the Old World."[1] Professional archaeologists of the twentieth century have rarely enjoyed such thrill and exultation in encountering striking physical remains.

It is important to bear in mind that these forerunners were amateurs. Archaeology had not yet become a science or even a profession, so they had no formal training for their work. They came from various walks of life. Del Río and Dupaix were military men, Galindo was a political adventurer, Waldeck an artist, Stephens a lawyer, Brasseur a priest, Le Plongeon a self-styled physician, and Edward Thompson had no particular trade or profession. The errors they made were the mistakes one might expect of untrained seekers. Their common bond was the strong desire to find and describe the structures and artifacts of the past.

As amateurs they also worked under disturbing handicaps. At the outset, they brought to the task of interpreting the remains the European tradition of classical antiquity, which proved to be a stumbling block because pre-columbian culture had no connection with early Egypt, Chaldea, Greece, or Rome. Not until the amateurs realized that they were dealing with an indigenous culture, original and unique, were they able to dismiss their preconceptions and study the remains with open minds. Moreover, they lacked scientific methods of investigating and reporting their finds. No matter how conscientiously they measured, described, and sketched, they adopted no accepted methodology, no professional vocabulary, no common objectives except to unravel the mystery of the ruins. As a result, they often asked the wrong questions, and grappled with the big problems before solving the smaller ones. As for their lack of methodology, modern professionals shudder at the casualness of their excavations and bemoan their ignorance of stratigraphy and their disregard of the valuable information that can be derived from potsherds. In posing questions as guidelines for their work, the amateurs neglected the prosaic details of the customs, beliefs, and daily lives of the people. These failures indicate that the early investigators had no conception of the complexity of the subject they were studying—another hazard common to pioneers.

Less important, but not to be overlooked, was the difficulty they experienced in making full use of the work that *had* been done, for the literature on the subject was often hard to come by. For example, Palacio's report was not printed until 1840, and the reports of Calderón and Bernasconi not until the twentieth century. Moreover, numerous brief accounts by investigators appeared only in newspapers or periodicals, which were difficult to locate as the years passed by. Although Dupaix's report and Castañeda's drawings were published, they appeared in limited and expensive editions. In 1840 a reviewer doubted that more than one copy of *Antiquités Mexicaines* was to be found in the United States, and three years later B. H. Norman asserted that there was only a single copy of Kingsborough's *Antiquities of Mexico* in the country.

Despite these handicaps the amateurs performed a significant task. They began the investigation of Maya archaeology, they assembled the information, elementary and incorrect as it was, that eventually provided the factual groundwork for the work of their successors, and they made the public conscious of an entirely new dimension in Middle America.

Were the amateurs peculiar individuals? When they are recalled today, it is often with contemptuous references to the wild theories they put forth. Even in their own day critics leveled charges against them. In 1840 Lewis Cass, referring to writers who sought to connect ancient Egypt with early Middle America, asserted that "before we can find indications" of transoceanic contact, "we must seek the facts." He characterized these writers as "*exaltés*, a class of historians whose imagination supply many of the facts and almost all of the conclusions."[2] A generation later, C. E. Haven, Secretary of the American Antiquarian Society, was struck by the "excitement that apparently bewilders the imaginations of all explorers of the marvellous remains of aboriginal life" in Middle America.[3] Was he correct? Did the templed pyramids, carved bas-reliefs, intriguing stelae in the round, and elaborate facades of Uxmal and Chichén have a way of attracting enthusiasts who could not resist strange and fanciful theories about the ruins?

The chapters that follow emphasize the personal aspects of the individuals. Previous accounts of Maya archaeology have too often subordinated the explorer to his archaeological contributions. Here the human element receives major attention. Sometimes the sources have been scanty; in the case of Antonio del Río, for example, we must rely almost entirely on his formal report. But most of these men left enough autobiographical writings to provide fairly clear pictures of their personalities. Finally, we have real people here, not unblemished heroes, and so we shall encounter human foibles as well as outstanding achievements.

2

Antonio del Río and Guillermo Dupaix

Two of the earliest Maya archaeologists never dreamed that posterity would consider them pioneers. Antonio del Río and Guillermo Dupaix were assigned official missions to carry out and fulfilled them to the best of their abilities, without thought of reward or acclaim. They filed their reports with the authorities, certain that the documents would never go beyond that graveyard of outdated papers, the official archives. Of course, these two men could not know that after several decades their reports would be sent abroad and printed for the benefit of serious readers. It was the accident of publication that gave del Río and Dupaix their unique place in the early history of Maya archaeology.

There are a few points of similarity between the two men and the work they performed. Each one served in the military: del Río was on active duty as a captain of artillery, and Dupaix was a retired captain of dragoons when chosen for the official commission. Although del Río was stationed in Guatemala and Dupaix lived in Mexico City, they happened to examine the same site, Palenque, located in Chiapas, Mexico. Beyond those few coincidences, each man displayed distinct individual characteristics, and the two explorations, separated by two decades in time, provided different contributions to the early knowledge of Maya archaeology.

Palenque, a ceremonial site nestling on a ledge of hills in the rain forest of Chiapas, had once been a large settlement spreading over several miles. By the eighteenth century many of the structures had crumbled, but those which attracted the attention of the first explorers and of all visitors since then include the Palace, the Temple of the Inscriptions, and the Temples of the Sun, the Cross, and the Foliated Cross. The Palace, standing on an earthen platform 300 by 240 feet, contains a maze of halls, rooms, courtyards, underground quarters, and a tower, all in varying states of preservation. Stucco decorations, executed with remarkable artistic ability, adorned the walls of the Palace. The four temples, mounted on truncated pyramids, also contained elaborate stucco figures and decorated roofcombs; each temple, however, soon became famous for the finely executed tablet or plaque that it contained. That of the Temple of the Inscriptions is restricted to hieroglyphs, but each of the other structures held an elaborate pictorial tableau, representing a religious or symbolic ceremony.

Interest in the ruins of Palenque began several decades before del Río appeared on the scene. In the mid-eighteenth century, when Padre Antonio de Solís became curate of nearby Tumbalá, his relatives explored the surrounding country and brought news of the curious "stone houses" they had found. Although Solís died before he could investigate for himself, the story was circulated in the families of the relatives. Years later a boy, Ramón Ordóñez, overheard the tale from a schoolmate, and when Ordóñez grew up and became a priest in Ciudad Real, he sent investigators in 1773 to look into the ruins. Acting on their reports more than a decade later, he told Josef Estachería, President of the Royal Audiencia of Guatemala, about the structures.

Estachería was a man of broad interests, and his curiosity was aroused by the news. So in 1784 he commissioned José Antonio Calderón, a local official of Santo Domingo de Palenque, the settlement closest to the site, to make a report on the ruins. Although Calderón was a faithful public official, he had no talent for archaeological work, and his examination during three rainy days produced a brief, perfunctory report with four drawings in folk-art style. Estachería was intrigued but dissatisfied. In the following year, 1785, he chose a professional, Antonio Bernasconi, the royal architect in Guatemala City, to carry out the task.

The comprehensive orders prepared for Bernasconi reveal the intelligent curiosity of Estachería or one of his aides. The topics listed for investigation are summarized here because the same orders were doubtless later given to del Río. In regard to the ruins and the civilization they represented, the investigator was asked to ascertain the age of the settlement, the extent of the population, the origin of its founders, the presence of defensive walls, and the causes of its downfall. Questions about the structures requested the style, the measurements, and an indication of the building materials.

The result disappointed Estachería. Bernasconi performed little better than the untrained Calderón; if the few drawings he submitted were more professional in appearance, his report was a sketchy affair only half the length of the questions prepared for him. Estachería sent the two reports to Spain, where Juan Bautista Muñoz, royal historiographer then at work on the story of the Spanish American colonies, read them and demanded more specific information. Once more Estachería had to find a man to examine the ruins. Calderón had proved incapable; Bernasconi had died after turning in his report; and two army officers who had qualifications were on other assignments.

At this point—it was now 1786—del Río entered the story. Estachería learned through acquaintances of this captain in the Spanish army stationed in Guatemala. But del Río had no qualifications for archaeological investigation beyond the recommendation that he was careful and intelligent. The president hesitated, hoping for a more appropriate candidate; when none appeared he reluctantly appointed del Río. To provide a visual record of the expedition, Ricardo Almendáriz was chosen as artist to accompany the captain; Almendáriz's name, however, never appeared in the later report, either through an oversight or because his services were held in low esteem.

From the beginning, del Río had troubles. Months passed before he arrived at Palenque on May 3, 1787, and the rainy season accounted for only part of the delay. At the village of Santo Domingo he commandeered Indians to guide him over the passage of three leagues to the ruins; the trees and undergrowth were so dense that one person could not see another five feet away. When he reached the ruins, he found the Palace hidden under a dense tangle of trees and vegetation.

The site had to be cleared before he could undertake serious work, so he returned to Santo Domingo and appealed to Calderón, who sent forth a call to nearby villages for 200 natives equipped with axes and machetes. Ten days passed before any Indians appeared, and then only seventy-nine with no more than twenty-eight axes among them. Calderón then commandeered twenty more axes from his village, and del Río agreed to make a second attempt on Palenque.

Having arrived at the ruins, he was determined to carry out his work unimpeded. For sixteen days he had the Indians cutting down trees and slashing away at bushes; then the refuse was disposed of in a grand bonfire. Del Río contemplated the clearing with satisfaction and declared that once more he could breathe healthy air and begin the investigation.

Naturally, he turned first to the Palace, the most imposing structure in the group. Once more, he put the natives to work clearing the building, which had a maze of rooms, corridors, and subterranean quarters. When they finished, he proudly reported "that ultimately there remained neither a window nor doorway blocked up,"[1] and that he had had excavations made in all parts of the structure. Later commentators shuddered on reading the statement, assuming that he had assaulted and ravaged the Palace like an enemy fortress. Actually, he was only carrying out orders. His report indicates that he was guided by instructions prepared for Bernasconi, and one of those queries asked if the walled-up doorways had been designed to fortify the place.

Totally unacquainted with the nature of the remains he had uncovered, del Río, like any neophyte stumbling upon the artifacts of a strange, silent civilization, could do no more than guess at the significance of what he saw. The Palace naturally received much attention. Almendáriz sketched the various forms of the windows and some of the decorations. Del Río, who apparently possessed only a rudimentary education, found it difficult to explain the structure. His limited knowledge of architecture led him to characterize the building as durably constructed but uncouth and reminiscent of the Gothic style. As for the decorative figures, especially the stucco reliefs for which Palenque became famous, the Indians offered no explanation, and the explorer once more resorted to guessing. He surmised that the portrait medallions pictured lords and rulers. Since he was an army captain, it is not surprising that he interpreted the figure of a man with a staff as a soldier bearing the flag of his legion and displaying signs of valor in his headdress. When del Río encountered a grotesque figure like the face with a crown and a chin beard, he could explain it only as the god of a superstitious people. A series of four plaques, each with two human figures in varying positions, suggested a sad drama of sacrifice required by a cruel and bloody religion. Sometimes he reverted to Roman deities as a parallel to what he saw, but he was obviously not fully convinced of the explanation. In two instances the appearance of the letter "T" suggested Greek influence. But he gave up the attempt at explanation when he came to the Temple of the Inscriptions and viewed the large stucco figures of women holding children in their arms.

As he moved on to the three smaller temples and gazed at the elaborate tablets of the Sun, the Cross, and the Foliated Cross, he was equally at a loss to understand them. The first he considered an allegory; this was obviously an ignorant guess, though he added lamely that the tablet might have memorialized their heroes or victories in war.

The second tablet elicited no comment whatever, and the third brought to mind the "idolatry" of the Phoenicians, Greeks, and Romans. Unlike many of his successors, however, he did not succumb to the lure of identifying the crosses with Christianity.

Other observations reveal del Río as a man of normal awareness with a limited background. The ruins he encountered before reaching the Palace he considered mere obstacles blocking the passage to the center of the site. He noticed the aqueduct only for its solid construction. He burrowed into the base of the tower and determined that it too was solidly constructed. Like most Spaniards, he had a low opinion of the Indians, and he attributed some of the less polished decorations to their rude, uncultivated style. In addition, he was aware that the ancients had not used metals, and he had a faint glimmering that the hieroglyphs were a form of writing. At appropriate places in the report he gave measurements, which were perhaps sufficient to satisfy the request of his orders.

At first he concluded that it was "indispensably necessary to make several excavations"[2] in order to turn up medals and inscriptions that throw light on the inhabitants and on the age of the settlement. But although he had Indians dig into the floor of the Palace in many places as well as in the underground area, nothing appeared. In four of the smaller buildings he unearthed what were probably dedicatory caches with a few pottery vessels, some flint lances, and a few other objects, including a small pot with bones and teeth, all of which meant nothing to him, though he dutifully forwarded the objects with his official report. When he trod the gallery of the Temple of the Inscriptions he never dreamed, nor did his successors, that many feet below lay the greatest find of all, a "royal tomb," discovered by Alberto Ruz Lhuillier 165 years later.

In response to Muñoz's request for artifacts, del Río extracted other items from the ruins. This archaeological loot included small plaques of hieroglyphs, pieces from several bas-reliefs—a head from one and a leg and foot from another—samples of lime, the few bricks he found, and artifacts from the excavations; as curiosities he added a bow and seven arrows used by the unconquered Lacandón Indians living in the neighboring mountains. Altogether he took away thirty-two items.

When he attempted to answer the questions about the origin of the ancient inhabitants and the nature of their civilization, his only recourse was outright speculation, though he was judicious enough to keep the remarks brief and tentative. He cited a manuscript of Fray Jacinto Garrido, who referred to the ruins of Ocosingo and attributed Greek and English influence to the natives of North America, but del Río dismissed the narrative as mere conjecture. More fruitful was his encounter with Fray Tomás de Sosa of Mérida, who described the ruins of Yucatán and convinced del Río that the same civilization had flourished there as in Palenque. Moreover, del Río was so impressed with the fertile soil, the favorable climate for agriculture, and the network of rivers in the area that he saw visions of an extensive commerce that had flourished between the inhabitants of Palenque and Yucatán. As he contemplated the advantages of the land and the sturdy buildings that had been constructed, he exclaimed that these ancient people had enjoyed a more peaceful and happy life than that of the inhabitants of the large sophisticated cities of his own day.

In the meantime, Almendáriz prepared a pictorial report in twenty-five plates containing thirty subjects. His record included the major works of decoration like the Beau Relief and the tablets of the Sun, the Cross, and the Foliated Cross. He omitted a floor plan and elevation of the Palace and a map of the site, probably because Bernasconi had already provided them. It is disappointing to find that he did not sketch the facade of structures like the Temple of the Sun nor provide a bird's-eye view of the assemblage of buildings in the center of the site. In view of the novelty of the subject he had to deal with, Almendáriz made an earnest attempt to capture the spirit of the decorations; he must be forgiven the haphazard depiction of the hieroglyphs because neither he nor del Río understood their significance.

It is too easy to note the faults of del Río's report and to fail to recognize his accomplishment, especially in view of the conditions under which the expedition was carried out. He was a military officer lacking qualifications as an archaeological explorer except for the traits of carefulness and intelligence. It is evident from his report that he had no prior acquaintance with pre-hispanic culture and that, unlike his successor Dupaix, he nursed no strong personal curiosity about it. The long list of questions and the requests of Muñoz guided the nature of his examination of the site. His report demonstrates the faithfulness with which he carried out the requirements of the commission.

In addition, he has not been given adequate credit for the frankness of the few speculations he included in the report. He couched all references to the transatlantic origins of the pre-hispanic people in conjectural, not dogmatic, terms. The fact that these statements are tentative even in the English translation suggests careless reading on the part of later commentators. Curiously, del Río's strongest declaration occurs in a passage omitted from the English version. In speaking of some of the decorations, he admits that he indulged in conjecture, aiming only to remain within the realm of probability.[8] He did not deceive himself nor did he intend to deceive his readers.

He completed the report at Palenque in June 1787, returned to Guatemala City, submitted it to Estachería—and disappeared into oblivion, leaving no information for posterity except this single document. Estachería had an engineer, Josef de Sierra, prepare a clean copy of the sketches to accompany the report, and he thoughtfully had a duplicate of the report and drawings made for his official files. In some unknown way still another copy came into a convent at Ciudad Real, probably through the intervention of

Ordóñez. More than a year after del Río completed his task, Estachería sent the report, drawings, and artifacts to Spain, where they were deposited in the Royal Cabinet of Natural History. Normally, that would be the end of the story—an expedition ordered and carried out, and the report of it filed away and forgotten in the archives.

Shortly after del Río had completed his assignment, two men wrote speculations on the transatlantic origins of the pre-Hispanic people of Middle America. Fray Ramón Ordóñez of Ciudad Real, the instigator of the explorations of Palenque, had long collected information about the early inhabitants, and he compiled a manuscript entitled *The History of the Creation of Heaven and Earth.* In Guatemala City an Italian by the name of Paul Felix Cabrera was interested in the same subject, and in the course of his research he consulted del Río's report and had the loan of Ordóñez's manuscript. Cabrera called his essay *Teatro Critico Americano.* Although neither book was published at that time, Ordóñez felt that Cabrera had borrowed too freely and charged him with plagiarism. Here, however, we are interested only in Cabrera's essay because of its later association with del Río's report.

In the ensuing quarter of a century unrest and revolution against Spain spread through Latin America. Doubtless because of the confusion and disruption of authority, one Dr. McQuy managed to secure a copy of del Río's report and drawings and of Cabrera's manuscript. Although the identity of McQuy has never been satisfactorily established, the important fact is that he took the papers to England.

Henry Berthoud, a London bookseller, bought the papers, had them translated, and published them in the fall of 1822 as *Description of the Ruins of an Ancient City, Discovered near Palenque . . . from the Original Manuscript Report of Captain Don Antonio del Río: Followed by Teatro Critico Americano . . . by Doctor Paul Felix Cabrera. . . .* The small book of 128 pages sold for £ 1 8 s. a copy. Berthoud employed Jean Frédéric Waldeck to engrave the sixteen plates that accompanied del Río's report. Thus, the modest volume introduced Waldeck, future artist-archaeologist, to the public, provided the earliest published firsthand description of Palenque for the scholarly world, and incidentally elevated del Río to the status of a recognized pioneer in Maya studies.

The volume suffered from several handicaps. Although the English translation was reasonably correct, it was freely rendered, contained some minor errors, and omitted a portion of the original manuscript. Also only about half of the illustrations were reproduced, presumably because they were the only sketches McQuy had secured. Curiously, however, the volume contained three pictures not in the original set. For the reader, the most serious imperfection appeared in the failure of the references in the text to be correctly keyed to the pictures. Subsequent events showed that Berthoud made a mistake when he decided to present the two works in one volume. Del Río's essay, though it appeared first, covered only twenty-one pages, while Cabrera's discourse filled the remaining hundred pages, and bore the pompous promise of being "A Critical Investigation and Research into the History of the Americans." That stale discussion of transatlantic influences too easily diverted the reader from the significance of the firsthand findings described by del Río.

Today it is surprising to realize that the *Description of the Ruins of an Ancient City* gained scant notice at the time of publication. Was the edition too small or the subject too novel to gain wide circulation? The only known contemporary review of the book probably had much to do with its obscurity. When the London *Literary Gazette* gave it a notice, the reviewer dismissed the report "upon a certain mass of ruins in New Spain" in order to criticize Cabrera's theories. He concluded that the volume "is obscure, and in parts unintelligible," and for good measure he added that the printers had been careless.[4] Thus, del Río's published report got off to a bad start at the hands of an ignorant reviewer who was more interested in speculations than in archaeological facts.

Interest in the volume picked up slowly in the fifteen years following its appearance. Two German translations were published, one in 1823 with the title *Huehuetlapallan,* which obviously emphasized Cabrera's essay, and another one nine years later that followed the English title more faithfully. B. D. Warden, an enthusiast of Americanist studies, prepared a French translation of abstracts of the English volume, which the Société de Géographie issued in Paris in 1825; Warden implied that the illustrations, separated from the text, were by Castañeda, the artist who accompanied Dupaix's expedition.

The English edition of 1822 received three belated notices. John Ranking, who had definite opinions on the origin of the American Indians, gave the first extensive summary of del Río's report in an article on Palenque in 1828. Ranking looked into the book solely to find support for his theories. And he found it: "Guatemala and Yucatan have been proved, by thc *remarks* on the ruins at Palenque, to bear strong evidence of their having been peopled by Asiatics; Turks, Mongols, and Calmucs." Then with an air of finality he concluded that "the arrival of the Tartars in America in considerable numbers from 544 to 1283, the earliest and latest dates recorded, are sufficient to account for everything of importance that is yet known with regard to America."[5] He too was dealing with Cabrera rather than with del Río. The second extensive summary of the book appeared in an American journal in 1832. In this case the reviewer conceded that the book contained the most minute available description of Palenque. Still another commentator, who showed general familiarity with the literature in the field, remarked that the little-known volume had been "scarcely published," and had fallen into oblivion. He maintained, however, that it "supplies more curious and valuable information than Humboldt on the subject,"[6] a correct statement but hardly an adequate recognition of the significance of the report. J. M. A. Aubin gave a more generous and more accurate opinion when he called del Río the founder of the archaeology of Yucatán.

Del Río's book was published ahead of its time. By 1822 the scholarly world was not prepared to make the most of the description and illustrations in the modest volume. Not until John Lloyd Stephens and other explorers in the 1840s emphasized the peculiarities of Maya ruins did del Río's book begin to gain stature as a work of historical interest; those explorers discovered that it was the first published account of Palenque.

Thus chance and accident combined to push Antonio del Río forward as an unintentional pioneer who informed the public of the strange ruins at Palenque and thus initiated the modern study of Maya archaeology. Other investigators had preceded him. Ordóñez had secondhand knowledge of the site, and Calderón and Bernasconi had investigated it at firsthand. But revolution, a mysterious Dr. McQuy, and an adventurous publisher combined to bring the captain's record and the artist's pictures to the literate world.

Guillermo Dupaix

Guillermo Dupaix was active in the first decade of the nineteenth century. He enjoyed considerable advantages in his work and in the personal gifts he brought to it. Appointed to carry out a royal commission, he explored a large area extending from Mexico City to Palenque, and his artist produced an impressive and varied pictorial record of 145 sketches. Also, Dupaix had a strong sympathetic interest in pre-Hispanic culture and had studied it extensively before he undertook the exploration. Over the years he acquired a private collection of artifacts, and he examined sites like El Tajín to satisfy his curiosity. Moreover, there are evidences that he had received more than an average education. As a young man he had traveled in Italy and perhaps in Greece, and he knew ancient Egyptian architecture from books and prints. Alexander von Humboldt, who knew him in Mexico and inspected his collection, considered him well informed.[7] Perhaps his most important advantage lay in his personal attitude: he was careful and patient in his work, the ruins excited his admiration, and he was reasonable in the small amount of theorizing he attempted. In other words, he avoided the zealous enthusiasm commonly associated with nineteenth-century Americanists.

Little is known about his earlier history. Alcina Franch, who has investigated the man in recent years, finds that he was born near the middle of the eighteenth century in Salm, in the Austrian Netherlands, that he belonged to the nobility, and that records credited him with some thirty-three years of service in the Spanish army, until his retirement about 1800. Dupaix explained that he spent twenty years in Mexico before he accepted the commission. All evidence suggests that he was reared a Frenchman and never divested himself of the French language and manners which were part of his personality. When Charles IV ordered an examination of the pre-Hispanic remains of Mexico in 1804, Dupaix, then a retired captain of dragoons, received the appointment, doubtless because of his interest and his knowledge of the subject.

He carried out the investigations of 1805–8 under favorable circumstances. The party accompanying him consisted of José Luciano Castañeda as artist, Juan del Castillo as secretary, and one or more dragoons. Castañeda was later vaguely identified as a professor of drawing and architecture. Dupaix was empowered to call on local officials for aid in locating ruins, and he could summon native labor to carry on excavations. By 1808 he was receiving 2400 pesos a year, his artist 1800, and the secretary 970. In his report he praised the accuracy of Castañeda, but he never mentioned his secretary. By temperament a self-sufficient man who took the hardships of travel in his stride, he was not given to complaints or excuses.

Although the plan of the annual expeditions was not announced in advance, the routes he took indicate an attempt to move progressively southward. In the first season he made an orbit of Orizaba, Cholula, and Xochicalco. The following year he visited Xochimilco, Lake Chalco, Ozumba, and Oaxaca. And in the final season he concentrated on Tehuantepec, Guiengola, Ocosingo, and Palenque.

In many ways his personal attitude was more significant than the factual information he recorded. As an older man with a deep interest in pre-Hispanic culture, he showed historical concern as he deplored the disintegration and eventual destruction of the ruins. Man and nature, he complained, unwittingly combined in wiping out the vestiges that remained. The religious zeal of an earlier age had taken its toll, and where trees and expanding roots had not loosened and crumbled the masonry, men carried off the squared stones to build their own houses. Only those ruins hidden in inaccessible mountains or far removed from the haciendas, he observed, were safe from the grasping hand of modern man. Also, he had seen fragments of the pictorial records on maguey paper and on *lienzos,* and he regretted the widespread disappearance of those annals of the past.

Moreover, he went about his mission seriously because of inherent interest in the task and a conscientious drive to examine everything of significance.[8] On arriving in a village, he called on the local official and sometimes on the priest to direct him to ruins in the neighborhood; he inspected occasional artifacts natives preserved in their homes; and when he learned of carved stones imbedded in the walls of modern houses, he went off to examine them. One can easily imagine him, notebook in hand, eagerly recording each item, whether he understood it or not, and then directing Castañeda to sketch those that seemed worthy of being recorded. Because his report takes the form of a commentary on the illustrated objects, appearing in the order in which he encountered them, the reader finds an array of miscellaneous items—geometrical figures, carved human heads and skulls, coiled snakes and various animals expertly cut out of stone, a jasper mask, and clay molds to print designs on cloth and maguey paper. Interspersed among these items are comments on musical instruments and examples of early applied science.

The more Dupaix traveled, the more he became aware of the scientific achievements of the pre-Hispanic people. First the symmetrical forms of their structures and their carvings, the careful measurements of their buildings, and the accurate division of the circle that was displayed in many a carved stone, gave evidence of knowledge of mathematics and geometry. At one place he noted how two stone heads of animals had been constructed to form a fountain, operated by water brought through an aqueduct and raised so as to flow through the openings in the faces. This convinced him of the builders' knowledge of hydraulics. When he visited an island in Lake Chalco, he was amazed at the three mile causeway that connected the island with the mainland. The broad road was so well built with stone, sand, turf, and stakes that it had served for centuries. At Mitla he noted the well-cut and splendidly finished masonry—the large stones were absolutely smooth, without the mark of a chisel—and praised the ingenuity of the builders. And on several occasions he came upon artifacts that convinced him the people had had a knowledge of astronomy.

Curiosity led him to investigate the instruments used to quarry the stones and raise them to proper position at the site. But a search for cutting implements left him none the wiser. Two multiedged chisels presented an answer to the question, but he was not convinced. He clung to the idea that metal of some kind had been used, though he realized that copper was too soft for the purpose. On one occasion he sent natives into the fields to search for the elusive instruments, and though they brought him many handworked stones, he was disappointed at not finding any metal objects. Once he admitted that iron was probably not known; later he assumed that iron instruments could have decomposed over the centuries. He never answered the question. Likwise, after inspecting a quarry, he could not determine the methods used to detach and transport building stones and to hoist them into position at the site. With no evidence at hand, he reasoned that some form of lever had been employed at the quarry and a pulley-like device at the site.

The few small-scale excavations he carried out yielded no information about the early people, because he was not equipped to interpret the finds. The human bones and potsherds he cast aside as worthless, noting only a whistle and a small clay head with a beard on the chin, which he found in a mound at Quilapa. The excavations, few in number and casually performed, added little to his report.

Dupaix was successful, however, in another direction, for, more than any of the early pioneers, he brought to his investigation a strong feeling for artistic expression. Familiar with the classical European forms of art, he managed to carry his esthetic sensitivity over to the early cultures of Middle America. His awareness sharpened noticeably as he moved from place to place. At first he noted only symmetry, the use of geometry, and accurate measurements. But as he moved out of the Aztec realm into other cultures that displayed more art, he sometimes departed from the calm, businesslike tone of his report. One of the early examples of his use of superlatives occurred near Puebla where he found in an Indian hut a green agate mask, "the most perfect in material, execution, and proportion" he had ever beheld in America.[9] On inspecting sculpture in relief and in the round, he often praised the realistic representation of flowers, animals, and vegetables.

Once he paused to explain his criteria of judgment. "The intrinsic value of works of art," he declared, "depends not upon size; they are not to be measured by the yard, nor estimated by their weight in the balance. Invention and finished execution are the true tests of excellence; . . . a figure of clay may be of more value than one of gold; and a work of diminutive proportions more worthy of admiration than a Colossus."[10]

Because he usually wrote with restraint, even moderate terms of praise indicate the emotions he felt on beholding certain artifacts. Of a monstrous head, he admitted that "the workmanship is excellent, and does credit to the artist." The ancient Zapotec pottery vessels struck him with "the brilliancy of their colours and the clearness of their varnish." On examining a carved human figure on a teponaztle, noted that "The head is remarkable for the singular beauty of its proportions. . . ."[11]

At Mitla, some twenty-five miles from Oaxaca, five groups of palaces appear at a distance to be low, undistinguished structures. Closer examination, however, discloses wall decorations of carefully cut tesserae painstakingly arranged to form a rhythm of geometric designs. Photographs or sketches fail to capture the achievement; in fact only personal examination can fully reveal the way in which skillful workmanship of detail produces a magnificent composition.

Dupaix had good reason for the use of strong words at Mitla. The structures displayed "a lavish magnificence worthy of ancient Rome," and demonstrated "the investigative genius of the artist who planned and executed them." Although he esteemed "the nice and perfect squaring" of the wall stones, the ingenuity of the mosaics raised him to fever pitch: ". . . these admirable structures, combining grace and beauty, display a style of architecture which it is impossible could be more original since in truth we here behold a gigantic piece of mosaic work such as antiquity never produced."[12]

When he came upon forms of artistic expression that were difficult to interpret, he drew upon his knowledge of other cultures. For example, he was puzzled by carved human beings with distorted proportions. But he found an explanation: the old proportions were due not to the artist's inability to draw or carve correctly, for Dupaix had seen many well-proportioned figures, but to political and religious conventions which dictated a uniform style for deities, as was the case in ancient Egypt.

When he could find no way to explain the meaning of a figure, he wrote it off as pure decoration. At Cholula the statue of a man with a ludicrous mask prompted the thought that some carvings were no more than the product of luxury and were intended only for ornament. And later he considered some "fanciful figures" as representing "only the extravagant invention of the artist."[13] But when he attempted to distinguish between the forms that were worshiped and those intended for decoration, he admitted a lack of sufficient data. He persisted, however, in believing that the decorations he failed to interpret were no more than mere esthetic expressions for their own sake.

So far we have considered Dupaix's personal traits in relation to archaeology; another facet of the man appears in the way he responded to the vexations of traveling through the country. Since he was generally reluctant to intrude personal items into the official report, the few occasions when he did so indicate the serious nature of the experiences. Delays occasioned by sickness and bad weather he apparently took for granted: they received only the briefest notice. But the dangers of travel were another matter.

Several times he noted accidents on the journey. On the way from Zongolicán to San Sebastian the corporal's horse slipped off the narrow path and fell into the trees below. Later the same day Castañeda's mount had a similar accident. In both cases the riders escaped unharmed, and local Indians rescued the horses and returned them to the party. Dupaix's turn came on the road up to Monte Albán. The July rains flooded an arroyo, and he and his horse fell into the swirling waters; they were soon fished out by the natives, and he continued to the summit to examine the ruins.

A proud man, he had no pity or understanding for a

group of Indians who mistook him for a common robber. Arriving near his destination one night, he got lost. The neighborhood had been victimized by marauders, and a party of Indian natives, believing him to be one of the thieves, seized his horse and sword and bound him with ropes, despite his protest that he was a captain seeking the center of the city. Finally an elderly native who comprehended the situation had him released. But Dupaix was so angry over the affront to his dignity that when he met the local official he slapped his face. Profuse apologies and news that the guilty Indians had been imprisoned were the best recompense he could receive for the mistake.

The most difficult experience occurred on the third trip during an eight-day passage from Ocosingo to Palenque. Here is his account: "The space which we had to traverse is scarcely passable for any other animal than a bird; the road winding through mountains and over precipices, which we crossed sometimes on the backs of mules and sometimes on foot. Our only vehicle was a litter or a hammock, and we were compelled to pass the streams which intersected our route by bridges rudely formed of trees. The country through which we travelled, though fertile, is uncultivated and unpeopled, except by the inhabitants of a few scattered huts; hence we had no other bed than the earth, nor covering than the heavens. Our baggage was transported by the help of some Indians of extraordinary strength and agility. Loaded with a weight of two hundred and fifty pounds, enough for the back of a mule, they proceeded on with unslackened pace, and climbed like deer the passes of the mountains."[14]

As a seasoned soldier, Dupaix could bear the hardships of travel far better than the vexations of the last months of the final expedition. By the time he reached Ciudad Real, political changes in Europe and Mexico cast suspicion on the purpose of his mission. Napoleon had invaded Spain, detained King Ferdinand VII, and placed Joseph Bonaparte on the throne. When Mexico learned the news, fears of

French domination seized the people. In the capital Viceroy Iturrigaray was suspected of being a traitor and was replaced by the aged Pedro de Garibay.

Dupaix and his party arrived in Ciudad Réal in May 1808, but the rainy season and dangerous roads prevented travel and exploration until October. Just as they were about to move on, news of the political changes reached the town and stirred the populace to suspect Dupaix as a spy. His royal commission of 1804 from Charles IV commanded respect, but the papers he carried, signed by Viceroy Iturrigaray, recently removed as a traitor, raised suspicion that the retired captain was Iturrigaray's tool. Moreover, the people considered him a Frenchman, and one local official claimed that Dupaix could scarcely speak Spanish. Nor did it help matters when one or two members of his own party made secret attempts to desert him and obtain passports to return to Mexico City.

The entire party was detained in the town for several months while the suspicions were investigated. A local junta of seven worthies examined luggage and papers of the captain and his artist without finding incriminating evidence. When the junta failed to exonerate Dupaix, he sent an indignant letter to the town official. Man has nothing more valuable than his honor, it began; it is more than life because death is better than infamous existence. He declared that the examination of his effects was so shameful that he did not know how he lived through that experience. In view of his innocence he demanded a written vindication, signed by each member of the junta. But the members refused to sign, for some of them believed that he had been tipped off in advance and might have hidden questionable documents.

Only an official statement from Mexico City finally settled the problem. A town functionary appealed to the new viceroy, and Garibay completely vindicated Dupaix. He testified to his fidelity, explained that he was an Austrian and not a Frenchman, and justified the value of his scientific work. Not until December did Dupaix and his assistants leave Ciudad Real to continue their explorations.

But his troubles had not ended. After examining Palenque, he proceeded to Villahermosa. There the governor approved his credentials, but the people quickly showed their dislike of him because he appeared to be French. Dupaix had had enough of this trouble and he decided to clear out of town at once. At the time his legs were swollen by insect bites and he could not travel overland by horse, so he stowed his party and baggage on a two-masted *bongo* and floated down the Grijalva toward the Gulf of Mexico.

At Alvarado he faced a churlish populace once more. Again the local governor greeted him in friendly fashion and treated him well during the first day. At nightfall, however, a wine dealer led a group of drunken, machete-armed muleteers to his house, forced an inspection of his papers and the drawings, and then sent a courier to Veracruz to report the suspicious character. Next day the governor hustled the visitors out of town so as to avoid more trouble; at the same time a detachment of dragoons arrived and escorted Dupaix and his party to Puebla; soon they were back in Mexico City.

Palenque was the only Maya site of significance that Dupaix visited during his explorations. When he reached the neighborhood of Ciudad Real he met Ramón Ordóñez, lifelong champion of the ruins, who doubtless aroused the captain's expectations, for Dupaix soon referred to the place as "the celebrated city."[15] After he arrived at the ruins he set up a makeshift camp in the area before the Palace and began the examination. What he saw amazed and perplexed him. Although pages of the report describe the structures and the stuccoes, his personal reaction is more interesting than the technical details. Here his artistic sensitivity responded to the esthetic perfection of a pre-Hispanic culture such as he had never experienced before.

The decorations fascinated him. Although the paintings

of birds, flowers, and fruit displayed taste and correct design, the bas-reliefs provided the unique feature of the settlement. Even the stucco of the plaques was hard and beautifully white. Dupaix's description of the bas-reliefs reveals his sense of wonder: "Most of the figures are erect and well proportioned: all of them are in profile, portly, and almost colossal, their height exceeding six feet; while their attitudes display great freedom of limb, with a certain expression of dignity. Their dress, though sumptuous, never wholly covers the body; their heads are decorated with helmets, crests, and spreading plumes; and they wear necklaces, from which are suspended medallions. Many of the figures hold a kind of rod or staff in one hand; at the feet of others smaller figures are placed in reverential postures, and some are surrounded with rows of hieroglyphics."[16] The air of authority and the rich clothing led him to conclude that they represented kings, and that the plaques related the history of the settlement. Although this was a reasonable conclusion, once more he repeated the contention that some of the figures might have been only decorative with no particular religious or political significance. He was upset to discover that no more than twenty-four of the original eighty plaques had survived.

In other observations Dupaix showed uncertainty. He was unable to comprehend the total plan of the "city," doubtless because of heavy vegetation. The absence of walls and fortifications suggested the peaceful existence of the inhabitants of long ago, but he did not visualize a utopia as del Río had. Curiously, he was puzzled as to the use of the aqueduct. Nor did the several excavations he undertook yield anything he could understand. In the Temple of the Cross, which he called a sumptuous building, the Christian symbol surprised him; however, he quickly gave up the attempt to interpret the elaborate tablet.

In two respects he was certain of his conclusions. The glyphs did not resemble those of Egypt or even those of the Valley of Mexico. And the flattened heads of the humans depicted on the walls convinced him that this was a race unknown to historians; those curious heads also led him to conclude that the contemporary Indians in the area could not have been direct descendants of the builders of Palenque.

In at least one instance he succumbed to the temptation of taking archaeological loot. He removed a stone with hieroglyphs from a wall of the Palace and carried it away as a "memorial of my journey, as well as a testimonial of the correctness of my draughtsman. . . ."[17] Later the national archaeological museum acquired the souvenir.

Palenque marked the climax and also the end of his investigations, and the impact of his experience there prompted him to turn briefly to the origins of the pre-Hispanic people, especially of this settlement. At Mitla he had posed the question of origins only to dismiss it for lack of sufficient information. At Palenque, however, he devoted several pages to the topic. He condemned the hasty generalizations of foreign travelers in Mexico as well as the far-fetched speculations of armchair theorists. The claims that so many different nations had colonized the country or had left traces of their culture on the early inhabitants appeared to him ridiculous; he added archly that only a direct route from the moon was missing from the range of speculation. For twenty years, he explained, he had lived in Mexico and studied the early people—and he was unwilling to speak with certainty on the subject.

But the artistic perfection of Palenque forced him to reconsider. How could one account for this achievement? He compared the style with that of ancient nations, and concluded that Palenque owed nothing to Gothic, Arabic, Chinese, or Carthaginian influence; nor did it have any relation to the style of the Zapotecs and Aztecs to the north. He determined that it was an original style. Moreover, because the envolutionary nature of art requires centuries to achieve perfection, the settlement represented the culmination of a long period of development. If the original inhabitants of that site came from Atlantis or some other land to the east, they could have brought their art with them or they could have developed it indigenously. Thus Dupaix did not quite abandon theories of transoceanic influences, but he certainly came close to an indigenous theory. The subject of origins was less significant to him than the product —perfection and originality—he beheld at Palenque. Here was an independent style of art flourishing at the height of its development.

After the third expedition Dupaix and Castañeda disappeared from public notice. When William Bullock, the English antiquarian, visited Mexico City in 1823, he met Castañeda and found that the artist had many of the original drawings. Bullock arranged to make copies of them but he never published them. Almost nothing is known of Dupaix, who probably died about 1818 or 1820.

The official report and drawings had been filed in the Cabinet of Natural History in the Mexican capital. However, the Napoleonic Wars in Europe and the movement for independence in Mexico forestalled any attempt to deliver them to the Spanish sovereign in fulfillment of the original commission.

Like del Río's report some years earlier, this one was also copied, taken abroad, and published. Lord Kingsborough secured the material in some way and presented the text and pictures in his *Antiquities of Mexico.*[18] Three years before these volumes appeared, H. Baradère arranged with the Mexican government to use the report and drawings in the Cabinet of Natural History, and he published them in *Antiquités Mexicaines.*

The published versions have been criticized. The English translation in the Kingsborough volume is careless and incomplete; and it was claimed that Aglio, Kingsborough's artist, made the drawings from copies in France rather than from the originals. In regard to the Baradère edition, Waldeck learned in Mexico that the illustrations were incomplete and that the text had been copied in a rush job by an Italian amanuensis who in fact made only excerpts.[19]

Judged against the background of his day, Dupaix was a pioneer of considerable merit. His report and illustrations provided the most comprehensive, though somewhat miscellaneous, account of archaeological remains in Mexico for years to come. Even the scholarly Humboldt could not boast of as much firsthand inspection of ruins in the same area. More important than the extent and scope of his work were the qualities he brought to it. He was conscientious in his search and sympathetic to the subject; he was alive to the artistic qualities of the early cultures; and few amateurs equaled his calm, almost scientific, spirit of reporting. His examination of Palenque convinced him of the unique character of Maya civilization. Although he confined himself mainly to description, he performed the necessary task of collecting facts about the physical remains, and along with del Río he helped to provide a point of departure for the study of Maya culture.

3

Juan Galindo

For more than a century Galindo flitted through the history of Maya archaeology like a lost soul; he was a part of that history, to be sure, but his identity was shadowy and uncertain. Actually, his work as an amateur explorer was subsidiary to the larger role he played in the military and political activities of Central America for more than a dozen years. Until recently his background was a mysterious blank: it was known only that he was an Irishman. As late as 1946 someone guessed that his real name was John Gallagher, which was incorrect. Since 1960 the mist has cleared away thanks to the painstaking research of William J. Griffith and Ian Graham, two scholars who ransacked newspapers, interviewed descendants, investigated letters in the British Foreign Office, and discovered his numerous communications and drawings in the Bibliothèque Nationale. As the result of this research Galindo now emerges as a man of flesh and blood who united two simultaneous careers in a rather brief lifetime. He was an adventure in Latin American politics and at the same time a conscientious reporter of the ruins of Palenque and Copán. Like a good actor, he played each role so completely in character that we might think these were two different men, did we not know that each one was Juan Galindo. As a military-political opportunist, he boasted and swaggered, sought quick wealth, and maneuvered himself into untenable positions. On the other hand, he turned out archaeological reports marked by careful and deliberate investigation; as a draughtsman, he curbed his imagination and depicted the remains with honesty and fidelity; and he indulged only moderately in theories about pre-Columbian people.

What tied the two careers together, what common element can be found in these several facets of the man? What impelled him to seek both position and wealth in Central America and, in addition, the applause of a small group of European scholars specializing in American antiquities? Insatiable ambition drove him forward; he hungered for fame. He knew that destiny had grand things in store for him, because the repetitive cycle of his genealogy made him a marked man. As he traced his family origins back to Clovis, king of the French, and the dukes of Aquitaine, he was convinced that every eleventh generation of his family blessed the world with a great personage, and he was the forty-fourth generation. Who could devise a more convincing argument to cultivate ambition and egotism?

His background gives little suggestion of the roles he was to play in America. Born in Dublin, Ireland, in 1802, he was given the name of John; his surname betrays the Spanish strain in the family, which began in the early eighteenth century when his great-grandfather migrated to England. John's father, Philemon Galindo, was an actor, performing in the theater at Bath for a number of years in the late 1790s, and it was there that he met Catherine Gough, of a formerly substantial Anglo-Irish family, whose reduced circumstances forced her to take to the stage for a living. They were married in Dublin in 1801. At that time Philemon was thirty-one and had shown little evidence of promise or stability. His acting never rose above the mediocre, and his later intrigue with the forty-seven-year-old actress Sarah Siddons tainted his reputation and troubled his family life.

John's early years remain obscure. Nothing is known of his training or education, though he later displayed a knowledge of French and ability of draughtsmanship, acquirements he probably obtained with the encouragement of his mother, who enjoyed a good education when her family was still prosperous. Later it was claimed that in 1818 he joined the expedition of Lord Cochrane, a colorful and controversial British naval commander who went to South America to fight for Chile's independence. If the statement is true, the young fellow was only sixteen years of age at the time; it is more likely that he went to Jamaica, where his uncle had a sugar plantation. Why he left England at all is one of the questions in his record that remains unanswered. We are on certain ground only from 1827, the year he turned up in Central America.

After arriving in Guatemala, he rose to important positions with considerable speed. At first he lived with John O'Reilly, the British consul, serving most of the first year as secretary and translator. By the latter part of the next year he had acquired the post of superintendent of improvements at the port of Itzapa and had also become a major in the Honduras battalion. He made one of the few wise choices in his life in 1829, when he joined the invading Liberal army of General Morazán, who set up the Central American Confederation. By this time he had changed his name to Juan, secured naturalization, and become a strong supporter of the confederation.

His interest in the cultural and economic life of his adopted nation appeared early. When the Sociedad Económica of Guatemala was revived, it employed him to translate English books for use in Central America; and by the end of 1830 he became a member of the organization. A little later he was sending tea and quinine from the Petén to England for analysis of their commercial quality.

His appointment as governor of the Petén, the huge northern part of Guatemala, opened his eyes to the natural resources that could be profitably exploited in that area. On his own initiative, he made an exploratory trip down the Usumacinta River, crossed westward, and reached Palenque in April 1831. He promptly turned his attention from economics to archaeology, from desire for personal gain to dreams of acclaim for revealing the glories of ancient America. He set up headquarters in the central entrance of the Palace, examined the major buildings, and by the end of the month wrote reports of his findings for the purpose of advertising his exploit in Europe. Later that year a London journal and the Geographical Society of Paris published his description of the region and his account of the ruins. A shorter notice, abstracted from these articles, appeared in an obscure French newspaper in New York City; and the following year the Royal Geographical Society reprinted the description of Palenque as a supplement to this article on the Usumacinta River. In view of the restricted nature of the subject and the small scholarly interest in American antiquities in 1831, he was fortunate to receive notice in four different publications.

His report on Palenque was a respectable performance. He described the major structures, indicated their orientation, provided measurements, drew plans, and sketched a number of the decorations. He gave attention to the stucco figures for which the site is famous, though he made no attempt to interpret their meaning. When he discussed the Tablet of the Cross, he noted that the emblem was the same as that used by the Christians without inferring a connection between the two religions. The hieroglyphs he correctly surmised to be a form of writing. Also he noted the tower and the aqueduct, two unusual features of the place; and like his predecessors, he was struck by the absence of warlike weapons in the decorations or among the detritus. Casually he mentioned that he found in the ruins metates and rollers like those used by contemporary natives for grinding corn.

He reached some conclusions by simple reasoning. On surveying the geographical location of the site, he decided that it had been astutely chosen to serve as the center of a flourishing trade with neighboring regions. He believed that the rooms in the structures must have been dark, "if the doors were of wood and kept shut." In a room in the Temple of the Cross he found no door, "but from the pillars . . . inserted in the walls, I conjecture it had curtains."[1] Unlike del Río, he saw a resemblance between the figures in the decorations and the Indians of his own day, and he concluded that the natives had descended from those who had built the structures.

A remarkable feature of his report that has not received the credit it deserves is his strenuous effort to avoid dogmatism. On a number of occasions he qualified statements with the word "apparently"; he identified assumptions as distinct from fact; and sometimes he indicated that he might be in error.[2] He left no doubt, however, of his unqualified belief in the superiority of Maya civilization to all other pre-Columbian cultures of the Americas.

In two of his early communications he added a brief description of a forty-five-foot stone tower on an island in Lake Yaxhá. He found it completely different from the towr at Palenque, and considered it more recent, because it still retained the door beams and other wooden fixtures.[3]

In order to impress Englishmen with the unique nature of Maya culture, he sent a small display of objects to the Royal Society in London in the fall of 1831. For the purpose he detached four plaster hieroglyphs from the Temple of the Inscriptions at Palenque and collected a vase and several small heads from Yaxhá. He succeeded in his aim, for illustrations of the artifacts, accompanied by a brief letter from him, belatedly appeared in *Archaeologia* in 1834.

In striking contrast to conventional archaeological writing, Galindo's reports reflected strong nationalistic overtones. Ancient Maya culture, he declared, marked the most civilized achievement of pre-Hispanic America, for surpassing the cultures of Mexico and Peru, and thus "saving ancient America from the reproach of barbarism." Momentarily, he betrayed a belligerent tone when he told the Société de la Géographie that he wrote "to make known to Europe our rights to its consideration."[4] On the other hand he shuddered in disgust at the local ignorance of the ruins.

At Palenque, when he asked who built the structures, the Indians attributed them to the devil, a priest thought they might be antediluvian, and the alcalde insisted that a colony of Spaniards had erected them before the Conquest! As a patroitic duty, Galindo determined to inform the learned world of the ancient wonders of Central America.

The first publication of his report for transatlantic readers appeared in the London *Literary Gazette* in October 1831, with unfortunate results. The sketch of two glyphs he supplied was obviously redrawn by a staff artist who knew nothing about the subject; one figure emerged too neat and symmetrical and the other contained a classical leaf cluster instead of the hieroglyphic character. Far more damaging was the misleading manner in which the report was presented. The editor, who assumed that he had a unique discovery on his hands, referred to Palenque as completely unknown. Galindo himself might have been guilty of the misconception, because he began the third paragraph with the words, "The principal edifice I have discovered,"[5] referring to the Palace. To make matters worse, Juarros was the only previous writer on pre-Columbian America to whom he referred; he thus completely ignored del Río's report, published in 1822. These blunders aroused a later writer in the *Foreign Quarterly Review* to condemn Galindo as a self-styled discoverer of ruins already described by others.

His country called for his services before he could make additional excursions into archaeology. As governor of the Petén, he was assigned the task of bringing the Lacandón Indians within the jurisdiction of Guatemala. Those natives, who had stubbornly resisted the white man, he considered timid, harmless, and uncivilized; he described them as existing by hunting, fishing, and the cultivation of tobacco, cacao, and maize. He managed to draw up an agreement with them, which officially completed his assignment, but for some reason it proved unsatisfactory, for the government had to negotiate another treaty five years later. About the same time, when rebels occupied the city of Omoa in Honduras, Galindo was dispatched to British Honduras to seek aid in suppressing the revolt by offering trade concessions to the English. Although he failed to gain the foreign help, he joined the Guatemalan forces, captured the port city, and received a medal for his meritorious service. Then he was appointed commandant of Trujillo.

He reached the summit of his career in 1834, when he received a large tract of land in the Petén, undertook a diplomatic mission to England, and returned to archaeology. The Guatemalan government granted him a concession of a million acres in the eastern Petén as part of Gálvez's ambitious program to develop the economy of the nation by giving away most of the public land to concessionaires who would promise to colonize and improve their grants. Galindo's tract, the smallest of those eventually given away, had peculiar strategic significance, because it included the western part of British Honduras. Gálvez intended to use the grant as a lever to force England to acknowledge Guatemala's claim to that region. Naturally, Galindo realized that he must make good his claim to the concession in order to uphold the national honor and also to derive the personal wealth he expected to gain in exploiting the area—and he relished the challenge.

He made one error, however, that proved fatal to his dreams of future money and prestige. When he had worked for Consul O'Reilly, he heard that official explain that the English government intended to recognize Guatemala's claim to part of British Honduras. After receiving his concession, the confident Galindo proceeded to Belize and attempted to assert authority over his land, only to discover that the officials there had no intention of recognizing Guatemala's claim. With unwavering optimism, he assumed that the local officials in Belize were uninformed as to England's real intention, and he concluded that Guatemala must deal directly with the Foreign Office in London. On that basis he induced his government to send him to England to gain the desired boundary.

In 1834, when he enjoyed the greatest favor from his political patrons, he was also busy with other activities. The Confederation decided to counter British influence in the Chiriquí area of Panama; at once he began to concoct a scheme to colonize the island of Bocas del Toro for the same purpose he entertained in colonizing the Petén. During the year he also served as temporary commander-in-chief in San Salvador and carried out his second major venture in archaeology.

He undertook the expedition to Copán almost by accident. In January 1834, the Guatemalan government provided for a program requiring firsthand examination and detailed reports on all pre-Hispanic structures in the nation; Galindo, Manuel Jonoma, and Miguel Rivera y Maestre were designated to carry out the assignment. Jonoma was to go to Copán, but he begged off because of the threat of cholera. Rivera y Macstre examined Utatlán and later made his findings available to John Lloyd Stephens. Then Galindo was sent to Copán, and in five months he submitted his report, though he probably spent less than eight weeks at the site.

In the part of the report that dealt directly with Copán, he noted the major characteristics of the ruins. They extended a mile and a half along the river and were supported by a retaining wall that showed signs of dilapidation. No building had survived undamaged, but he was able to determine the major plazas and the principal edifices. In addition, he identified stelae, altars, grotesque carved figures, and the intriguing stone table decorated with the figures of sixteen seated Mayas, which later archaeologists interpreted as a congress of scientists. He explored some distance from the settlement and found more stelae, the quarry which supplied the building stones, and Cutilca Cave, which gave no indication of human habitation. Details did not escape him: He detected traces of red color on the stelae and identified the hieroglyphs as phonic writing (a view not shared by later scholars). He assumed that human sacrifice took place at certain temples, though he offered no proof to support his assumption.

The great retaining wall facing the river contained several openings, and he entered one of them and carried out an excavation. "First I encountered the opening of this window," he explained, "and excavating to a greater depth, we entered a sepulchral chamber, the floor of which is 4 yards and 9 inches lower than that of the small plaza. It is 2 yards and 6 inches high, 2 yards wide, and 3 yards and 19 inches long, extending directly from north to south, in accordance with the compass, which in these countries has a variation of 9° to the east. . . . It has two niches on each side which are 18 inches high from the floor and which are 16 inches deep, 19 inches high and 28 inches wide, and both the niches and the floor of the sepulcher were filled with pieces of red earthenware coated with tar, such as dishes, wash-bowls, frying-pans, and pitchers. I took out more than 50 of superior workmanship, and some of these were full of human bones, mixed with lime, sharp razors, and with a material that the Mexicans call '*itzli,*' with a small head . . . , which seemed to represent the head of a corpse, the eyes almost closed, the lower jaw fallen, and protruding lips, there being many symmetrical holes in the back, as for hanging or shaking the same, the whole head being made of a fine stone covered with green enamel [jade], the same as two strings of beads which I also found in the vault, together with many shells of snails and oysters, which undoubtedly were brought from the sea in compliance with some superstition. Besides, there were stalactites brought from some cave to be deposited here. The whole floor of the subterranean vault was filled with the fragments of bones, and under them there was a layer of lime on the solid pavement of stone. The stones from which this vault is constructed are 10 inches thick and 10 inches wide and long, and were not set in mortar."[6] If this is not glowing prose, it is nevertheless a serviceable piece of archaeological reporting for that day. The head carved in jade was a miniature, two inches high, of which he made a drawing to accompany the report.

He showed a scholarly inclination as he considered the similarities and differences of the two sites he had examined. "Comparing these ruins with those of Palenque," he wrote, "it can be seen immediately that their similarity suggests a similar origin, in spite of the fact that they differ in essential points.

"Palenque was ruined and forgotten before the conquest, while the Spaniards found Copan in all its splendor; and yet the buildings and other works in Palenque are in a better condition than in Copan, owing to their superior architecture. Here in Copan there are no houses standing, as there are many in Palenque. Its building-stones are of diverse character, while those of Palenque are not more than 2 inches thick. The roofs in Copan were made of inclined stones, while those of Palenque are always horizontally placed. In Palenque they are cemented with mortar, while in Copan they are not.

"In ancient times, with the exception of Palenque, Copan was undoubtedly the most remarkable city of Central America, since, if the capitals of the Quichés and the Cakchiqueles equaled it, there would have been left some signs of their superiority.

"There is more fineness and perfection in the human figures there [Palenque], and they are nearly always placed in profile, while those on the contrary are most commonly found in front views. I did not see obelisks nor carved tables at Palenque.

"The circular stones of both places are very similar, and also I always find their writings always placed in almost square blocks containing faces and hands and other identical characters."[7] Galindo was the first investigator to draw and identify hieroglyphs as distinctive Maya writing.

He opened his report with an aggressive claim for the significance of the pre-Columbian inhabitants of Central America. Three years earlier he had asserted that they had achieved a civilization superior to all other native cultures in the Americas and that this achievement rescued the New World from the charge of barbarism. In the report on Copán he extended his claim by suggesting that ancient Central America had been the cradle of all civilization. First, he assumed that civilization and power had always moved westward, and that the Indian was the oldest of the six races of the world. In some distant primitive age the aborigines had set up the first civilization in Central America. It was later so completely destroyed by some calamity that no tangible evidence of it survived. A small number of inhabitants, however, escaped the catastrophe and migrated to eastern Asia, where they "prepared the enlightenment of Japan and of China." Because the major ancient civilizations—the Chinese, Hindus, Persians, Chaldeans, and Egyptains—displayed similarities, the fact suggested a common source, and the source "may be looked for in America."[8] When these other civilizations were rising, America fell into barbarism until the fifth century A.D., when the Toltecs, bearing "some enlightenment and a partial civilization" inherited from the first primitive age, moved southward and founded an empire in the Valley of Mexico. They then spread their conquests farther south, and Galindo "deduced" that they set up a colony at Copán, which became the capital of a kingdom embracing the present nations of Guatemala, Honduras, and El Salvador. He came to this conclusion because the same language, Chorti, was spoken by the natives of those regions.

After this praise of the early inhabitants of Central America, Galindo turned about and disparaged the pretensions of the white man. The Caucasians were not the "mother of the Indian race" nor did they originate the civilization of the aborigines. The latest of all races to appear, the whites spread over Europe, and, "aided by the strength of their youth and talent,"[9] they more recently invaded Africa and Asia. The Spanish conquerors of America were so barbarous as to snuff out even the memory of a cultural achievement like Copán. Only the priests, especially Bartolomé de las Casas, defended the Indians.

But what of the Indians in Galindo's day? He acknowledged that they were weak, ignorant, incapable of learning when they had the opportunity, and yet they were the descendants of the builders of Palenque and Copán. He attributed their present situation to fate. The Indians had gone through the stages of youth and civilization, and were now in decrepit old age, helpless and degenerate. The new independent nations of Central America "endeavored to have them share the benefits of civilization," a policy which was destined to fail because the race had almost come to the end of its cycle of existence and was about to disappear.

If Galindo's theory of history is read against the contemporary setting, it stands out as a bold manifesto of nationalism. Near the end of the report he suggested this idea when he declared: "Now that the governing class of this hemisphere has a direct interest in its fame and a filial love for its history, the ancient history of America will begin to be properly considered and written. The study of the history of their own country will give the people of Central America a more refined patriotism and a character peculiarly its own."[10] Three years earlier he had explained that this knowledge of the pre-Columbian people would demonstrate to Europe that America had a glorious past. Now he declared that the Central American Federation occupied the very soil where civilization originated. His thrust at "the mistaken and foolish pride"[11] of the white man was directed against Europeans. The reader could easily understand the implication: if civilization and power always moved westward, Europe and England were on the decline, while the independent states of Latin America, headed by a new breed of enlightened leaders, were waiting to assume primacy in the world picture. He disposed of the contemporary natives of his area by explaining that their race had run its course. His theory of history was no academic exercise; it was carefully tailored to justify his own pride and that of his adopted country.

There is a curious story about Galindo's four reports on the ruins of Copán. He sent one letter to the London *Literary Gazette,* and a year later when he was in the United States on a diplomatic mission, he dispatched a letter on the same subject to the American Antiquarian Society. These two published accounts are informative but not as detailed as the official report he submitted to his government and the copy of it he sent to the Société de Géographie de Paris. These latter documents, each with a set of twenty-six illustrations, were not published during the nineteenth century. It is still a mystery why the Geographical Society failed to print the communication in its bulletin, for it was superior to his report on Palenque. The manuscript slumbered in its archives, which were later transferred to the Bibliothèque Nationale in Paris, where Ian Graham discovered it a few years ago.

The history of the official report is more intriguing. In 1834, Galindo explained that his government intended to publish it with the illustrations, but it never appeared. Eighty-five years later Sylvanus Morley sought it for use in his volume on Copán; he and Adrián Recinos naturally searched for it in the archives in Guatemala City, but on not finding it, they presumed it lost. When Morley was going over galley proofs of his book in 1919, he happened to visit William Gates, an Americanist who owned a fine collection of Central American documents. Gates showed him the original report in Galindo's hand, but the pictures were missing. Although Morley included an English translation of the document in his book on Copán, the original Spanish version was not printed until 1945, and today the complete set of illustrations remains unpublished. Galindo's attempt to give the world his full account of Copán was dogged by his usual bad luck.

When Galindo had completed his task at Copán, he hurried on to other projects in his zeal to achieve reputation and wealth in Central America. Officials in British Honduras refused to recognize the larger part of his concession as belonging to Guatemala, and the fragment of the grant which they did not contest was too isolated for exploitation. In the meantime, a new British consul, Frederick Chatfield, arrived in Guatemala City. Although friendly at first, Chatfield developed an abnormal hatred for Galindo, collected every bit of unfavorable news and gossip about the man, and forwarded the data to the home office in London. Eventually those letters played a part in ruining Galindo's venture into diplomacy.

Self-confident and optimistic, Galindo set out on the foreign mission in January 1835. On the way to England, he stopped off in the United States, hoping to secure aid for his cause by a little horse trading. Washington was interested in a canal or railroad route across the isthmus, and in turn Galindo wanted American support for Guatemala's boundary claim against British encroachments.

He never got to first base with his plan. On arriving in New York in May, he informed Secretary of State Forsyth of his presence. When illness immobilized him in the city for some weeks, he made more communications to the secretary, including a collection of documents bearing on the isthmus project and a private letter detailing the boundary controversy. By June 23 he was in Washington, and Forsyth granted him an interview two days later, carefully restricting the agenda to discussion of a route across Honduras. During the next six weeks the secretary had the documents translated, and he then returned the originals with a short, noncommittal note. The Guatemalan boundary controversy, the matter closest to Galindo's heart, never entered into the official discussions, and the special agent from Central America left the United States empty-handed as he approached the harder task that lay ahead.

He proceeded to England, where his diplomatic mission ended in ignominious failure. Lord Palmerston met with him unofficially several times, and finally Galindo realized that England had no intention of withdrawing from the boundary it had always claimed. He was stunned to discover that he had been working on an erroneous assumption, and he wrote a strong anti-British report to his government. Time dragged on as he attempted to achieve his ends by various methods. Eventually Palmerston learned of the adverse sentiment in Guatemala engendered by Galindo's report, and in a final interview Palmerston dealt him the ultimate blow: Galindo could not represent a foreign power because he had been born a British citizen and could not give up his citizenship, an interpretation originally suggested by Chatfield. This marked the end of Galindo's effectiveness as a diplomatic agent.

In yet another direction, Galindo found that he was no match for powerful England. Wherever he advertised for colonists to settle his land, alert British agents quickly issued public warnings that the promoter had no legal title to the land. He never did attract colonists. Thus, he was defeated on the boundary issue and also in the attempt to colonize his concession.

While he was in London, he put another iron in the fire by developing the colonization project in Panama. He sent his father Philemon and a group of settlers to Bocas del Toro, and induced his uncle James in Jamaica to try his fortune in the same venture.

After two years abroad Galindo returned to Central America with nothing to show for his diplomatic efforts. By the time he reappeared in Guatemala in 1836, local changes had weakened his position. His political supporters had been driven from office, and the new leaders failed to patronize him as had Gálvez and Morazán. Grasping at straws, Galindo managed to secure a grant to a mine in Costa Rica as one more way to gain wealth, but that project soon proved worthless. When his concession in the Petén was officially withdrawn by the government—a loss that was only nominal, it is true—it demonstrated his fall from political favor. Within a year the Panama project also collapsed, because no provision had been made to take care of the settlers, who drifted away; Juan's father returned to England, and his uncle James, after begging help from Chatfield, went back to Jamaica.

Little is known of Galindo's personal life except that he failed to establish stable domestic relations. In 1834 he had a child by a native woman of the Petén, if we can credit the gossipy Chatfield. We know nothing more about his private affairs until four years later, when Guatemala City officially granted him permission to adopt two orphan children. Sometime during the following year he boasted that he was engaged to the daughter of a wealthy Guatemalan. That venture also failed, because the girl's father apparently cooled toward the proposed match; there is no record of a marriage.

Political and military events brought his declining career to an end. The Liberal Party he supported was now on the losing side in the changing scene. In a last-ditch effort to rally support, Galindo put on a one-man campaign to rouse the populace against England; but the government was not interested in anti-British sentiment at that time, and the appeal elicited no popular response. Once more he returned to the army with what was left of the federal forces under the Liberal leader Trinidad Cabañas, who attempted to reestablish the Morazán regime in Honduras. In January 1840, the Liberal army met the combined forces of Honduras and Nicaragua near Tegucigalpa, Honduras, and was defeated. Soon afterwards Galindo, a fugitive attempting to find his way out of enemy territory, was murdered by a group of Hondurans.

As an amateur Americanist, Galindo made modest contributions to Maya archaeology. The scope of his examination was restricted to two major sites, Palenque and Copán, and possibly to Topoxté in Lake Yaxhá. He sent an undetermined number of artifacts abroad, though few of them can be identified today as having come from him or from the sites he visited. His published articles on the geography of Central America fail to rise above routine performances. Brasseur de Bourbourg reported that Galindo once owned the first part of Ximénez's manuscript account of native languages; this is one more suggestion of Galindo's serious interest in the indigenous culture of the region.

Generally his work, which probed a number of fields, received no more than moderate notice. His attempt to supply firsthand information on Central America resulted in reports on archaeology, linguistics, and geography; in addition he prepared maps and pencil and watercolor sketches of Guatemalan life. His manuscript letters and drawings now in the Bibliothèque Nationale have attracted only two investigators, E. T. Hamy in the 1880s and Ian Graham in recent years. In succeeding generations, archaeological opinions of his performance have ranged from hostility to limited praise.[12]

His failure to gain widespread recognition for his contributions to archaeology can be traced in part to unfavorable circumstances. He appeared too late to be credited with the discovery of Palenque and Copán. As early as 1822, del Río's report on the first site was published, and in 1831, the year Galindo visited Palenque, Dupaix's report and Castañeda's illustrations appeared in Kingsborough's volumes and a few years later in *Antiquités Mexicaines.* Galindo's report on Copán bore a stronger claim as an original contribution, because it provided the public with the first informative decription of the site. The earlier remarks by Fuentes, incorporated in Juarros' history of Guatemala, were too brief and untrustworthy to be of service; and the sixteenth-century report of Palacio was not printed until 1840. Moreover, Galindo's record suffered because his articles appeared only in periodicals and annual reports, which were too easily filed away and forgotten. No book bearing his name was ever published. And unfortunately his official report and drawings also failed to appear in print. Then in 1841 John Lloyd Stephens issued two volumes on Central

America, broad in scope, attractively written, and superbly illustrated, which in the future completely overshadowed the work of Galindo.

His speculations become less significant if they are judged not as a serious attempt to advance knowledge of the pre-Hispanic people of Central America but as a cultural instrument to support the nationalism of the new nations of that region. The major theories he put forth, it should be noted, dealt only with the historical background of Palenque and Copán; rarely did he theorize about the structures, decorations, and artifacts. Impressed by the physical remains, he responded to the current romantic impulse by attributing a glorious antiquity to the land of the new nations; in fact, he went so far as to identify the region as the source of world civilization. We should also realize that he advanced this theory in 1834 when he enjoyed generous political patronage, dreamed of wealth from his concession, and displayed the greatest self-confidence. The entire report on Copán, to which his theory of history and of the races of mankind forms the introduction, rings with a tone of self-assurance lacking in his earlier report on Palenque. With his future prospects closely identified with those of Central America, his discovery of the great past fortified his own ego and provided a cultural nationalism to reinforce the pride of the people of those new nations. Although this explanation does not make his views of history and of races acceptable to the twentieth century, it makes his theorizing understandable as a product of the peculiar conditions of time and place.

All told, he produced respectable archaeological reports for his day. When we know that he was an opportunist seeking political preferment and wealth in Central America, the reports appear better than one might expect. This is the more interesting because there is no indication that he engaged in archaeology before he visited Palenque, and his knowledge of previous writers on the subject was probably very limited. However, he demonstrated a quick grasp of the essentials, as he instinctively realized that measurements, detailed descriptions, and drawings provided the fundamentals of examination and reporting. In addition, he exhibited growth, moving from the carefully qualified statements in the report on Palenque to assurance and confidence in the description of Copán. Regardless of his motives, he made a conscientious attempt to awaken the world to the intriguing ruins of Maya civilization.

4

Jean Frédéric Waldeck

Over the years Waldeck has failed to receive adequate recognition for a striking achievement. Several generations have praised him as an early explorer of Palenque, as the author of a pioneering book on Yucatán, and as an intriguing artist of archaeological ruins. But somehow his admirers have ignored the outstanding role he played as a public relations man on his own behalf, successfully "selling" his version of his early life to the learned world. It was a remarkable feat, for even without the aid of an autobiography his self-portrait of a romantic, adventurous personality went unchallenged for seventy-two years after his death. Simply by planting incidents from his past in minor articles and by relating episodes from personal experience frequently and disarmingly, he became a legendary figure long before his death at the age of 109. When he celebrated his hundredth birthday in Paris in 1866, he was already an acknowledged curiosity—a hale, hearty man, an avid girl-watcher at sidewalk cafés, and a charming conversationalist. Few men have enjoyed a celebrity of their own making as long and as abundantly as did Waldeck.

Although he never considered his lengthy existence as anything more than an endless series of entertaining anecdotes, his biography can be divided into three different periods. His "youthful" wanderings extend to 1822, when he reached the age of fifty-six. Then, for most of the next fourteen years, he was an amateur in Middle American archaeology. During the remainder of his life—thirty-nine years, to be exact—he cultivated the art of growing old without apparent aging and continued to enjoy lively parties and good conversation.

The incidents of the first period, according to his recollections, are marked by colorful adventure, though it is doubtful that many of these adventures actually took place. There are several versions of his origins. He claimed to have been born in Paris, Prague, or Vienna on March 16, 1766, the son of a German with noble connections either in the family of Waldeck or of Waldestein-Württemberg. On this basis Jean Frédéric assumed the title of count or, more rarely, that of duke in his later years. Also, his nationality varied from time to time, for he claimed German, Austrian, French, or English citizenship on the basis of residence or travel in different countries. At the age of fourteen, in 1780, he supposedly joined the party of François Levaillant on an expedition to study the natives and birds of South Africa. He returned to France in 1785, gave up ornithology for art, and put himself under the instruction of Jacques Louis David, the foremost painter of the day. Other versions say that he trained under Joseph Vien, David's teacher, or under Pierre Prud'hon, who later achieved fame as a painter. Since Waldeck's drawings show a strong neoclassical style, he could have come under the influence of Vien or David but hardly under Prud'hon, who followed an earlier style. Incidentally, he gave no information about his education as a young man, which is a peculiar omission in view of the cultured tastes he displayed in his second period.

He developed a flair for associating with prominent personages. In fact, he appears to have been on friendly terms with George III, Fox, Pitt, Lord Byron, Beau Brummell, and Baron von Humboldt. He was also acquainted with Marie Antoinette and her circle; he visited her when she was in prison, and three-quarters of a century later he painted from memory a portrait of the unfortunate queen. How he came in contact with these distinguished people is not clear, but one must assume that his title of nobility and his attractive personality opened all doors.

When the old regime was crumbling in France, he saw the handwriting on the wall and adopted the teachings of the new movement. The artist David moved over to revolutionary ideas, and in his studio Waldeck imbibed those views. Eventually he associated with Marat and Robespierre.

Once more he showed astute political judgment when he joined the Napoleonic movement. He later claimed to have been a soldier with the Little Corporal at the siege of Toulon in 1794, to have followed him on the Italian campaign the next year, and then gone on with him to Egypt. Waldeck's role in Egypt is not clear, for it seems that he was no longer a soldier. But he was rumored to have associated with Etienne Goeffrey Saint-Hilaire and Edme François Jomard, both young men in their twenties who would later make names as scientists, and even to have gained some social attention from Napoleon himself.

But when the Egyptian campaign collapsed, Waldeck proceeded to other adventures instead of returning to France. He and four companions wandered across Africa in an ordeal that he alone survived. Even after this experience, he claimed, he did not hesitate to join Robert Surcauf's privateering expedition into the Indian Ocean.

Then for almost two decades we have no record of the man. Some unexplained disappointment, occurring about the time of Napoleon's coronation, soured him on France, and he did not return to Paris until 1837. When questioned as to the reason, he replied with a smile that he had developed a taste for travel in other countries.

He embarked on still another expedition in 1819, when he joined Lord Cochrane, a colorful and controversial officer who had been expelled from the British navy. Cochrane brought a group of young men to South America and operated a navy for Chile in its war for independence from Spain. But before Cochrane completed the task and moved on to a similar command in Brazil, Waldeck had troubles with the commander and left his service. He wandered northward entirely on his own, following the Marañon River and reaching Central America, where he spent a month sketching the ruins of Copán.

At this point the story stumbles in chronological confusion. Did he leave Cochrane in 1819 or 1821? Both dates are given. Since 1819 was the year he joined the expedition to Chile, two years of service and the trip to Central America would place the end of his first American experience in 1821. But he explained later in his diary that he married Maria Iarrow (probably Jarrow) in Dublin, in February 1820. At the time she was thirty and, according to his calculation, he was fifty-four. He already had two children by a previous marriage. At the end of 1820, a son, Fritz, was born to the couple.

It is clear that he was in London in 1822 and had become acquainted with Berthoud, the bookseller and publisher. A Dr. McQuy had just sold Berthoud the manuscript and drawings of Antonio del Río's report on Palenque, made in 1787, and he employed Waldeck to engrave the plates for the English translation of the book. The volume appeared late the same year, and those illustrations marked the artist's introduction to the public. The claim that Waldeck met Edward King, otherwise Lord Kingsborough, in London about this time is no more than speculation, but King was a member of Parliament and already interested in pre-Hispanic America, so a meeting of the two men was possible.

Jean Frédéric enjoyed relating these adventures in his later years. If anyone raised a doubting eyebrow, no facts were at hand to controvert the genial artist's version of his past. And later generations continued to repeat the tales until Dr. H. C. Cline published a disquieting paper in 1947. Cline industriously checked contemporary evidence to determine those aspects of Waldeck's life that could be verified up to 1822, and the results exploded the delightful adventures and incidentally revealed an important trait in the personality of the artist.

Because Cline had to deal with negative proof, he was circumspect in his statements, but the cumulative effect of his findings turned Waldeck's story into fantasy. The date and place of his birth could not be verified. This is significant because a birth date about 1766 is necessary to accommodate the chronological sequence of his adventures and of the people he claimed to have known. In another way the date of his birth was significant because he intimated that he retained considerable masculine vigor in the later years, a claim that added a titillating fillip to the story of his long life. Nor could his nationality be established with certainty. Although he was never accused of lying about his age, thoughtful persons must have had grave doubts.

Cline proceeded to investigate other statements about the early years. He found no proof that Waldeck had any legitimate connection with nobility; he was not a member of a noble family, and this in turn undermined his right to use the titles of count and baron. Cline considers it more than coincidence that members of the French nobility of his day never recognized him as one of their group. Also, the records of Levaillant's expedition to Africa and of Surcauf's privateering jaunt in the Indian Ocean fail to disclose his name or even the possibility of service under an assumed name. Likewise, his service under Napoleon in Italy and Egypt has not been confirmed. More significant is the flat contradiction of his early association with Jomard, for we find Waldeck writing a letter to that scientist in 1832, introducing himself for the first time.

Several points about his early experience in America also appear doubtful. The chronology of his activity from 1819 to 1822 is confusing at best; a hostile critic would consider it impossible to reconcile the dates and events of those years. Equally mystifying is the geography of his travels from Lima by way of the Marañon River to Central America. Moreover, the month he supposedly spent sketching ruins at Copán curiously left no impression on him; he attributed his inspiration to study Maya archaeology to the engravings he made in 1822 rather than to firsthand experience at an outstanding site only a year or two earlier.

In conclusion Dr. Cline considers the early adventures apocryphal and Waldeck a poseur who innocently fed his vanity and gained attention by repeating the tales. Perhaps we can go one step farther and consider the entertaining stories as a reflection of his artistic imagination. That interpretation has the advantage of explaining the delightful impossibilities he injected into his Americanist studies.

In the second period he cut a far different figure from the dashing adventurer of the earlier years. Now we learn about him from his diaries rather than from anecdotes, and he emerges in a more natural light. He was a normal human being who had to struggle to make a living, experienced his share of hopes and disappointments, and found his natural gift for artistic expression.

If he decided to enter archaeology in 1825, he used a roundabout way to achieve the purpose. He signed up as a hydraulic engineer at £400 a year for an English silver-mining company operating in an isolated spot in Mexico. It is doubtful that he looked toward Americanist studies at this time, for he did not mention the subject during his first year in Mexico. It is more likely that money attracted him to the country. Ravifinoli, the Italian manager of the mine, had to advance cash so that he could outfit himself for the journey and his stay abroad. Either Waldeck was in poor straits or he husbanded all of his resources to support Maria and Fritz during his absence.

He spent almost three months en route from London to the little village of Tlalpujahua on the eastern border of Michoacán. Several other employees accompanied him on the ocean voyage, which was an uneventful two months at sea except that he got sick and had disagreements with his friends. After landing at Tampico, he lived for a week at

Pueblo Viejo, where he received his first taste of the exotic atmosphere of Mexico. He was thrilled to see the quaint village church, the barracks, and the public fountain, and to admire the beauty of the young women in their native costumes. He whipped out drawing paper and sketched the fountain, a girl washing clothes, a stately figure carrying a jar on her head, and a beauty who resembled an antique statue.

Finally he and a guide set out for a journey of three weeks over the mountains to Tlalpujahua. They traveled by horse and mule, slept in hammocks, sometimes under the open sky, and were treated sometimes well, sometimes indifferently, at the villages and haciendas on the way. When he arrived at his destination, he found a half-ruined town with a cathedral, four churches, and a monastery with one monk, all in a forsaken spot more than a hundred miles north of Mexico City.

Although he served less than a year as engineer at Tlalpujahua, those months produced misery, depression, and disappointment. Ill health plagued him off and on, and debility from tropical sickness left him in low spirits. From the time he entered Mexico, mosquitoes, niguas, and garrapatas tortured his flesh. If the natives had been picturesque subjects for sketching, now they irked him: "never have I seen lazier people than the Indians; they work but two hours a day, if that, and the remainder of the time they squander in talking and laughing among themselves."[1] To make matters worse, they took everything not under lock and key; once he had a horse worth eighty pesos stolen from him. Nor did his opinion of the country rise when he discovered that furniture ordered from Mexico City exhibited poor workmanship—"the Mexicans are entirely in their infancy and I believe it will take much time before they can make passable things"[2]—and that his boxes of drawing paper and books arrived in battered condition.

The volumes he had so carefully selected and brought to America reveal something of his taste. He chose Voltaire's

Philosophical Dictionary in fourteen volumes, Diderot's *Encyclopédie* in twenty-eight volumes, Montesquieu, the Odyssey, Xenophon, Plutarch, a Greek lexicon, an ancient history, a natural history, and numerous prints. In addition, we know that he was familiar with Volney's ancient history, and that he acquired several volumes by Humboldt. His tastes also extended to the theater. Before leaving London, he saw *Der Freischütz* and *Othello* and similar productions. Later, in Mexico City, he eagerly attended ballets, operas, and plays. In addition, he had some knowledge of architecture and some interest in biology. Although he never mentioned the source of his education nor how he became competent in engineering, it is clear that he was accustomed to the cultural advantages of urban life and enjoyed conversation with informed people, all of which made the transition to the mountains of Mexico a shattering experience.

At Tlalpujahua he suffered most from the lack of news about his wife and child. He had written Maria four letters during the ocean crossing, but after arriving in Mexico he received no replies from her. Weeks passed, even months, and still no word from Maria. For a time he suspected her of infidelity, and he was upset to learn that she had called at the company's office in London for money but left no letters for him. He continued to write; at least one of the letters was bitter and reproachful: "a heart which suffers like mine has a right to complain."[3] Finally, in November, nine months after he had left home, he heard from her. She in turn complained of lack of news from him since his arrival in Mexico. At once he suspected a plot: someone was holding up their correspondence. Were the officials in the London office reading his letters? It was all very strange. Also, during those nine months he suffered from disturbing dreams about Maria and Fritz, especially about the boy, who always appeared in some form of danger.

To make matters worse, he failed to get along with his superiors and associates at Tlalpujahua. They did not consider him worth his salt, for, even after many months, he had little to show for his employment. He said that he lacked the instruments to carry out his tasks. When he succeeded in constructing the model of a machine to crush stones, it was dismissed as wasted effort because the Indians were incapable of building it. Every day there were snide remarks and innuendos. He tried to control his temper and wisely confined his opinions to his diary: he noted that one man was an imbecile, another an egotist, and a third a traitor.

Actually, the men knew him better than he knew himself. It was plain to everyone that his heart was not in his work and that personal interests absorbed most of his time. He sketched scenery and native costumes; he spent Sundays painting views of Tampico and Tlalpujahua, a new road to the mine, or an Indian offering a cigarette to a woman. He wrote an essay on native customs, and planned a book of drawings and text, convinced that the volume would sell well in England. And he worked on his Phantasmagoria, a device in which changing optical effects were produced by a magic lantern, equally confident that it would be a moneymaker if he could exhibit it in the capital. Some of the friends he castigated in the diary went out of their way to help him find a more congenial position in Mexico City, but nothing came of the efforts, even after he spent eighteen days there looking for a job.

At the end of nine months he could take no more of Tlalpujahua and the engineering work. He gave up his post, received £100 in lieu of a return trip, and had the money paid to Maria in London. Then he spent two and a half days riding down to Mexico City with £117 in his pocket. Surely a man with his qualifications would find work in the metropolitan center.

He never dreamed that he was destined to live there six years, eking out a living, cultivating pre-Hispanic studies, and trying to finance an expedition for personal examination of Maya sites. First, he sought a position in which he could use his abilities and gain a regular income. At times several attractive posts were open, such as manager of the national theater, head of government lithography, and president of an academy of fine arts, but in each case he was passed over. Next he attempted to capitalize on his Phantasmagoria by scheduling performances at his home. The first show was announced as a benefit for charity, but thereafter we hear nothing about that enterprise. The £117 would not last forever, for he had to care for Maria and Fritz in addition to himself, and so reluctantly he followed the only course that remained open: he became a free-lance artist. In the newspaper he announced that he would paint portraits and miniatures, decorate house interiors, and give lesson in drawing and painting.

Although he depended entirely on his own initiative and lived on an uncertain income during these years, he managed to support himself and send occasional remittances to Maria, and at times he indulged in the luxury of buying artifacts and pre-Hispanic documents. Whatever a patron demanded he was willing to produce; portraits, religious subjects, and classical decorations all came from his brush. Now and then he gave private lessons in sketching, which he apparently found congenial, for he would have welcomed more pupils.

Sometimes the going was difficult. Waldeck's diary indicates that November 9, 1829 was one of those unfortunate days. "Went out for a portrait, nothing determined. Ran about to get some students, without results." He could always turn his collection of artifacts into money, though he vowed that he would not give up a single item unless it was a duplicate. After failing to find a patron or a pupil, he "took to Ackermann's home an idol which I had bought of Stasson the past year; was offered only 50 piastres—and I prefer to keep it at that price for it is a capital and rare piece. It is a basalt."[4] On other occasions he was hard pressed for cash, even for food. In November 1830, he confessed, "I ran about to get some money. Without success."

A month later: "Ran about all day to find some money. No one pays and I'll lose all that is owing to me."[5]

At times people who were curious about his artistic work called to inspect his studio, and he welcomed the relief from routine, always hoping to find a patron among the visitors. Two of the numerous callers appeared so intriguing that he mentioned them in the diary. The Prince of Wittenberg, a large man of about thirty-five, paid a call one day, giving little attention, however, to Waldeck's paintings and drawings. The prince made it clear that he was interested in natural science, and he rattled on endlessly, parading his fragmentary knowledge and dogmatic opinions. Waldeck did not interrupt the monologue, "persuaded that a Prince ought to know everything better than others."[6] If the prince was a bore, the other visitor, William Maclure, "so-called American philanthropist,"[7] was a rare character. The wealthy Scotsman had studied geology in the United States, established an agricultural school for poor farmers in Spain, returned to the United States to participate in Robert Owen's settlement at New Harmony, and had recently settled in Mexico to improve his health. Waldeck quickly discovered that his guest was no connoisseur of painting, so he let him talk about his own interests. At first Maclure announced a highly favorable opinion of Mexicans, which did not go down well with Waldeck. Then he explained how he dispensed his fortune for the good of humanity, scorned conventional religion and the institution of marriage, and believed in the free association of the sexes. Waldeck kept a straight face, and made no comments of his own when he recorded this interview.

Maclure's praise of Mexicans, however, did appear superficial to Waldeck, for his experiences intensified his dislike for the people and their culture. When a friend suggested that he draw Mexican caricatures, he wisely dismissed the idea, saying that they would be too costly to produce and probably would not sell. Perhaps he realized that he smoldered with too much bitterness. On coming to Mexico

City, he had expected to find a lively cultivation of the arts and belles lettres; instead, he discovered an ignorant elite and a community notorious for its neglect of cultural life. What was worse, he had to toady to these provincially minded patrons for small commissions. One day when he was in low spirits he snorted that "to deal with Mexicans is to deal with the wind, which is uncertain."[8] Nor did the politics of the nation increase his respect. Late in 1829 a military riot raged in the city for days in a change of political power. "We have fortified our doors with great beams. . . ." "Packed up my paints, the most useful thing for earning a living in case of accident and if I escape the general disaster that is expected.'"[9] He despised Santa Ana and accused Alamán of all the sins in the political book. To complete the catalogue of his dislikes, he distrusted ecclesiastics, and Mexico was overrun with them. Although some well-informed priests kindly aided him in his archaeological research, those acts never eased his suspicion that they were somehow crafty and underhanded in their dealings. Late in 1829 he exclaimed, ". . . I mistrust more than ever Mexicans and especially priests . . ." Some days later he declared in regard to ecclesiastics, "Already I have had enough disagreements with them.'"[10]

The unhappy man continued to worry over Maria and Fritz back in London. He received her letters more regularly than at Tlalpujahua, and he responded immediately with long replies. But eager and impatient as he was to hear from her, the letters rarely lifted his spirits, as they were written in an unpleasant tone. Early in 1830 he recorded an unusual item: "Received a letter from Maria that spoke to me for the first time of my work in a somewhat consoling manner. . . .'"[11] Apparently finances were one cause of trouble; sometimes Maria complained that though he earned money, he neglected to send remittances. He always felt the duties of a husband and wanted to aid her; sometimes he did so, but there were other periods when he lacked the cash. Maria managed to send Fritz to school in

St. Omer, and the father was pleased; although he no longer had those disturbing dreams about Fritz, he had not lost his concern for the growing boy.

Waldeck endured the frustrations of his way of living, the bitterness he felt toward the people, and the agonizing absence from his family for only one reason: the city offered the best opportunity for an introduction to the study of the pre-Hispanic culture of Middle America. As he investigated the history of Anáhuac in books, studied and collected artifacts and documents, and visited ruins in the central part of the country, his interest rose to a passion. He dropped plans for the volume on Mexican costumes, he gave up going to the theater, and he begrudged every moment he had to devote to hackwork for the despised patrons. He lived only for pre-Hispanic history. With a clear conscience he spent money to acquire more artifacts and early documents. He valued his collection of antiquities and books at a thousand piastres. Despite the distraction of painting portraits and giving lessons, he devoted endless hours to the early history of Mexico. Many an entry in his diary tersely states that he worked all day sketching an idol or a vase. He permitted few recreations to interfere with his labors. At most, he dined with friends and occasionally went horseback riding to Chapultepec, Tacubaya, or San Angel. Never did he complain of weariness or monotony; rather, he bubbled over at every new bit of information he encountered about the early people.

Soon after he arrived in the city he cultivated friends, especially Isidro Icaza at the National Museum, where he set to work drawing items in the collection. The officials were enthusiastic, and prepared to publish this pictorial record of their holdings. Willingly Waldeck engraved the illustrations, hoping, one can be sure, that he might become known as a lithographer. A four-page leaflet, carrying an ornate title page and presenting sketches of a dozen objects, appeared under the title of *Colección de las antriguëdades mexicanas que existen en el Museo Nacional* in 1827. The publication marked an auspicious beginning of the project; unfortunately, it also marked its demise, for lack of funds halted the appearance of additional installments. A decade later he admitted that the *Colección* "was very imperfect, in consequence of the extreme difficulty of working the stones . . ."[10]

As she pursued archaeology, he enjoyed the stimulating company of a small circle of friends who shared his interest, men who collected antiquities or were writing books about Mexico. Perhaps his closest associate was Adolf Karl Uhde, a man of means who assembled a fine array of small sculptured artifacts that were later housed in Heidelberg and eventually presented to the University of Berlin. Uhde loaned books to Waldeck, dined with him, and suggested ways for him to make money; in return Waldeck agreed to make a collection of insects at Palenque for his friend.

Another intimate was Carl Nebel, a European artist gathering material for a book about travel and archaeology in Mexico. He employed Waldeck to decorate a room in his house and to restore a work of art. But Waldeck was apparently jealous of his proposed book. Then in 1831 he suspected that Nebel would get to Palenque before he did, which proved to be a false alarm. Several years later Waldeck wrote to a European correspondent that Nebel was the only person in Mexico in whom he had confidence. When Nebel published his *Voyage pittoresque,* a sumptuous volume of colored plates, in 1836, it was evident that he had produced a book similar to the project Waldeck had earlier planned. Nebel did not mention Waldeck in his publication.

In his social and professional activities Jean Frédéric encountered other interesting persons. Mark Beaufoy, a top official in the mining project at Thalpujahua, was scarcely a close friend, though Waldeck made at least one drawing for him. His name appears rarely in the diary, and when Beaufoy published his book on Mexico in 1828 he failed to mention the artist. During the early years in the capital Waldeck hobnobbed with Count Linati, who issued a brief work on Mexican costumes, also in 1828, and this publication probably cooled Waldeck's interest in a similar project. With Count Peñasco the artist had only formal relations; the wealthy landowner had a fine collection of antiquities and native *lienzos,* but Waldeck had little access to them. Just before the Palenque expedition, the count offered to exchange three of his mules for the copy of Diderot's *Encyclopédie,* but after examining a volume he changed his mind because the reference work was not up to date.

From the start Waldeck developed strong opinions about Middle American archaeology. When he examined an "Etruscan" vase someone had found at Mitla, he doubted the identification, and speculated as to how a vase of that origin could have reached central Mexico. Already he was convinced that persons from Asia had influenced the culture of Middle America, and he insisted that Xochicalco, which he had seen, and Palenque, which he had not yet examined, were Asiatic in style. When he sketched "a vase that has a head similar to that of a Tartar,"[13] he saw no reason to doubt the attribution. His failure to appreciate predecessors in the field appeared on his return from Xochicalco, when he declared that the pioneer description by Alzate was so incorrect that it was difficult to believe that the man had seen the place. Fully confident of his own knowledge, Waldeck hastily wrote a history of Anáhuac, based on information from books and artifacts and from the eighteen documents on maguey in his collection. Like the work on Mexican costumes, it was never published.

In the course of his research on Central Mexico, he determined to visit Palenque and Yucatán for firsthand study of the ruins. He solved the problem of financing the expedition by gaining official support for a project to attract donors. In October 1831, Vice-President Alamán, historian and founder of the National Museum, announced the plan. It invited citizens, ecclesiastics, and states of Mexico to pledge subscriptions totaling 10,000 Mexican dollars. In exchange for the use of part of the fund, Waldeck agreed to spend two years exploring Palenque and Yucatán and to publish a book with 200 illustrations. In addition he agreed to make molds of decorations at the sites, exhibit them in London and Paris, and then turn them over to the National Museum. Each subscription share was priced at $250. He also had his eye on a prize offered by the Société de Géographie of Paris for the best book on Palenque. In the early stages of the project he was so enthusiastic that he declared, "If I cannot find money to make the Palenque journey. . . I am determined to make the trip on foot. . . ." Then came the sobering second thought, "It is too much for my age, but will Providence help me? It is for my family that I expose myself to all of the hard work."[14] There were fits of despair, as he spent time, often fruitlessly, buttonholing well-to-do persons for subscriptions. Signatures came in so slowly that sometimes he doubted that the plan would ever materialize. When a third of the total sum had been raised and the remainder seemed to be forthcoming, he set out for Palenque in March 1832.

The expedition to Chiapas provided a new scene, new problems, and the promise of discovery. On arriving at Santo Domingo de Palenque, he found 42 whites, between 100 and 120 Indians, and not more than a dozen habitable huts covered with palm leaves. His stay extended from May 1832, to July 1833. Later, he usually referred to the visit as having lasted two years, and, conversely, unfriendly critics said it amounted to only three months. Actually, he lived in the village for almost a year and made frequent trips to the ruins; then, early in 1833, he built a hut on the site and lived there for some four months. The time of his stay and the place of his residence are not as significant as the work he accomplished; several months before he left, he counted ninety drawings he had made of the ruins.

The achievement cost him much in patience and endurance. He supervised the Indians in clearing a road to the site and removing the dense vegetation around the old structures. Officials in the capital had promised native labor free of charge at Palenque, but he quickly learned that he not only had to pay for the service but pay in advance, and on occasion the Indians did not appear at the appointed time. In addition, he had trouble with the domestic servants. Perhaps the natives feared the white men, as he learned soon after arriving, but it is more likely that he failed to make himself understood. When he moved to the ruins, he was optimistic enough to believe that he could retain at least one domestic around the clock, but he found that on occasion he was completely deserted.

Palenque had the undesirable features of a tropical location. Its record for rainfall is one of the heaviest in the Western Hemisphere, and here it was that this man, who complained that he could not stand moisture in hot climates, decided to study Maya archaeology. In the rainy season the tropical downpour continued day after day, and the humidity almost smothered him. When he lived in the village he could do nothing but draw and write at home during these periods; after he moved to the ruins, he managed to copy some decorations in the shelter of a temple structure. Once more he was bothered by insects, especially the pestiferous garrapatas, and occasionally at night he heard wild beasts prowling about his hut.

At the beginning of his work he complained of the destruction of many of the decorations and of the pilfering of objects from the ruins. The stucco figures on the walls of the buildings were already badly disfigured, a sharp disappointment to the artist. Anything that could be carried away had been stolen, he declared angrily, and he noted that carved stones from the Temple of the Cross were imbedded in the walls of a private house in the village. The most notorious case of pilfering was in progress when he arrived. Portions of the Tablet of the Cross had been removed from their setting and left face down on the ground because a wealthy doña of the village had connived to export it to the United States. Waldeck assumed that he was responsible for the ruins and indignantly complained to state officials; later he boasted of having prevented the theft.[15]

The letters he wrote to friends radiated enthusiasm, announced progress, and intimated that startling discoveries were about to be made. After he recovered from his initial amazement over the ruins, he settled down to prosaic details. He cleaned the decorations, sketched them, explored the surrounding country, drew a map of the settlement, and began the laborious work of making molds of some of the figures.

During his stay he associated on friendly terms with Francis Corroy, another amateur archaeologist. Corroy was a French physician who had come to the island of Santo Domingo in the ill-fated expedition of General Leclerc at the beginning of the century. After that fiasco, Corroy moved on to Mexico, practiced medicine in Villahermosa, and headed the military hospital of Tabasco. After 1819, he developed a taste for antiquities, visited Palenque, collected some artifacts, and assembled information on the early inhabitants of the region.

When Waldeck appeared at the ruins, he and Corroy became close friends. They spent many an evening together discussing their mutual interest over the dinner table. Although Waldeck laughed at the physician's belief that the ruins were antediluvian, he found him a jovial companion. Corroy loaned artifacts to the artist, and Waldeck in turn made some drawings for him. They exchanged letters, and, back in Villahermosa, Corroy arranged for a shipment of plaster to Palenque for Waldeck to use in making molds.

If Jean Frédéric was aware of his friend's voluminous manuscript material about Palenque, he did not fear that it would compete with his own endeavors. At one time he observed that Corroy aspired to be the historian of the site. Nor did the physician's few publications upset him. Some articles in a Veracruz newspaper and a few brief notices in the bulletin of the Société de Géographie offered no competition. Only after Waldeck left Palenque did he learn of Corroy's attempt to publish a two-volume treatise in New York.

For several years, including the period when the two men were friends, Corroy had written a number of lengthy letters to Samuel Latham Mitchell, a well-known physician, college teacher, and public figure in New York. When Mitchell died, in 1831, the papers were turned over to Dr. Samuel Akerley, who continued to receive letters from Corroy. Then in September 1833, Akerley told the New York Lyceum about the Frenchman, and published the dedication Corroy had made to Akerley. Corroy's ideas about the ruins were a confusing rehash of current views. In one letter he reported Palenque to be 4,600 years old, and in a later communication he said the civilization fluorished 1,300 years ago and had been founded by Phoenicians, Egyptians, Greeks, Asiatics, Arabs, and Chinese. He referred to a plan of the Palace, drawn by Waldeck and "corrected" by Corroy, and in the next breath he suggested that no entire buildings existed and that only fragments and ruins covered the site.

Akerley had discouraging news for the would-be author. Harper's publishing house refused to print the work on the plea that illustrations would make it too expensive, and suggested that he try London or Paris. In addition, Akerley advised the physician to dedicate the book to some well-known scholar in Americanist studies.

On learning of these developments, Waldeck turned about and denounced every aspect of Corroy's work with charges of ignorance and plagiarism. The doctor did not examine artifacts carefully, he lacked knowledge of the Toltec language and of geology, and he was completely incapable of drawing. Moreover, he made unauthorized use of Waldeck's excavations and appropriated some of his sketches. Corroy's boast that he had spent $4,300 in his researches brought the retort that over fourteen years the doctor had not been at Palenque for a total of more than sixteen days.

Angry and indignant, Waldeck set forth these charges in a letter to Akerley to which he never received a reply.

Ever since Waldeck had conceived the project of examining Palenque and publishing the results, he had feared that some competitor would anticipate him. When his friend Nebel suddenly left Mexico City in 1831, Waldeck imagined that he planned to get to Palenque ahead of him. Now Corroy was the arch-villian, contriving to publish a large work before the artist could complete his own project. There was, of course, an element of practical competition in the picture, for the Société de Géographie had offered a prize of money and a gold medal for the best book on Palenque; as early as 1827 Waldeck had clipped the notice and kept it among his papers. During the ensuing years the offer was renewed, and though he did not discuss it in his diary, it lurked in the back of his mind. In the case of Corroy, however, Waldeck overrated the danger of rivalry, for the physician had nothing substantial to offer to the learned world. Nevertheless, hatred for the man persisted, and a generation later Waldeck went out of his way to condemn Corroy as an iconoclast, though it is not clear what he meant by the word.

The attack on Corroy was more than an isolated incident of egotism, for that trait ran through Waldeck's personality and cropped up on numerous occasions. He habitually condemned the work of all pioneers in Middle American archaelogy—Alzate, Humboldt, del Río, Dupaix, Castañeda, Aglio, Galindo—and later he attacked Stephens and Catherwood. He was willing to award merit only to the sketches by Max Franck. Apparently he assumed that his firsthand examination of the sites and his ability as an artist to portray the figures accurately made him the final authority on the subject. Up to the end he displayed undiminished self-confidence; in one of his last published statements he informed the world that he had been the first competent man to study Middle American ruins, or as he put it, he was "le premier Américaniste."[16]

As he explored the buildings at Palenque, he announced interesting discoveries. In the beginning he was astonished by the finely finished masonry. "I've seen one window with its frames of double molding," he observed, "perfectly equal and as correct as if they were of wood and made by a good carpenter. . . ."[17] When he unearthed a burial, at once he believed he had uncovered the remains of Mox or Ofri or Votan or his son; he was uncertain, because he did not have historical reference books at hand. In the Palace he encountered two gigantic figures with European profiles, each fourteen feet high; the giants in the courtyard, he added, "are infants by comparison."[18] In the subterranean area of the same building he found an Egyptian monument, and as he wandered about the grounds he discovered two perfect pyramids, thirty-one feet high and ending in a point; this was a remarkable find, for all other pyramids in Mexico were truncated, with a flat surface on top to accommodate a temple.

Of all his discoveries, the most controversial was the claim that he found carved elephant heads in the sculptures and hieroglyphs of Palenque and later in the wall decorations at Uxmal. He reproduced these heads in several sketches, copied from pieces of stucco he picked up in the rubbish of the Palace. As an additional proof, he detected elephant heads in some of the glyphs.[19] When doubters insisted that he had mistaken tapirs for elephants, he triumphantly pointed out that the tapir could not throw its snout upward in the air as depicted on the protruding curves on the wall decorations at Uxmal. Later he prepared an essay to prove his contention about the elephant figures, but it was never published. In the twentieth century the elephant controversy reappeared in a larger context when G. Elliott Smith revived Waldeck's "elephants" as proof of the diffusionist theory Smith championed. The diffusionists assumed that knowledge of the elephant could have come to pre-Hispanic Mexico by contact with people from Asia and Africa. Opposing the diffusionists were those who held that the

Mayas had developed an indigenous culture uninfluenced by contacts from abroad, and they denied the depiction of elephants in Middle America, accusing Waldeck of an overactive imagination. Later archaeologists identified the long-nosed figure as the mask of the rain god.

From his investigations he also acquired certain ideas about the history of Palenque. The ancient inhabitants were "formed by a mixture of various nations of the old continent; to all appearances the Chaldeans were the original stock, and the main body consisted of Hindoos." However, "The astonishing sculptures, which still remain, are of a quite different character from all that has hitherto been known."[20] The Toltecs had been ignorant of this settlement, he declared, since he could find no resemblance between the religion, hieroglyphs, or architecture of the two cultures. Although he did not indicate how long Palenque had flourished, he claimed that it fell before the assault of a neighboring power about 600 A.D.

If constant sketching and molding kept him busy, there were times when he became lonely and vaguely apprehensive. As usual, he thought of Maria and Fritz. Once he wrote to the head of the school at St. Omer to inquire about his son; three weeks later he read in the newspaper of a plague raging through that town, killing many people, and he worried anew over the fate of Fritz. Eventually, Maria wrote that both were in good health; though he welcomed the news, it did not end his apprehension. Other matters also preyed on his mind. Cholera morbus appeared in Villahermosa, seventy-five miles from Palenque, and also in Campeche, his projected first stop in Yucatán. His leg broke out in boils, and for a time he suspected that he had a venereal disease.[21] To add to his troubles, he also learned that the project providing money for his work at Palenque was encountering difficulties in the capital.

He had left Mexico City confident that he had escaped the burden of earning a living while pursuing his Americanist studies, but soon he found that the expected funds from the capital had ceased. He had started on the expedition with only one-third of the total sum available; additional subscribers failed to appear, and then the political situation in Mexico City turned against his friends. On the way to Palenque he had a satisfactory interview with Santa Ana. But six weeks after he reached the ruins, he made an appeal to Lord Kingsborough for subscriptions, and followed it with another appeal two months later. In the meantime the political wheel turned, Waldeck's friends were ousted from power, and he had to rely on his own resources. 'This devil of Santa Ana has ruined all my hopes,"[22] he exclaimed early in 1833. In an effort to economize, he gave up his house in the village and built a hut at the ruins, expecting to raise his food and shoot game for the table. On occupying the one-room building, he exclaimed, "Here I have finally arrived! How will my enterprise end?"[23] By the time Lord Kingsborough subscribed to ten shares, the project had expired, and Waldeck had to request direct financial aid from the Irish patron.

Before completing the examination of Palenque, he made an exploratory trip to Ocosingo to investigate the ruins at that site. He complained of the awesome route over the mountains, apparently unaware that Dupaix had gone through the same ordeal a quarter of a century before for the same purpose. Waldeck marveled at the ruins, pronounced them important, and resolved to see them again, but as time passed he lost interest and finally dismissed them as pure Aztec in style!

While he waited for news and money from Lord Kingsborough, he left Palenque for Yucatán, little realizing that he would be ten months on the way. He stopped off for a time at Frontera and Tabasco, and pushed on to Champotoón, but was driven back by an epidemic of cholera. The plague was everywhere, spreading, receding, and breaking out again. Suddenly he realized that he was in his mid-sixties and doubted that he had the physical stamina to resist the disease, so he wrote his will and packed up his drawings for a friend to forward to England. The next danger appeared when early in 1834 revolution flared up in Tabasco; he slept in his clothing several nights in fear of the army and pillaging. To make ends meet, he painted portraits—and waited and waited for a letter from Kingsborough.

Finally, he reached Campeche in May 1834. At least he was in Yucatán, though without funds to make trips to the ruins. He began to draw a map of the peninsula, and he was swamped with commissions for portraits, which he turned out as fast as possible to make money, though he detested painting to earn his bread. "I have no taste for portrait work. I do them with difficulty although it is the only resource I have to make a living. I would wish to be occupied only with antiquities; it is the only solace that I find in my work! Why has fortune not allowed me that which I was born with?"[24] At times he was sick, and the summer heat was unbearable. He counted the months and even the days since the last letter to Ireland.

In September the news arrived. Kingsborough granted him 4,387 piastres for archaeological research and sent a hundred livres to Maria for Fritz's education at St. Omer. The only condition the patron imposed was a request that Waldeck send all medallions he found to Oxford University. That institution, however, gained nothing, because no medallions turned up. Deeply appreciative of the aid, he named the Pyramid of the Dwarf at Uxmal after Kingsborough and later dedicated his first book to him.

As soon as the rains ceased, he pushed on to the ruins of Uxmal, inspired by a brief mention of the site in Buchon's atlas of the two Americas. Always enthusiastic and optimistic, he announced to friends that the ruins of Yucatán were more elaborate than those of Palenque. Although he traveled about the country, he concentrated his work at Uxmal, where the lavish ornaments challenged his ability to capture the details on paper. To impress a freind with the intricate decoration, he explained that he spent thirty-five days sketching the facade of one of the structures atop the Pyramid of the Dwarf and forty days copying the intricate serpent panel in the courtyard of the Nunnery.

The discoveries he reported intrigued and amused later readers of his book. It is strange, for example, that his measurements of the House of the Turtles are about double the actual figures, an error that might be ascribed to faulty transcription of notes. It is more difficult to account for several unusual finds that he reported. The courtyard of the Nunnery, he asserted, had been paved with 56,946 square stones, each one bearing a carved turtle. In the *Voyage pittoresque* he included a sketch of a cluster of four of these carved turtles to support his contention; as an afterthought he added that most of the stones had been removed to make way for later construction. On another occasion he put the number at 43,660. Only a few years later John Lloyd Stephens spent a morning digging about the courtyard and was unable to find a single one of the turtle paving-stones. Could Waldeck have mistaken the carving of a conventional flower with four petals for turtles? In the same courtyard he found on the walls many examples of what he called symbolic elephant heads.

Americanists were amused by his analysis of the use of the Nunnery. When he drew the floor plans of the structure, he concluded that the rooms had been deliberately arranged so that the priests could maintain surveillance over the "nuns" who supposedly lived there. But there is no evidence that nuns ever inhabited the building; he naively accepted the name given to the structure by the first Spaniards, who knew nothing about the use of the building.

He also contended that the Mayas had indicated the age of a building by the use of certain stones. He maintained that each stone in the checkerboard design of the Nunnery represented twenty years and that the hut carved in stone over each entrance denoted 832 years. Later archaeologists were not convinced that the builders had adopted a system of dating so convenient for the information of posterity.

The Pyramid of the Dwarf likewise had its revelations. In one of the upper structures he found seventy-two small circles cut in the walls, and in this instance he provided two explanations, which wre obviously no more than guesses: the circles had been made by prisoners awaiting execution or they furnished an exact record of sacrifices. He made a striking sketch of the facade of one of those structures, showing four sculptured giants, two on either side of the doorway. Each man was clothed only above the waist. Waldeck explained that the figures were not *in situ* but had fallen to the ground, and that he had been able to piece one of them together. Fearing that Mexican authorities might seize the remarkable work, he buried it. Later explorers never found the hidden statue nor any evidence that the four huge figures had ever adorned the facade.

The rains drove him back to Mérida, where he received a letter from a friend in Chiapas warning that the Mexican government planned to seize his Palenque drawings. He made two hurried visits to Chichén Itzá and then set to work copying the drawings, and he hired a secretary to transcribe his manuscripts, hoping to send the originals to England before the blow fell. Fortunately, his plan succeeded; he was able to dispatch the papers to a British official in Jamaica before the authorities arrived. Then on January 16, 1836: "The act of indignity which I foresaw for a long time took place today at 11 o'clock in the morning," he explained. The alcalde, Felix Guerero, and attending officers "came with a government order to seize my papers and sketches. I did not make any resistance . . ."[25] He believed that "the surveillance that they make of my house all day" indicated "that I am going to be arrested," he observed on the 21st.[26] Some time later Governor Toro informed him that the authorities were interested in artifacts that Waldeck might try to export; the artist kept a straight face because a jasper idol, the only object he possessed, had escaped detection. Toro also hinted that Waldeck's complaints against governmental authorities had prompted the drastic action, but Waldeck never elaborated on the complaints he had made, so the precise cause of the incident remains hazy. In later years he maintained that Toro considered him a spy for the British government. He was allowed to leave Yucatán for Veracruz, and from there he went on to England and Europe.[27]

One can surmise the sources of friction from other evidence. An official newspaper declared that he had vandalized Palenque and showed discourtesy to Mexico by seeking foreign aid for his archaeological work and by publishing accounts of his discoveries abroad. Although there was some basis for this charge, it was probably used to mask other resentments. Doubtless Waldeck had offended the Mexicans by his lack of *simpatía*. His diary reveals strong criticism of the people and their customs; in Mérida, for example, he noted the immorality of the women and claimed that the Governor of Yucatán maintained a harem. It is likely that he talked too much and made his feelings too clear; somehow he became persona non grata.

On leaving Yucatán, he went first to England for a reunion with his family and then on to Paris to arrange for publication of the long-promised book. The *Voyage pittoresque et archéologique dans . . . Yucatan . . . 1834 e 1836* appeared in 1838. It is an attractive folio volume of over a hundred pages of text, with a map and twenty-one plates, a third of which show contemporary Mexican costumes. For several years he had been telling the public about its contents, explaining that it would treat statistics, commerce, customs, Maya vocabulary, a history of the Mayas, and information about the ruins. The volume takes up those subjects, it is true, but it is a bit disappointing to a twentieth-century reader. The text devotes more attention to the picturesque than to the archaelogical side of the story, and offers no more than a sampling of the various topics he promised.

To be fair, we should realize that he never intended to produce a scientific monograph. Rather, he aimed to entertain the informed circles of Europe by giving them a taste of contemporary Yucatán and the intriguing aspects of the ruins. In addition, he used the book as a convenient vehicle to display his drawings, which are an attractive part of the volume. There is another reason why the text is weak. He could not write effective, sustained prose. His notebooks contained a hodgepodge of material that he was unable to organize. He appealed to a friend, Frédéric Lacroix, to select the topics and shape them into acceptable form and style, but even Lacroix could not give unity to the eclectic material. In view of these considerations, it is only fair to evaluate the book on the basis of the author's intentions rather than of our expectations.

The text reveals his strong feeling against Mexicans, which he made no effort to suppress. It is true that he was unhappy from the first day he landed at Tampico in 1825 until his sudden departure after the seizure of his papers in 1836. But why the uncomplimentary remarks? He spoke of the ignorance and barbarity of the people, called their customs dissolute and their women superficial, and he revealed his anti-Catholicism and his suspicion of the clergy. Was this forthright honesty, or was he perhaps attempting to amuse his European readers? His personality appears to provide an easy explanation: he deliberately used the printed page to take revenge for the years of unhappiness he suffered in the country. As might be expected, the Mexicans never forgave his gratuitous insults.

The fate of his second wife, Maria, is unknown, but in 1850 when he claimed to be eighty-four, he married his housekeeper's niece and became the father of a son, Gaston.[28] The faithful wife cared for him the remaining quarter of a century that he lived. Unfortunately there is little information about these later years.

He hungered for public notice. When an article on the natives of Central America appeared in Charles Dickens's magazine in London, he used it as an excuse to send a lengthy letter to Dickens, claiming to be the first person to have written about a mysterious contemporary Maya city that had escaped penetration by the white man. At the end of the rambling account he extended several invitations to examine "my drawings of the different races of that country and others on natural history no less interesting," and indicated that Dickens might use the letter "as you deem proper." But there is no evidence that the novelist showed any interest in Waldeck's "fourteen years spent in researches on the subject of the Ancient population of Central America."[29]

He still possessed many drawings made in Mexico, and he tried to persuade the French government to buy them for a lump sum. The deal was made in 1860 for 188 of the sketches, and the government, according to a well-known story, was conscious of the artist's advanced age and insisted on paying him in the form of an annuity. The arrangement angered Waldeck so much that he determined to live long enough to get the better of the deal.

Some of those drawings have another story, because they appeared in his second and final book under unusual circumstances. By the 1860s, the government of Napoleon III was cultivating Mexican antiquities as an artistic and scientific by-product of the Maximilian regime and was publishing a number of serious studies on the subject. Waldeck was able to ride the crest of the wave in a restricted way. A commission of six scholars examined the drawings and, after comparing them with Charnay's photographs of the same subjects, gave a favorable report on fifty-six of them. They noted his penchant for restoration and his interest in elephants, but they were unwilling to trust him with writing the text in the proposed publication. Only a few pages were allotted to him for a commentary on the plates, and Brasseur de Bourbourg received the task of writing the text. Ironically, over 60 percent of the plates illustrated Palenque, a site which Brasseur had not yet visited. It appears, however, that the authorities were intuitively correct in not trusting the artist with the text. So Waldeck made his second major bow to the public entirely through his illustrations, which were his greatest achievement.

Recherches sur les Ruines de Palenque is a handsome piece of bookmaking, and receives too little attention today. Of folio size, with generous margins and attractive typography, it reflected the government's munificent patronage of art and science. On opening the book, the reader gasps as he comes upon the drawings. In clean, clear outlines the designs stand forth with commanding sharpness. The Beau Relief is so appealing, especially since the original disappeared some time after he had copied it, that it is commonly reproduced today. The double-page spreads of the Tablet of the Cross and the Tablet of the Sun are arresting tableaux of ceremonial drama.[80]

His other publications consisted only of a few short articles, appearing in the later years and based on material he had accumulated in Mexico in the 1820s and 1830s. He described the Tablet of the Cross at Palenque and the pyramids of Teotihuacán, and wrote articles on architecture and Aztec history. These items gained little notice because by the time they appeared other explorers had made reports that superseded his information.

In all of his archaeological performance Waldeck made his poorest showing when he dealt with the origins of early civilization in Middle America. At first he committed himself to a belief in Asiatic sources. After seeing Palenque, he added Egyptian and Near Eastern influences, relying on the elephant as an important part of his proof. Moving on to Yucatán, he saw in Uxmal the product of Asiatic luxury and slavery—and he saw more elephants. In his later years, he turned his interpretation upside down and declared that Middle America had preceded Asia and Africa in developing civilization. It is doubtful that he took these views seriously; he never constructed careful proof to support his ideas. In fact, one wonders about his judgment when he declared that the head of a thirteen-year-old native girl of Palenque had Chinese traits and resembled the profiles carved on the ruins! His aptitude was for art, not for the theoretical aspects of archaeology.

He was happy and amiable in his last years. He lived in Montmartre, at 2 Chaussée des Martyrs, in a few modest rooms four flights up. When Mary Darby Smith called on him in 1865, she was surprised to meet a man six feet tall, well proportioned, and healthy looking. He appeared to be about seventy, though he claimed he was ninety-nine. He told her that he engaged in exercise, by which he probably meant walking, and that he ate well, lived temperately, and flourished on seven hours of sleep a night. To what did he attribute his physical fitness? Eating horseradish for six weeks every spring! Another visitor, who saw him some years later, described the simplicity of his life. Unable to afford servants, the artist graciously opened the door to all callers, and his wife prepared the meals. He enjoyed talking about his longevity and referred to himself as a biological curiosity. "I have passed the age when man dies," he remarked with a twinkle in his eye. "Now there is no reason that my life should end. My archaeological studies make me believe that I have reached a state of petrifaction which can endure centuries after centuries."[31]

He was still active with various projects. Over the years he had compiled an encyclopedia of American archaeology in three volumes, which he hoped to publish by subscription.[32] He died before it was printed, and the manuscript remains with his other papers in the Newberry Library. He also planned a glass diorama spreading all history and science before the spectator, and he sought a loan of 10,000 francs to bring the exhibit to New York to make a fortune. Through an intermediary he approached P. T. Barnum to help exploit the device, but the great showman replied that both men were too old to begin new projects.

If Waldeck lived on limited means in his last years, he continued to enjoy an easygoing, carefree Parisian life. The fall of Napoleon III ended his pension, but he continued to receive 1,500 francs annually from the Institut de France He was a common sight on the streets of Paris, strolling the boulevards during the day and enjoying gay dinner parties late into the night. As a raconteur, he was reputedly at his best when surrounded by an adoring female audience. In 1875 he enjoyed the celebration of his 109th birthday and the momentary publicity it received.

According to legend, his long life ended with a characteristic act. Six weeks after his birthday, as he was sitting at a sidewalk café, he turned to look at a pretty girl passing by, suffered a stroke, and died. It is a typical Waldeck anecdote, and one suspects that he might have invented it, if that were possible. Like so many incidents in his life, it is but a legend. His wife gave a more prosaic, though probably more truthful, version: on the way home from an evening party, he fell, developed an abscess from the injury, lingered a few days in bed, and died.

Although archaeologists generally viewed his work with an unfavorable eye,[33] Waldeck deserves a place in the roster of pioneers in Maya studies. His theories, the least important part of his achievement, should be dismissed as having come from a man with no ability for the theoretical aspects of the subject. And one might add that even in his explorations he lacked the cautious approach, was hasty to invent quick explanations, and failed to display the scholar's care for serious and sustained study. His natural gifts directed him to seek out the lavish ornamentation of Maya architecture in order to capture it in his drawings. That was a worthy objective, for even today the accurate sketch often reveals more than the photograph. Unfortunately for archaeology, his artistic temperament sought perfection, and he too easily glided into the realms of reconstruction, exaggeration, and, one must add, fancy.

Perhaps it is best to accept him simply for what he was, an artist who revealed the esthetic aspect of Maya archaeology in dramatic illustrations.

5

John Lloyd Stephens

It is impossible to write about John L. Stephens without using superlatives. He covered more territory and examined more Maya sites than any previous archaeologist. With the aid of Frederick Catherwood, the able artist who accompanied him, he produced four volumes of narration and description so attractively presented that no other amateur's writings have approached them in the wide public appeal they have enjoyed since they appeared in the early 1840s. More significant than the popularity of his writings is the quality of his contribution: he provided accurate descriptions and measurements of the structures, he admired the achievements of the ancient Maya without succumbing to "enthusiasm," and he indulged in a minimum of speculation, which was always guided by careful reasoning.

He did the job that needed to be done in the early stage of Middle American studies. He explored the country, examined the sites, and provided a sober, accurate report. He set the record straight, disproving rumors and relying only on what he had seen for himself. In all of his travels he overlooked but one important area, the Petén, which he described on his map as "Parts said to be very thinly inhabited." It is unlikely that he could have penetrated that region even if he had wanted to.

He put the remarkable achievements of the ancient Mayas on the cultural map. After the appearance of his volumes, no one could plead ignorance of the subject. At the same time that Prescott laid before the reading public the ancient civilization of Central Mexico, Stephens revealed the lesser-known area to the south, disclosing a culture that surpassed that of Tenochtitlán. Moreover, he concluded that Maya civilization (of course, he did not use the word "Maya") had been a purely native development, thereby giving Middle America a history of its own rather than a culture borrowed from Asia or Africa.

Family and education gave Stephens unusual advantages in preparing for his future work. He was the son of a well-to-do New York City merchant; and though he was born in Shrewsbury, New Jersey, in 1805, his family soon moved to the metropolis. There he attended Joseph Nelson's Classical School for three years, mastering Latin and other subjects under the strict surveillance of a rigid teacher. At the age of thirteen he entered Columbia College and, following the prescribed curriculum, he graduated in 1822 at the age of seventeen. His family background and his collegiate training destined him for one of the professions. In order to prepare for law he went to Litchfield, Connecticut for fourteen months of intensive study in the small but excellent school founded by Tapping Reeve. When he returned to New York City at the age of nineteen, the natural wanderlust of a young man prompted him to travel into the backcountry of the new West on a trip that finally took him down to New Orleans, where he embarked for the homeward voyage.

It was now time to settle down to business, and he hung out a shingle at 67 Wall Street as a practicing lawyer. During the nine years he occupied that office, politics rather than briefs and court sessions attracted his attention. He threw his support behind the popular Jacksonian movement from 1828 on, and continued to give public speeches for the Democrats until he began to suffer from a throat disorder.

When his physician advised a trip to Europe, Stephens had no objection; in fact, he spent two years wandering through the lesser known parts of the Continent. It was more than the ordinary grand tour. In addition to England,

France, and Italy—the countries Americans customarily visited—he also toured Greece, Turkey, Russia, and Poland. Then he traveled down the Nile to inspect the ruins, and, donning native costume, he trekked across the desert to ancient Petra and Palestine. The jaunt was exciting and exhilarating, showing him monuments of the ancient world as well as contemporary life in the more backward parts of Europe.

On returning to New York, he resumed his old habits by reopening the law office and plunging into the political whirl, until an accidental encounter changed the whole course of his life. One day he dropped in at Harper's publishing house and learned in a casual conversation that travel books were the most popular works with the general public. At once he dashed off two volumes of his experiences in Egypt and Arabia, and the books gained immediate popularity. Harper's had to issue six editions within a year to meet the demand, and Stephens welcomed the $15,000 in royalties, which made him independent of his father. The next year he followed his success with a sequel, again in two volumes, relating his adventures in Greece, Turkey, Russia, and Poland. This work also proved popular, not only in the United States but abroad; three editions appeared in the British Isles, one in France, and another in Sweden. There was no need for more tangible evidence that he could write what the public wanted to read.

These experiences in traveling and writing led directly to Stephens's adventures in Central America. Now thirty-two years old, he had had ample experience in getting along abroad, and he realized that news of little-known regions had the greatest appeal to the public. With that in mind he laid careful plans for the next trip. It is not clear when or how he chose Central America, though John Russell Bartlett, proprietor of a bookstore Stephens frequented, claimed to have directed his interest to that region by calling his attention to Waldeck's recent folio volume, which had just arrived from Paris. Francis Hawks also insisted that he had influenced him in the same direction. At any rate, Stephens prepared himself by reading all of the standard works—those of del Río, Dupaix, Zavala, Galindo, and Humboldt—standard only because nothing more was available on the subject. He learned of Palenque from del Río and Dupaix, of Uxmal from Zavala, and of Copán from Galindo. Humboldt had never traveled in the Maya area, and Kingsborough's large, expensive volumes would have given him no additional information, even if he had had a copy.

In the meantime Frederick Catherwood came into the picture. Six years older than Stephens, he had the background and experience that made him an ideal partner for the proposed trip. Coming from a well-to-do English family, he had received a classical education, and at the age of sixteen he began training for architecture as an apprentice to Michael Meredith, after which he spent a brief period in Sir John Soane's classes at the Royal Academy. Like Stephens, he traveled abroad, spending three years in Italy and Greece, and gaining firsthand acquaintance with ancient classical remains; he added another year in Egypt, where he sketched the ruins along the Nile. On his return to England he set up as an architect, but failed to gain sizable commissions. When another trip abroad beckoned, he jumped at the opportunity and became a member of Robert Hay's archaeological expedition to Egypt, where he sketched more ruins. After that he went to Arabia and Palestine, still making pictorial records, which would prove useful in England.

At Burford's Panorama in London he exhibited a huge canvas of Jerusalem, with an accompanying lecture. When Stephens had completed his European tour in 1836 and was on his way back to New York, he stopped at Burford's and met Catherwood. The two men immediately became friends. In the course of their conversation Catherwood called Stephens's attention to del Río's little-known book on Palenque, and it seems that they discussed the idea of a journey to Central America. Sometime after Stephens's return to the United States, Catherwood left London and settled in New York, opened an architect's office in Wall Street, and soon established his own panorama, in which he showed canvases of Jerusalem, Thebes, and Baalbek. When Stephens finally decided to go to Middle America, he quickly persuaded Catherwood to accompany him as artist of the expedition.

At the last moment Stephens acquired an unexpected role, that of diplomatic agent to the Central American Confederation. The post had a dubious reputation, because previous incumbents had died while in service, and the last appointee, William Leggett, a leader of the Democrats in New York, had died before he was able to leave the United States. Stephens applied for the post, and since his party loyalty was unquestioned, he received the appointment. While a tailor was making a ceremonial coat for Stephens with gold braid and all the decorations, Catherwood put his panorama into the hands of a partner, and bought artist's supplies and a camera lucida. Early in October 1839, the two men sailed out of New York harbor on the *Mary Ann.*

On arriving at Belize, Stephens sought the quickest way to Copán. He sailed down to Punta Gorda, over to Lívingston, down the Río Dulce to Lake Izabal, then overland through Chiquimula and Esquipulas to Copán. Even today the ruins are not conveniently accessible except by plane. As he went along, he took ample notes. Now he was an author-explorer, recording vivid firsthand experiences while they were fresh; later he wrote the material into a smooth narrative describing picturesque scenes—a feature expected by readers in that romantic generation—incidents of travel, curious personalities, and, of course, the ruins. Just before reaching his goal, he had his first unfortunate experience with petty local officials, who came close to shooting him because he would not surrender his passport.

Copán, at last! The place was swallowed up in luxuriant tropical growth that obscured its features and increased its mystery. "We ascended by large stone steps . . . ," he wrote, "and reached a terrace. . . . Our guide cleared the way with his machete. . . ." "Working our way through the thick woods, we came upon a square stone column . . . , sculptured in very bold relief, and on all four of the sides, from the base to the top. The front was the figure of a man curiously and richly dressed. . . . The back was of a different design, unlike anything we had ever seen before, and the sides were covered with hieroglyphics."[1] It was one of the famous stelae, which make Copán unique in Maya art. Fortunately for Stephens, he encountered this gem at the start of his investigation as a thrilling indication of surprises to come. In addition to other carved stelae, he came upon curious altars, a pyramid studded with a row of sculptured figures, a great plaza surrounded with rows of steps, and a colossal portrait head. Clambering up a wall of steps, overgrown with trees, he entered the terrace a hundred feet above the river.

Catherwood had trouble adjusting to the new task. "The designs were very complicated," Stephens explained, "and so different from anything Mr. Catherwood had ever seen" in his experience in Egypt "as to be perfectly unintelligible. The cutting was in very high relief, and required a strong body of light to bring up the figures; and the foliage was so thick, and the shade so deep, that the drawing was impossible."[2] Trees and brush had to be removed to admit the sunlight. The strange figures and the enigmatic hieroglyphs tried the artist's skill and patience, but as the days passed he managed to capture the spirit of the carvings with remarkable accuracy. Other problems also plagued him. On one occasion Stephens found his partner standing in the mud and wearing gloves to protect his hands from mosquitoes while he drew his sketches.

As the days passed, he and Catherwood wandered over the place, with its complex of terraces, pyramids, stelae, and stairways—some preserved, others dilapidated. They discovered that the remains extended two miles along the river. When Stephens published his two volumes on Central

America, he included thirty-one of Catherwood's engravings of Copán, about two-fifths of the total number of illustrations in the work.

The next objective was Palenque, but it was far off. As they went along the route, Stephens inquired for other ruins and visited those within reach. Although he missed Quiriguá because of a diplomatic side trip, Catherwood learned of the site and visited it in order to sketch some of the stelae, which are similar to those of Copán. Then the two men traveled through Guatemala, heading for Chiapas, Mexico, with Palenque as their goal. On the way they visited the former capital of the Cakchiquels at Tecpán and the chief city of the Quichés at Utatlán, but those places were without ornament, carving, or hieroglyphs and yielded little information on architecture. Further on at Huehuetenango, the result was scarcely better, though the hasty excavation of a mound revealed a burial with several vases. Next they came to a site near Ocosingo, where among the confused assortment of ruins they encountered some stucco ornaments, which, although they were unaware of it at the time, foretold the artistic style of Palenque.

After a tortuous mountain trip through a region of inhospitable natives, they reached Palenque. First, the Palace came into view: "through the opening in the trees we saw the front of a large building richly ornamented with stuccoed figures on the pilasters, curious and elegant; . . . in style and effect unique, extraordinary, and mournfully beautiful."[3] The structure, in a reasonably good state of preservation, was a complicated maze of corridors, rooms, courtyards, underground passages, and a square tower. Nearby stood small graceful temples perched on pyramid mounds. Stephens soon discovered that the crowning glory of Palenque was its stucco reliefs, which appeared everywhere, and the stone Tablets of the Sun, the Cross, and the Foliated Cross. Other features made the place unique. The window openings of the Palace took the form of crosses, half-crosses, and pointed arches. The sloping roofs of the temples led up to roofcombs suggesting Chinese lattice-work. A man-made aqueduct carefully conducted a stream through the settlement. And the delicately rendered stucco figures signaled a remarkable development of Maya art. The hieroglyphs, great tablets of them, molded in stucco or carved in stone, were masterpieces of precision and beauty.

Stephens little realized that Uxmal, third and last goal of his first season, would become the starting point for his second journey a year and a half later. Shortly after the two men reached Uxmal, Catherwood had a physical collapse and Stephens hurried him back to New York. But there was time to examine Uxmal briefly before they left. Unlike Copán and Palenque, the place had been cleared of brush, and the visitor could see the vast panorama at a glance. "We took another road, and emerging suddenly from the woods, to my astonishment came at once upon a large open field strewed with mounds of ruins, and vast buildings on terraces, and pyramidal structures, grand and in good state of preservation, richly ornamented. . . ."[4] First to attract his attention was the curiously shaped Pyramid of the Dwarf, topped with two structures loaded with carved stone ornament. Then he came to the Nunnery, the House of the Turtles, and the enigmatic House of the Pigeons. But it was the Governor's House that fascinated him: "It is the grandest in position, the most stately in architecture and proportions, and the most perfect in preservation of all the structures remaining at Uxmal," he exclaimed.[5] When he and Catherwood returned in 1841, the whole site was overgrown with weeds and bushes, and twenty-foot saplings waved from the top of the Pyramid of the Dwarf. They took up quarters in the Governor's House, and made a detailed examination of the surrounding mounds, buildings, and cultures.

The entire area abounded in ruins. If many of the structures were small and unpromising and others were too dilapidated to reveal significant information on brief inspection, several were worthy of careful scrutiny. At Kabáh the facade of the main building, 151 feet long, was a riotous mass of conventionalized masks of the rain god, which produced a weird rhythmic pattern and cast curious shadows in the sun. Zayil had a longer structure, three stories high, with a grand staircase in the center; simple columns topped by plain capitals provided doorways and supported the superstructure. Within a short distance they encountered Labná, which was a complete surprise to them, as they had had no advance notice of the place. The complex included a steep pyramid with a temple clinging precariously to the top, rows of rooms with an outstanding arched gateway, curiously ornamented facades, and the main palace, 282 feet long, ornamented with stone sculpture.

After penetrating the peninsula as far south as Iturbide and Macoba, visiting remains wherever he learned of them, Stephens moved north to Chichén Itzá. The site differed in details from the other major settlements. He explored the main buildings and had Catherwood draw them—the House of the Dark Writing with its mysterious carved lintel; the mass of masonry called the Nunnery, with the elaborately decorated Annex and Iglesia; the round Caracol, believed to be an observatory; the Red House, the Ballcourt and the Temple of the Jaguars, the Castillo, and the Thousand Columns. There were intriguing sculptures and murals in the Temple of the Jaguars and sharply etched figures atop the Castillo, all providing some of the finest pre-Columbian art of Middle America. Stephens had looked forward to Chichén and said that he was not disappointed by it, but somehow his account fails to register the same enthusiasm that marks the description of other major sites.

Pushing north to the Gulf of Mexico, he sailed to the eastern part of the peninsula. By this time the modest ruins of Isla Mujeres and Cozumel appeared commonplace, but Tulum on the rocky coast of the mainland, "amid the wildest scenery we had yet found in Yucatan,"[16] proved to be an imposing place. Inside the surrounding walls, Stephens and Catherwood came upon the buildings one at a time, because the thick growth hid everything from view. In the center stood the Castillo with its broad, majestic stairway; there were also watchtowers, oratories, temples with the figure of the descending god, and still other structures whose use could not be guessed. On the return to Mérida, they passed through Aké and examined the curious stone shafts, the large palace and the tremendous mound, and then to Izamal, where Catherwood fortunately sketched the huge stucco face that has since disappeared. After farewells to friends in Mérida, the two men took a boat at Sisal and reached New York on June 17, 1842.

In his extensive travels through Central America, Stephens was pioneering in the true sense, blazing a new trail for those who came after him. The few publications that he could consult told only about Copán, Palenque, and Uxmal—three of the forty sites he eventually visited. "I am entering abruptly upon new ground," he remarked. "Volumes without number have been written to account for the first peopling of America." "The monuments and architectural remains of the aborigines have heretofore formed but little part of the groundwork for these speculations.'"[7] Although he directed attention to the physical remains, which would eventually turn current speculation into new, more fruitful channels, his task was that of a pathfinder heading into unknown areas.

He had to learn everything for himself. As he began the task at Copán, he remarked: "The ground was entirely new; there were no guide-books or guides; the whole was a virgin soil. We could not see ten yards before us, and never knew what we should stumble upon next. At one time we stopped to cut away branches and vines which concealed the face of a monument, and then to dig around and bring to light a fragment, a sculptured corner of which protruded from the earth. I leaned over with breathless anxiety while the Indians worked, and an eye, an ear, a foot, or a hand was disentombed; and when the machete rang against the chiseled stone, I pushed the Indians away, and cleared out the loose earth with my hands. The beauty of the sculpture, the solemn stillness of the woods, disturbed only by the scrambling of monkeys and the chattering of parrots, the desolation of the city, and the mystery that hung over it, all created an interest higher, if possible, than I had ever felt among the ruins of the Old World."[8]

The lack of local traditions and the scant information in historical sources complicated his problem. At every site he queried the natives closely for stories about the place, and inevitably received the answer, "*Quien sabe?*" "Who knows?" In Rome and Athens, recollections of bygone ages were cherished but at Copán, Chichén, Itzá, and Uxmal, the past was a blank among the natives. Even the historical records of the early Spanish conquerors and their followers said next to nothing about these places. He concluded that an early account of the Spanish conquest of Copán was obviously in error as to the site; the bits of information about Uxmal he could extract from local records excited his curiosity rather than satisfying it.

The historical vacuum enveloping these strange ruins created a secretive, mysterious atmosphere. It was in this spirit that he recorded his first impression of Copán. "The city was desolate," he wrote. "No remnant of this race hangs around the ruins, with traditions handed down from father to son, and from generation to generation. It lay before us like a shattered bark in the midst of the ocean, her mast gone, her name effaced, her crew perished, and none to tell whence she came, to whom she belonged, how long on her voyage, or what caused her destruction; her lost people to be traced only by some fancied resemblance in the construction of the vessel, and, perhaps, never to be known at all . . . All was mystery, dark, impenetrable mystery, and every circumstance increased it."[9] After exploring the whole site and describing the remains, he returned to the same theme, referring to the monuments, "standing as they do in the depths of the tropical forest, silent and solemn, strange in design, excellent in sculpture, rich in ornament, different from the works of any other people, their uses and purposes, their whole history so entirely unknown, with hieroglyphics explaining all, but perfectly unintelligible . . . The tone which pervades the ruins is that of deep solemnity."[10]

These impressions are more than the superficial romantic stance expected of a writer in the 1840s. It is true that as Stephens progressed from site to site he stopped recording his musings of mystery and solemnity. But when he entered Copán, his first site, these statements expressed his initiation to the new problems. He was penetrating the unknown without aid, and, above all, he was tackling the problems that face every historian: How to explain the civilizations that human beings have created, how to interpret the esthetic expression and probe the thought of unfamiliar cultures, and how to measure their advances in civilization. Stephens fully realized that the task before him was to extract from the remains an answer to the question: Who were these people?

One of the first things that impressed him and continued to impress him was the high esthetic achievement evident in the structures he visited. On reaching Copán and seeing his first carved stela, he observed: "The sight of this unexpected monument put to rest at once and forever, in our minds, all uncertainty in regard to the character of American antiquities, and gave us the assurance that the objects we were in search of were interesting, not only as the remains of an unknown people, but as works of art, proving, like newly-discovered historical records, that the people who once occupied the Continent of America were not savages."[11] Somewhat later, at Palenque, the gigantic carvings in the Palace courtyard aroused his admiration despite some reservations. "The design and anatomical proportions of the figures are faulty," he wrote, "but there is a force of expression about them which shows the skill and conceptive power of the artist."[12] After inspecting Uxmal, he noted that the style of its ornament differed from that at other sites. "The designs were strange and incomprehensible, very elaborate, sometimes grotesque, but often simple, tasteful, and beautiful. Among the intelligible subjects are squares and diamonds, with busts of human beings, heads of leopards, and compositions of leaves and flowers, the ornaments known everywhere as *grecques,*" all of which formed "an extraordinary mass of richness and complexity, and the effect is both grand and curious."[13] With great care he explained how the designs were formed by placing small pieces of stone together, resulting in "a species of sculptured mosaic," as he termed it. The facade of the Governor's House at Uxmal also left a deep impression on him; that architectural expanse exhibited no rudeness or barbarity in proportion or design; "on the contrary," he remarked, "the whole wears an air of archietctural symmetry and grandeur."[14] The perfection of that structure still exerts its spell on the visitor to Uxmal, perhaps more so now than in Stephens's day, because it has been restored to its original form.

His visits to the various sites involved more than a tourist's view of buildings and monuments. In addition to selecting the subjects for Catherwood to draw and directing workmen to remove the underbrush so as to provide a clear view for the artist, he diligently recorded the measurements of all the important structures, a difficult task because of the vegetation and accumulated debris. When he reached a new site, he eagerly scrambled over pyramids and buildings, often at the peril of losing his footing on loose stones. At Labná and Uxmal he had natives let him down into chultunes so that he might study their construction and determine their use. In order to gain a view of the countryside and to discover other ruins, he missed no opportunity to scale the highest eminences. On a few occasions he engaged in excavation. At Huehuetenango he uncovered a burial; at Uxmal he boldly cut into the back wall of the Governor's House to determine whether the structure contained secret passages, and behind the same building he probed the middle of a pyramid, exhorting his laborers to dig for the entrance to a room, though in the end he encountered no more than a wall; near Ticul he uncovered another burial that netted a skeleton and a vase. Mindful of Waldeck's insistence that the court of the Monjas at Uxmal was paved with carved turtles, he spent a whole morning digging over the entire area and found not one turtle. Excavation was only incidental to his major purpose, so his failure to unearth striking objects did not hamper his progress.

His thrist for more knowledge of the Maya civilization almost took him into the Petén. When he reached Iturbide, the most inland point of Yucatán to which he had penetrated, he was tempted to strike due south to Lake Flores on the basis of the old, persistent rumor that a group of unconverted Indians, never visited by white men, lived beyond the lake and carried on the habits and practices of the ancient Mayas. Even intelligent persons of Mérida, he reported, held such a belief, and a priest of that city provided him with an itinerary for the trip. But he was unable to learn whether there were ruins in that area, and fearing that the journey might prove fruitless, he dismissed the idea. However, he continued to harbor the thought that a group of natives might still practice the old rites in the Petén. Had he struck south toward Lake Flores, it is difficult to imagine the result. The trip by land would have been far longer than the air distance of two hundred miles, and it is doubtful that he could have penetrated the region successfully, with its sparse population and inhospitable wastes. If he had been able to overcome these difficulties, he would have found one of the richest areas of Maya art and architecture.

His avid quest for information prompted him to search for historical documents that might reveal the early history of the sites he had visited. At Ticul he pored over the tattered archives of the monastery and found no more than an early record of marriages and baptisms; on another occasion he gained access to the title papers of the hacienda of Uxmal and learned that in the late seventeenth century natives still carried on religious rites at that site. At Maní the municipal archives produced more facts about Uxmal and also a curious map made in 1557.

In his feverish search for all kinds of facts about the early people of Yucatán, he had the good fortune to meet Juan Pío Pérez and Estanislao Carrillo, the best informed and the most helpful men he encountered in his whole journey. Both were in their early forties, but they differed entirely in personality and in the kind of knowledge they had acquired.

When Stephens stopped at Peto in March 1842, he had his first meeting with Pío Pérez, then *jefe político* of the department. He came from an old Spanish family in Mérida, where he was educated in elementary schools and at the Colegio de San Ildefonso, but he never prepared for a professional career. His knowledge of the native Maya language qualified him for the post of interpreter to the secretary of the government, and in that position he had to handle the old records. Those documents aroused his interest so much that he began to study and copy them, even after he lost his political appointment. Excessively modest about his research and his attainments, he never gained the scholarly recognition he deserved for preserving and interpreting native records. He imposed upon himself the task of copying several of the books of Chilam Balam; he made a copy of one of them for Stephens, who translated it into English and included it in his *Yucatán.* Equally important was a paper of his that Stephens also published; this essay, which explained the Maya calendar, proved helpful to Americanists for several decades. Pío Pérez likewise compiled a Maya-Spanish dictionary, drawn from older works and from his own research, but it did not appear in print until after his death. The selections of Maní, Ixil, and Kaúa that he copied from the Book of Chilam Balam were called the Codex Pérez; in later years that codex assumed increased significance, because the original manuscripts of two of the three books had disappeared.

After Pérez's death from tuberculosis in 1859, the codex eventually came into the hands of the Escalante family of Mérida and remained there until it was bought by the Mexican government in the twentieth century. Deeply grateful to the diffident Pérez for his generous and valuable help, Stephens deposited the manuscript copies at the New York Historical Society and induced several learned societies in the United States to honor the Yucatecan with membership.

Far different in personality was Fray Estanislao Carrillo, the curate of Ticul. An outgoing, kind, and intelligent Franciscan, he could appreciate the work that Stephens was attempting to accomplish. Carrillo's hobby was studying the antiquities of the country and wandering about Uxmal and other ruins in the nearby area; when the opportunity arrived, he generously shared his knowledge and extended his aid to Stephens. On learning that the North American wanted to excavate a burial, Carrillo selected a small mound, arranged the details, and directed the native laborers in the work of digging. He also told the explorer about Zayil and Kabáh, two significant sites unknown to the visitor. On learning that Stephens would visit Maní, Carrillo wrote ahead to the schoolmaster and paved the way for an examination of the old local records relating to Uxmal Later when it became evident that Stephen's transcription of the Maya documents was faulty because he did not know the language, Carrillo journeyed to Maní himself to make accurate copies.

Carrillo displayed the depth of his character at his first encounter with Stephens at Uxmal. Coming to visit Stephens as a fellow student interested in Maya ruins, the curate found the North American gravely sick with the fever. He insisted on taking him to his quarters in Ticul twenty miles away, and several days later Dr. Cabot, who accompanied Stephens and Catherwood on the second trip, and the native foreman also arrived at Ticul and became patients under his care. It was a touchy task for Carrillo to suggest to the American physician a native prescription for the fever, but he carried it out with consummate tact; his doses of sour orange, cinnamon, and lemon brought the ailing visitors back to good health.

In his books Stephens paid tribute to the Franciscan with this gracious characterization. He was "past forty, tall and thin, with an open, animated, and intelligent countenance, manly, and at the same time mild, and [he] belonged to the once powerful order of Franciscan friars, now reduced in this region to himself and a few companions. After the destruction of the convent at Mérida, and the scattering of the friars, his friends procured for him the necessary papers to enable him to secularize, but he would not abandon the brotherhood in its waning fortunes, and still wore the long blue gown, the cord, and the cross of the Franciscan monks. By the regulation of his order, all the receipts of his curacy belonged to the brotherhood, deducting only forty dollars per month for himself. With this pittance he could live and extend hospitality to strangers. His friends urged him to secularize, engaging to procure for him a better curacy, but he steadfastly refused; he never expected to be rich, and did not wish to be; he had enough for his wants, and did not desire more. He was content with his village and with the people; he was the friend of everybody, and everybody was his friend; in short, for a man not indolent, but, on the contrary, unusually active both in mind and body, he was, without affection or parade, more entirely contented with his lot than any man I ever knew. The quiet and seclusion of his village did not afford sufficient employment for his active mind, but, fortunately for science and for men, and strangely enough as it was considered, he had turned his attention to the antiquities of the country. He could neither go far from home, nor be absent long, but he had visited every place within his reach, and was literally an enthusiast in the pursuit. His friends smiled at this folly, but, in consideration of his many good qualities, excused it."[15]

The things Stephens saw raised continual questions. On viewing the quarry used by the builders of Copán, he wondered how the stones had been transported over the uneven ground and up a mountain two thousand feet high, but he could not discover the answer. Nor could he determine the instruments the ancients used to hew out the blocks of stone and then carve them in skillful design; he was convinced that there was no metal in the region. Though a native accompanying him pointed to stone flints, with the remark that they were the cutting instruments, Stephens mused that the flints appeared to have been shaped by metal. Another question arose as he gazed at the flattened foreheads on the stucco figures at Palenque; they differed so much from the natives he saw every day that he concluded that the earlier inhabitants of Palenque had been "a race of people now lost or unknown"[16] and believed that the hieroglyphs, when deciphered, would tell the whole story. He did not know that the earlier Mayas flattened the heads of their babies for esthetic reasons. Then there was the corbeled arch, evident in all of the ruins he examined. It intrigued him so much that he wrote a short treatise on the subject in the appendix of his *Yucatán*. He concluded that that type of arch did not indicate communication with people of the Old World, who had employed a similar form, because it was the natural mode that early people generally developed. On the question of the source of water at the ancient sites, he found no answer. As he traveled from place to place, the mystery of the supply of water increased, because he assumed that the extensive buildings indicated the existence of a large population.

Common sense dictated the answers to some questions. For example, he dismissed the name "Nunnery" given to the quadrangle at Uxmal by the Indians, suspecting that the early Spanish conquerors had supplied the appellation. Likewise, he rejected Waldeck's designation of the long hooked nose on the masks at Uxmal as an elephant's trunk, "for the elephant was unknown on the Continent of

America."[17] He doubted the accuracy of an early narrative describing the Spanish conquest of Copán, because the site had obviously not been built for defensive purposes.

He was constantly searching for broad associations and similarities among the sites with the hope of forming some conception of the time and nature of that curious civilization. Using Catherwood's report on Quiriguá, he considered the monuments there generally similar to those at Copán. After moving on to Santa Rosa del Quiché, he failed to find carvings or hieroglyphs; thus, "in the absence of such evidence we believed that Copán and Quiriguá were cities of another race and of a much older date."[18] This is one of the few cases in which a dubious line of reasoning led him to a reasonably correct conclusion. On the other hand, he scored an important point when he discovered that the glyphs at Palenque were the same as those at Copán and Quiriguá. Then he went one step further and concluded that, despite the great variety of native dialects in use through that large area in his own day, "there is room for the belief that the whole of this country was once occupied by the same race, speaking the same language, or," he added cautiously, "at least, having the same written characters."[19] Later on, he demonstrated the resemblance of the glyphs at Palenque and Copán to those in the Dresden and Vienna codices. After he received information about the calendar from Pío Pérez, he pointed to the similarity of that system to the one used by the ancient Mexicans and suggested that it indicated the common origin of the two peoples.

He stated his boldest generalizations in unequivocal terms. He was convinced that Maya civilization had flourished at a relatively recent date, not in extreme antiquity as was commonly assumed. By the time he had examined Palenque, he concluded that there was no reason to consider it as early as ancient Egypt. "What we had before our eyes was grand, curious, and remarkable enough," he remarked. "Here were the remains of a cultivated, polished, and peculiar people, who had passed through all the stages incident to the rise and fall of nations; reached their golden age, and perished entirely unknown."[20] Later, on reaching Uxmal, he arrived at another conclusion: ancient Maya civilization was unique, not derived from other cultures. It was not cyclopean; its pyramids were unlike those of Egypt, and its remains did not resemble those of Greece and Rome. These ruins "are different from the works of any other known people, of a new order, and entirely and absolutely anomalous: they stand alone."[21] To emphasize the point, he summed up his opinion in one statement: "It is the spectacle of a people skilled in architecture, sculpture, and drawing, and beyond doubt, other more perishable arts, and possessing the cultivation and refinement attendant upon these, not derived from the Old World, but originating and growing up here, without models or masters, having a distinct, separate, independent existence; like the plants and fruits of the soil, indigenous."[22] And finally, he believed that these ruins had been built by the ancestors of the Mayas who now inhabited the land. He went to considerable length to disprove the arguments that had been advanced against this point—the Indians' lack of traditions about their ancestors, their degeneracy at the present time, and the alleged absence of historical records about them—and concluded that they were the direct descendants of the creators of the ancient civilization.

He refused to be drawn into questions that he could not answer with conviction, such questions as who these ancient people were, where they had come from, and why their civilization had collapsed. But he supported the propositions he did advance with the tight arguments of a lawyer presenting a well-buttressed brief. All told, he displayed remarkable good sense. He managed to establish several simple conclusions, which are generally accepted today. Had his successors built upon his solid foundations, Americanist studies would have gained much of the time that was lost in nebulous speculation.

Although Stephens attempted to probe the mystery that surrounded the early Mayas, he also had an eye on the commercial potential of the ruins he investigated. Unfortunately, all his dreams of financial exploitation came to nothing; in fact, a singular fatality pursued every move he made in this direction. He believed that the American public would welcome the opportunity to see stelae, paintings, carvings, and ceramics from the former culture of Central America. At first, he planned to exhibit such objects in Catherwood's panorama; then he conceived the plan of establishing a Museum of American Antiquities, and after returning from his first season, friends offered to contribute $20,000 to the project.

Not accustomed to doing anything in a small way, he first attempted to buy whole sites, with the aim of transporting all the objects to the United States. For that purpose he purchased the land and ruins of Copán for $50. Next, he negotiated for Quiriguá but was unsuccessful in closing the deal, so he left an offer pending with the owners. His effort to acquire Palenque for $1500 collided with the Mexican law that required a foreigner to marry a native woman before he could buy property. Thus, for one reason or another, his wholesale purchase of sites failed completely, and he had to scale down his ambition to less spectacular acquisitions.

He attempted to secure plaster casts of monuments at Palenque. For this purpose he commissioned Henry Pawling, a former New Yorker then drifting about Mexico, to make the molds. Pawling carried out the job of completing thirty items after Stephens had continued his journey. But just as Pawling was about to pack up and transport the casts, the citizens of Palenque insisted on a payment of $4,000 or $5,000 for the right to carry away the duplicates of their monuments. Pawling left the reproductions in the town. When no money appeared, the disappointed citizens smashed the replicas to pieces.

Stephens finally became content with removing an occasional object for display in the United States. Some natives gave him items, like the three terra cotta figures he received at Santa Cruz del Quiché; and he acquired a few small objects in the several excavations he undertook. As he traveled through Yucatán, he appropriated some sculptured stones and a carved beam from Uxmal, and another carved lintel and two sculptured doorjambs from Kabáh, dispatching them to New York for Catherwood's panorama. At Keuic, however, the mural he took from a building proved too heavy to transport, and he was forced to leave it at the site.

Even these few items, the entire harvest of his extensive travels, were destined to escape him. Shortly after he returned to New York in 1842, Catherwood's panorama burned to the ground and the Maya objects perished in the conflagration. Fortunately, one shipment of stones arrived after the fire. But by then Stephens had given up the idea of a museum, and he presented the objects to his friend John C. Cruger, who sent them to an island he owned a hundred miles up the Hudson, where they were incorporated in a simulated ruin of the type popular with romantically inclined people of that day. It was not until 1918 that the archaeologist Herbert J. Spinden accidentally learned about the stones, and he paid Cruger's daughters $10,000 to transfer the relics to the American Museum of Natural History.

There is no doubt that Stephens profited handsomely from the books he wrote on Central America. They gained immediate popularity and continued to sell over the years. The two-volume *Central America* was reported to have sold 12,000 copies in four months; and profits from the sale abroad went entirely to the author through his arrangement to secure copies for that market at a special price from Harper's, the publisher. Two years later, when he produced the *Yucatán,* he was in a position to stipulate terms. The format and price were to be the same as those of *Central America;* the publishers credited him with $5,700 for the expense of preparing Catherwood's plates; and he received royalties of over 20 percent, an exceptionally high rate. In addition to several editions in the British Isles, the book was translated into six languages. Within a few years the author reputedly received $30,000 from this work.

The success of the volumes owed much to the excellent drawings of Catherwood. The *Central America* contained 78 plates and the *Yucatán* 127, a total of over 200. Although it is impossible to determine the precise part the illustrations played in the appeal of the volumes, two facts cannot be denied. In the first place, Catherwood's work was more than a mere contribution; it was part of an outstanding collaboration. The text and drawings of the volumes are inseparable, fitting together and complementing each other perfectly. The text can stand on its own as travel literature, but the archaeological descriptions are colorless without the illustrations; likewise, the plates, striking and incisive as they are, need the setting and the explanation that Stephens supplied. In the second place, Catherwood gave the reading public its first extensive pictorial view of the ruins. Earlier illustrated books on the subject were too scarce or too expensive to reach the general public. The moderately priced Stephens volumes sold widely in the United States and appeared abroad.

Catherwood suffered continued bad luck in all of his major undertakings. Although the illustrations in the four Stephens volumes are the greatest sustained achievement of his career, he failed to receive proper recognition. His name did not appear on the title page, and the volumes have always been referred to as Stephens's books. The artist was even less fortunate with the drawings he made on Robert Hay's expedition to Egypt; they remained unpublished, filed away in the British Museum. Nor was he happier in his business dealings as an architect; he received no outstanding commissions, and he never gained first place at the hands of judges of competitions.

The successful collaboration of author and artist never occurred again. Stephens dreamed up a plan for another book, an elaborate publication to be called *American Antiquities,* comprising 120 engravings by Catherwood and essays from the standard writers—Humboldt, Prescott, Stephens, and others—for the text. The work was to sell for $100 a copy, and would require 900 subscribers to finance it. Not surprisingly, the project failed for the want of sufficient subscribers. Then Catherwood went ahead and issued his *Views of Ancient Monuments in Central America, Chiapas, and Yucatan,* a folio of twenty-five plates, with a brief text and commentary on each picture. Since it was restricted to an issue of 300 copies, it received limited circulation. In dedicating it to Stephens, the artist indicated his continued high regard for the author. But after the appearance of this work in 1844 neither Catherwood or Stephens returned to the Americanist field except in the minor role of helping to create the American Ethnological Society.

The last years of the two men can be briefly summarized. Catherwood returned to his profession as architect and then moved into the field of engineering. First, he went to British Guiana to superintend the construction of a railroad; three and a half years of frustration, bickering, and tropical disease drove him away with nothing to show for the time spent and the hardships endured. Next, he tried working for Stephens in Panama, again on a railroad project, but malaria laid him low, and his friend sent him to California to recuperate. Arriving there in the midst of the boom created by the gold rush, he turned to building wharves and warehouses, and he became a consulting engineer for a local railroad. After a sojourn in England, he was returning to the United States in 1854 on the *Artic* when another vessel plunged into it at sea, and he went down with many of the passengers.

Stephens continued to try to make his fortune. He became deeply involved in the Ocean Steam Navigation Company and made a trip to Europe to establish service at Bremen. He also had an interest in the Hudson River Railroad. But Latin America beckoned once more, and he joined William H. Aspinwall, controller of the Pacific Mail Steamship Company, and Henry Chauncey, a capitalist interested in mining and railroads, in forming the Panama Railroad Company. Stephens secured the necessary concession from New Granada, and proceeded to Panama to supervise construction of the line. Miles of track were laid, but disease and death among the workers exacted a frightful human cost. Stephens, suffering more and more from malaria, was found unconscious one day and was immediately put on a boat for New York. Back at his home at 13 Leroy Place, he lingered through the summer, and he died in October 1852.[23]

The popularity of the Stephens's books produced an amazing sequel, for which the famous explorer was in no way responsible. A pamphlet appeared in 1850 in New York City with the title *Memoir of an Eventful Expedition in Central America; Resulting in the Discovery of the Idolatrous City of Iximaya, in an unexplored region: and the possession of two Remarkable Aztec Children, Descendants and Specimens of the Sacerdotal Cast, (now nearly extinct) of the Ancient Aztec Founders of the Ruined Temples of that Country, Described by John L. Stevens, Esq., and other Travellers. Translated from the Spanish of Pedro Velasquez, of San Salvador*. It enjoyed some popularity. Three different firms issued editions in New York in 1850, it appeared in London a few years later, and it was translated into French and published in Amsterdam and Paris.

After quoting Stephens on rumors of the existence of a hidden city of living Mayas who continued to practice the ancient rites, the editor explained how two men, Mr. Huertis, a wealthy American of Spanish-Cuban parentage, and Mr. Hammond, a Canadian civil engineer, determined to find and examine the intriguing place. They arrived at Belize in the fall of 1848 and proceeded to Copán, where they encountered Pedro Velásquez and invited him to join them. Velásquez, who knew the geography and native languages of the area, kept a journal that provided the information for the whole story. Finally, they discovered the city of Iximaya, located somewhere in the Mexican panhandle that cuts into Guatemala between the Petén and Alta Verapaz. The city of eighty-five thousand people, who spoke a Maya dialect, extended over twelve square miles and was protected by a wall sixty feet high. Its avenues were lined with gigantic satutes of the ancient kings of Assyria and their Aztec descendants!

The three white men and their attendants gained entrance to Iximaya only after outwitting the defenders some miles from the city. The native horsemen, patrolling the environs to keep strangers at a distance wore bright blue and yellow tunics, carried long metal-tipped spears, and used packs of fierce bloodhounds. After terrorizing these soldiers with modern firearms, Hammond, Huertis, and Velásquez defeated them but treated them honorably and insisted on being taken into the city. There they enjoyed the freedom of the place. Hammond, who had been wounded in battle, was cared for; Huertis studied the buildings; and Velásquez gradually interested Vaalpeor, a superior young native, in the outside world and induced him to engage in a plan to escape. In carrying out the project to get away, Vaalpeor brought with him two children, of whom he was guardian; they were the only survivors of an ancient, venerated priestly class, the Kaanas.

The two children gained modest public notice when they were exhibited in New York City in the early 1850s. An anonymous journalist described them as "scarcely larger than the fabled gentlemen of Lilliput (though one is twelve or thirteen and the other eighteen years of age), of just and even elegant proportions, of physiognomies striking and peculiar, but not different in intellect or refinement." As for the Velsquez account of the background of the children, the writer was noncommittal, remarking that "of the credulity of this account we express no opinion." though he believed that "the 'Aztec Children' have the phrenological and general appearance of the ancient Mexican sculptures."[24]

The dwarfs also attracted the attention of Horace Greeley, the colorful editor of the *New York Tribune,* who had ideas on everything around the city. He went to see the exhibit and handed down his opinion. "These children are simply abridgements or pocket editions of Humanity—bright-eyed, delicate-featured, olive-complexioned little elves, with dark, straight glossy hair, well proportioned heads, and animated, pleasing countenances."[25] Though he could not determine whether the Velásquez record was true or false, he was certain that the children were from Central America.

The whole affair was one of P. T. Barnum's hoaxes. It is significant that the great showman considered popular interest in Central American antiquities sufficiently widespread to warrant exhibiting the two children and having the pamphlet published to advertise his latest feature. The pamphlet revealed certain aspects of popular knowledge of the day. It did not distinguish between Aztec and Maya culture. Also, it pictured the people of Iximaya as descendants of ancient Assyrians and their architecture as Egyptian, all despite Stephens's insistence that Maya culture was indigenous. The writer of the pamphlet had some knowledge of the geography of western Guatemala, but the location of Iximaya was a geographical puzzle, as perhaps it was intended to be. The attempt to reconstruct the costumes of the people and the buildings of the city suggests to the modern reader the artificial glamor of a Hollywood scenario.

In England, Charles Dickens took note of the incident in a weekly magazine he edited. After summarizing the Velásquez tale, he observed that "in a country which boasts of a Barnum" the reader should consider the story and the children "with a caution."[26] If the exhibition came to England, Dickens hoped that the scientific societies would require some accounting of its veracity. Almost two years later, Jean Frédéric Waldeck, then living in London, came upon Dickens's article. He was so intrigued with the hoax that he wrote a lengthy letter to the distinguished editor, enumerating all the reasons why the story and the children could not be genuine.

There is no evidence that the hoax had any adverse effect on Stephens's reputation. Barnum and Stephens appealed to different audiences. The general public expected the great showman to fool them, and paid money to enjoy the experience. Serious readers, on the other hand, knew that they could rely on the veracity of Stephens and the accuracy of Catherwood.

Even today the collaboration of Stephens and Catherwood excels in information, clear illustrations, charming narrative, and perceptive comments—traits that make these men outstanding among the pioneers in Maya archaeology.

6

Charles Étienne Brasseur de Bourbourg

An American student by the name of Herbert B. Adams spent some time in Rome in December 1873, trying to decide where to begin his graduate study. Living at the Hotel della Minerva, he encountered a number of Catholic ecclesiastics, also guests at the hotel. He struck up an acquaintance with an English priest, who "talked Roman Christianity by the hour," and at one point introduced him to another guest, the Abbé Brasseur de Bourbourg, an ascetic-looking, bespectacled French cleric, who had the appearance of a scholar.

Adams was completely captivated by the abbé. "I found him the most interesting man I had ever met, for up to that time I had never encountered a true cosmopolitan." The conversation quickly revealed an unusual accomplishment. "The Abbé told me that he spoke twelve different languages and had a reading acquaintance with more than twenty. Judging from his perfect command of English, German and Italian, I thought him a master of tongues. I heard him converse with persons of different nationality and apparently with as much ease and facility of expression as when he talked English with me."

Brasseur frankly explained his relations with the church and with scholarship. "He talked a great deal about his travels and archaeological studies in Mexico and Central America. The point which impressed me most was that, in his opinion, many of the truths of modern science had been anticipated by the learning of those early peoples. He also impressed me with the fact that he never should have been able to obtain access to the rare collections of manuscripts and antiquities in Spanish America unless he had been a good Catholic. He said this with a kind of merry twinkle in his eye, which made me think he was something of a diplomatist and man of the world as well as a man of science and religion. He tried to persuade me to stay in Rome to study history, art and archaeology. He said one could have as much intellectual liberty in Italy as in Germany. It was only necessary, he thought, to have one's feet upon the rock of the historic church; one could then be as liberal and progressive as he pleased; the Church had room enough for scholars and scientific men; it was not necessary for a man educated at a Catholic institution in Rome to become a priest, or to devote himself to ecclesiastical interests. 'For example,' he remarked, 'I am an Abbé in the Church but my ecclesiastical duties have always rested very lightly upon me.' This too he said with a pleasant and rather amused expression."

Adams could not resist the engaging cleric. "You may imagine the personal influence which this most fascinating, scholarly Abbé exerted upon me, a young and inexperienced Puritan, fresh from Massachusetts and Amherst College," he confessed. "He was a strikingly handsome man, with a good head, keen eyes, a very intelligent and attractive face, tall stature and courtly manners. He seemed to me a kind of scientific Talleyrand. . . . Every day after my return from walks in and about Rome he would renew his charming conversation and tell me of his own travels in America. He never failed to lead the conversation back to Rome and the historic attractions of the eternal city. He gave me many valuable suggestions concerning objects of historic interest and places that I ought to visit. Sometimes we breakfasted together and I started out upon my morning rambles with words of helpful direction from the learned Abbé."[1]

Brasseur had been slow in developing an interest in Americanist studies. Born in 1814 in the town of Bourbourg in northern France, seven miles from Dunkirk, he early encountered French, Flemish, and English speech, a promising beginning for multilingual training. As a child he enjoyed reading the histories of Egypt, India, and Persia, and at the age of fifteen he first learned of America in the books of Antonio de Solís, Garcilaso de la Vega, and Count Carli, which described the pre-Hispanic civilizations of the New World. Three years later he came upon a newspaper report of the discovery of a tomb in Brazil with Macedonian relics and Greek inscriptions. And soon he was pursuing Antonio del Río's report on Palenque. "Today I cannot describe the astonishment mixed with pleasure that this reading caused me; it decided my archaeological vocation for the future," he remarked twenty-five years later.[2]

But as a youth in Bourbourg he had no opportunity to satisfy his curiosity. Life in the village was restricted, there were few maps, and no way to secure books on America. "I was far from hoping that my dreams and aspirations might be realized some day. My ambition was really limited only to the desire of seeing the capital, visiting its museums and libraries." ". . . I contented myself with travels in books, going to Switzerland and Italy in imagination, sometimes even America."[3]

Although the vision of Indians had been planted in his imagination, a decade passed before he could cultivate his youthful interest. In the interim, education and work filled his days. If he attended the Collége de St. Omer, as is sometimes stated, he failed to explain how long he stayed or its influence on his education. More important was his stint at journalism. By his early twenties he was in Paris, writing for various publications, among them *Le Temps* and *Le Monde*. He discovered that he could turn out fast, readable copy, and he was soon producing potboilers to supplement his income. Those romantic novels and moral tales bore the titles of *Les Epreuves de la Fortune et de l'adversité, Les Pêcheurs de la côte, Sélim ou le Pacha de*

Salonique, l'Exilé de Tadmor, and so forth. At least nine of these productions are credited to his pen.

After some five years as a journalist and romantic novelist in Paris, he gave up writing for a more serious profession. When family circumstances took him to Ghent, he enrolled in the seminary there for courses in philosophy and religion. The lectures in the classroom and a job in the library brought about a profound change in his outlook. When he was employed to reorganize the library, he learned to know and appreciate serious books. Although he left before completing the task, he was influenced by it to follow intellectual pursuits.

He was attracted increasingly to the church, not an unwise choice for a man of his inclinations. Already he had written several books on religious themes, like *le Martyr de la Croix* and *Saint Pierre de Rome et le Vatican,* and in 1843 he published *Jérusalem, tableau de l'histoire des vicissitudes de cette ville* under the pseudonym of E. C. de Ravensburg. He had been able to indulge a youthful desire to see other countries when he traveled through Germany, Switzerland, the Tyrol, and Sicily. Then he settled down in Rome to complete his training for the priesthood. At La Sapienza and the Roman College he had the good fortune to have classes under Passaglia and Perrone, well-known Catholic theologians, and Secchi and Brescani, reputable archaeologists of that time. In addition to this stimulation, he enjoyed friendships and exchanges of ideas with Cardinals Mai and Mezzofanti, both linguists and former directors of the Vatican Library. All told, Brasseur was one of the best prepared persons to enter Americanist studies in the nineteenth century.

On completing his formal training, he took orders in the church at the age of thirty-one and embarked on a career ostensibly religious but soon to turn largely into secular channels. After his ordination, he set out for North America, carrying letters for the Sacred College of the Propaganda, and settled in Quebec in 1845. There he became professor of church history in the seminary, later the University of Quebec, published a biography of the first bishop of that city, and examined the ecclesiastical archives for data for another volume on the church in Canada. After less than a year in Quebec, he left in the middle of 1846 for a visit to Boston. There he served as honorary vicar-general, but devoted much time to his interest in America, which he now had the opportunity to cultivate. He perfected his knowledge of English and read Prescott's *Conquest of Mexico,* a work which had appeared only three years earlier and was influential in acquainting the public with the Aztecs of Mexico. The volume, he remarked later, persuaded him that his scientific calling was in the Americanist field. Incidentally, the only complaint he ever uttered about his stay in Boston was against the dreariness of the long puritan Sabbath, when he could not even secure a carriage to visit a fellow priest in the neighborhood.

On reaching the age of thirty-two, he began diligent preparation for a career in Middle American studies. He returned to Rome at the end of 1846, and there he pondered over the Kingsborough volumes and similar books in the Vatican Library, and Cardinal Franzoni opened the library of the Propaganda to him, where the young scholar found the Codex Borgia the major attraction. After two winters in Rome, political upheavals drove him to France, and soon he was arranging another trip to America.

This time he decided to go to Mexico to study Indian history on the ancient soil of Anáhuac. On the way he indulged his passion for traveling by landing in New York and wandering westward. He sailed down the Ohio and the Mississippi, eagerly scanning the young cities on those highways of commerce. At New Orleans he embarked for Veracruz, and during the voyage he struck up an acquaintance with a fellow passenger, M. Le Vasseur, a French diplomat on the way to his new assignment in Mexico. The two men got along splendidly. At Veracruz, Le Vasseur invited the

1. Castañeda's rendition of the Palace and tower at Palenque. *Antiquités Mexicaines.*

2. Tablet of the Cross, Palenque. Almendáriz drawing, engraved by J. F. Waldeck. Del Rio, *Description of the Ruins of an Ancient City.*

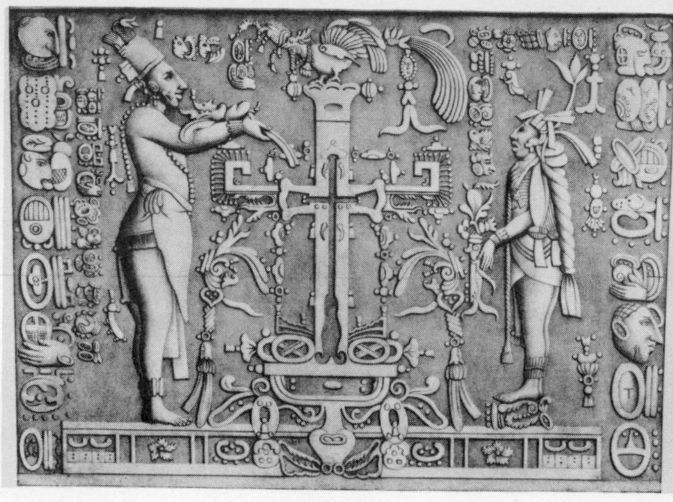

3. Castañeda's Tablet of the Cross, Palenque. *Antiquités* Mexicaines.

4. Castañeda's rendition of a stucco plaque, Palenque; Dupaix's third expedition. *Antiquités Mexicaines.*

5. Castañeda's rendition of the Beau Relief, Palenque; Dupaix's third expedition. *Antiquités Mexicaines.*

6. Colonel Juan Galindo. By permission of *Estudios de Cultura Maya,* Mexico.

7. One of the numerous stelae in the Ceremonial Area, Copán. Author photo.

8. Jean Frédéric Waldeck; sketch in Winsor, *Narrative and Critical History of America.*

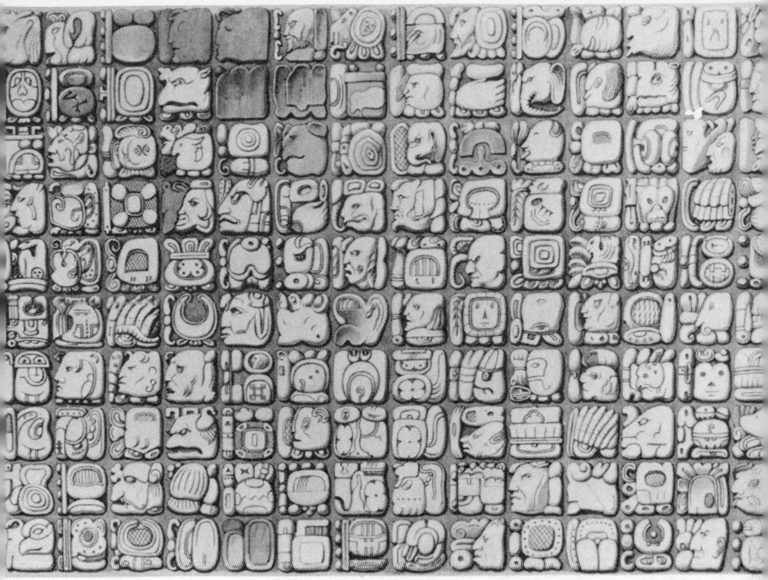

9. Waldeck's drawing of hieroglyphs. Note elephant heads: 2d row, 5th figure from right and 3d row, 7th figure from right. *Recherches sur les Ruines de Palenque.*

10. Hieroglyphs carved in stone, Copán. Details can be seen only in the glyphs in the top row; artists' line drawings of glyphs remain more satisfactory than photographs. Author photo.

11. Waldeck drawing, section of the Serpent Panel, Nunnery, Uxmal. *Voyage pittoresque.*

12. Waldeck drawing of a design in court of the Nunnery, Uxmal. *Voyage pittoresque.*

13. Waldeck's imaginative reconstruction of the Pyramid of the Dwarf, Uxmal. Note the four large, carved human figures flanking the entrance. Later investigators found no basis for this restoration. *Voyage pittoresque.*

14. Waldeck's drawing of one of the four figures he said adorned the entrance to the temple on the Pyramid by the Dwarf. Later archaeologists never found evidence of this figure. *Voyage pittoresque.*

15. Waldeck's view of the Temple of the Cross, Palenque, with his living quarters at the foot of the mound. *Monuments Anciens du Mexique.*

16. Portrait of John L. Stephens. From *Maya Explorer: John Lloyd Stephens and the Lost Cities of Central America and Yucatan,* by Victor Wolfgang von Hagen. Copyright 1947 by the University of Oklahoma Press.

17. Tablet of the Sun, Palenque, drawn by Catherwood. Stephens, *Incidents of Travel in Central America.* Compare earlier artists' renditions of tablets with hieroglyphs (e.g. figs. 2 & 3).

18. Nunnery, Annex. Chichén Itzá. Catherwood drawing. From *Maya Explorer: John Lloyd Stephens and the Lost Cities of Central America Yucatán,* by Victor Wolfgang von Hagen. Copyright 1947 by the University of Oklahoma Press.

19. Nunnery (left) and Temple of the Dwarf, Uxmal. Catherwood drawing. Stephens, *Incidents*.

20. Temple of the Dwarf, Uxmal. Author photo.

21. Charles Etienne Brasseur de Bourbourg. Portrait from *Lost Tribes and Sunken Continents,* by Robert Wauchope. Copyright 1962 by the University of Chicago Press.

22. Augustus Le Plongeon. From *Queen Móo and the Egyptian Sphinx.*

23. Alice Le Plongeon. From *Queen Móo and the Egyptian Sphinx.*

24. Temple of the Jaquars. Chichén Itzá. Le Plongeon's imaginative reconstruction. He called it Memorial Hall. From Le Plongeon, "Queen Móo's Talisman."

25. The Chacmool unearthed by Augustus Le Plongeon. Le Plongeon, *Monuments of Mayach.*

26. Edward H. Thompson, 1924. Photo courtesy J. O. Kilmartin.

27. Sacred Cenote, Chichén Itzá. The surface of the water appears at the bottom of the picture. Author photo.

28. Chichán-Chob, or the Red House, Chichén Itzá. This Classic Maya building bears decorations only in the two roof combs, one of which is visible. This is the way the early explorers saw the building, shrouded of course in a growth of trees and bushes. Since this photograph was taken, the Red House has been restored. Photo, *Pan American Union Bulletin,* 1911.

20. House of the Turtles, Uxmal. Restored. Three of the carved turtles appear near the top of the facade. The structure is noteworthy for its simplicity and proportion. Le Plongeon believed that it had been the private residence of the native ruler. Author photo.

30. Profile of two buildings, Nunnery, Uxmal. Waldeck and Le Plongeon contended that the decorations on the building to the left represented elephant heads. Today these forms are accepted as masks of the long-nosed rain god Chac. Author photo.

31. Death's heads, Copán. Author photo.

32. Ik God, Reviewing Stand, Copán. Restoration. Author photo.

33. Ball Court, Copán. Spectators' galleries appear in center and upper right; a portion of the third gallery can be seen in lower center. Reconstructed. Author photo.

abbé to accompany him on the overland journey from the humid coast up the mountains to the pleasant climate of the capital. As soon as the minister assumed his official duties, he appointed Brasseur almoner of the French embassy to help him meet the right people.

Now a serious and determined scholar, he sought the basic firsthand sources on the ancient inhabitants of Middle America. First, he went to the National Museum, carefully hiding his feelings about the paltry collection of objects housed there, and met the director, Rafael Isidore Gondra, who placed in his hands a rough draft of the first volume of Ordóñez's history. The manuscript included Ximénez's translation of a Quiché document, later known as the *Popul Vuh,* which Brasseur insisted he had been the first to discover. He also met Manuel Larrainzar, state senator from Chiapas and later minister to Rome, who presented him with a copy of Juarro's published history of Guatemala, even then a scarce item, and also some notes on Chiapas. José Maria de Lacuna, a cabinet minister, opened the viceregal archives, where Brasseur read the history of the Aztecs by Ixtlilxóchitl, a native who had used the official pre-Hispanic documents. Father Arriaga made the library of the university available, and José María Andrada offered his excellent private library for Brasseur's perusal.

For two years he immersed himself in the literature of ancient Mexico. Then he traveled by horseback through the central part of the country through Tula, Querétaro, and Guanajuato to the Pacific Coast, and took a four months' trip to San Francisco, California. All the time he was collecting books, manuscripts, and artifacts. He settled down in Mexico City to learn Nahuatl, the language of the Aztecs, and studied it under Faustino Chimalpopoca Galícia, descendant of a brother of Montezuma and then professor of law at the Colegio de San Gregorio. It was in honor of him that Brasseur named the valuable manuscript the *Codex Chimalpopoca,* known today as the *Anales de Cuauhtitlán.*

Before leaving Mexico, he published in French and Spanish his first book on American antiquities, *Lettres pour servir d'introduction à l'histoire primitive des nations civilisées de l'América septentrionale*. In the brief work he described two manuscripts by Ordóñez, as well as the Chimalpopoca and Gondra codices, and outlined the history of the Indians. Although the book appears rather superficial today, it should be noted that the author himself considered it a rapid and incomplete sketch. He later acknowledged that its appearance had the advantage of bringing him to the attention of two important persons. One was E. G. Squier of the United States, who had acquired a reputation for excellent archaeological work in the Ohio region and was already extending his research to Central America.[4] The other was J. M. A. Aubin, whom he met on his return to France at the end of the year through the kindness of Edme Jomard, the Egyptologist.

Brasseur had good reason to be grateful for the introduction to Aubin. In 1830 Aubin had been sent to Mexico on a scientific mission, but trouble with his instruments diverted him to collecting the manuscripts, now scattered, that Boturini had possessed. After a search of nineteen years in America and Europe, Aubin assembled one of the best private libraries on Middle American studies. He did little to exploit the rare works and kept all scholars at arm's length except Brasseur, who made full use of the collection from 1851 to 1854. Later on, the abbé joined several other scholars in founding the Société des Américanistes for the purpose of publishing Aubin's manuscripts.

In the meantime Brasseur continued his researches in Paris and in the Vatican Library in Rome, and wrote industriously on the history of pre-Columbian Mexico and Central America. When he realized that he lacked important materials, he planned another trip to America in 1854. At that moment his personal finances were so desperately low that he took time off from his studies to turn out some more potboilers, which he delicately described as works of "lesser importance," to replenish his purse.

His third visit, extending from 1854 to 1857, was one of the most fruitful of his career. He stopped off in New York and renewed his acquaintance with Squier, who strongly urged him to pursue his research. In Washington he encountered Buckingham Smith, an old friend and formerly the secretary of legation in Mexico, who introduced him to Henry R. Schoolcraft, well known as a scholar of North American Indians, and Peter Force, a devoted collector of Americana. Force loaned him manuscript copies of Las Casas and Durán, later standard histories, which had not yet appeared in print. On returning to New York, Brasseur ran short of funds once more and had to sell his portable missionary chapel and a vocabulary of the Maya language.

He left New York in the fall of 1854 to begin new investigations in Central America, though his plans and objectives appear to have been uncertain. Despite his scholarly inclination, he had a romantic affection for unusual scenery, which he indulged in his travels through Central America. On landing at Greytown, Nicaragua, he journeyed west and north by easy stages. Jogging along on a mule toward Lake Nicaragua, he admired the beauty of the Río San Juan and the "magnificent vegetation, an image of perpetual springtime."[5] Although the path bore the name of Camino Real, it was little more than "bearings scarcely traced in the forest." Everywhere, however, "the passage is full of charm: the aspects of nature are so great and varied, the woods, the rocks, the roaring waters, the volcanoes. . . . One proceeds without knowing where he is going, but the unknown itself is an additional attraction for the visitor."[6] In his published version of this trip he omitted unpleasant experiences. When he wrote to Squier, however, he mentioned the "sad things on account of the civil war still raging in these fine regions. The only incident I have to relate is that I have been a prisoner for a few days in the hands of a party belonging to the late Chamorro."[7] Passing by Lake Nicaragua and Lake Managua, he arrived at León, where he had a letter of introduction to Dr. Livingston, the former U.S. Consul, who entertained him for several weeks. From the towers of the cathedral, Brasseur surveyed the surrounding plain, "one of the richest and most beautiful in the world."[8] After a leisurely two months in Nicaragua, he pushed on to San Salvador and looked with amazement on the destruction of that city wrought by an earthquake the previous year. And on every side he saw volcanoes, some topped with white vapor by day and with fire by night.

As he traveled through these countries, he also gave attention to the Indians and their customs, and bridled at the remains of paganism. He deplored, of course, the forced conversions by the Spanish conquerors, but he could not condone the confusion of Christian and pagan practices. He declared that the natives were "sworn enemies of the Christian faith. They kneel before crosses and altars, but under these altars and behind these crosses they place idols to those to whom they render true homage."[9] On one occasion curiosity led him to investigate a secret rite. "In Xlopango they no longer sacrifice the four youths to the Water Goddess, but it is said generally that each year at the same time an unbaptized child is offered. I do not know if they cast it into the water, but it is certain that they place it at the entrance of a grotto on the lake; and that the Goddess, emerging from the waves in the figure of a beautiful woman, lifts it and carries it to the depths of the abyss. With curiosity to observe this fact, I went down to the lake shore. I took a canoe that was fastened to the trunk of a tree, and two Indians led me. I spoke to them of the traditions of the country, having them drink a glass of aguardiente. They smiled, looking at me and shaking their head, because it is rare that they respond immediately and openly to this kind of question. Firm in my object, I asked them if it were true that a victim had been offered a year before to the Mother-serpent. Why not, they answered, since it is the only way to obtain harvests, and the last one had been so good! The preceding year we were hungry, and the cause had been despising the Lady of the Lake. I thought then that they would conduct me to the grotto, but they refused with various protests."[10] He was equally unsuccessful in gathering data on antiquities in Nicaragua and San Salvador, and hoped for better results at his next stop.

Guatemala more than satisfied his expectations. The historical and linguistic riches he found there raised his spirits to a new pitch of excitement, as he made one discovery after another, and he remained in the country for two years. Much of his success came from the generous cooperation of scholars in the capital city. Mariano Padilla, physician, historian, and owner of a fine library, "became my first and almost only cicerone for the antiquities of his country."[11] Brasseur also associated with Juan Gavarette, an antiquarian and copyist of manuscripts, who had charge of the public archives.[12] Dr. Barrios, dean of the cathedral, placed a copy of Flores' Cakchiquel grammar in his hands. The resident archbishop, Francisco García Paláez, a historian in his own right, had published several volumes on the pre-Columbian history of the nation a few years earlier.

Paláez befriended him in an unusual manner. Brasseur was seeking some kind of employment, but during his visits to the United States, Nicaragua, and El Salvador he had had no success,[13] despite the letters of introduction he had presented along the way. Paláez appreciated the abbé's ability and the significance of his work, and generously appointed him curé of Rabinal, sixty-five miles north of the capital, in the heart of the Indian country, where he could learn the Quiché language.

As Brasseur journeyed to Rabinal, once more he was overwhelmed by the grandeur of the scenery. He crossed the Montagua and ascended the steep hills of El Chol. The land "rises without interruption among rocks and great groves of pines," he wrote, "until reaching the summit of the mountains. . . . I cannot explain to you the grandeur of the spectacle which from those towering heights is offered to the sight of the traveler. . . . Like the eagle hovering in space, I towered above all the volcanoes in Guatemala. . . ."[14] He took a few more steps and then gazed down on "a magnificent valley with its banana and sugar cane plantations, and its great orange trees," "surrounded entirely by a circle of high mountains, crowned with live oaks and pines. In the center appears a small village with its great church and Moorish cupola. It is Rabinal. . . ."[15]

He spent over a year in that town of seven thousand natives, direct descendants of the inhabitants of the ancient Quiché kingdom. "The place appears picturesque," he explained, "but there is in it something, I know not what, that disposes one to absentmindedness and contemplation. It is because everything here invites man and the historian to meditate on the great past and the vanity of earthly glories. Will it surprise you that this happens in this solitude? Well, I experienced it after reaching Rabinal and its surroundings."[16]

Brasseur, however, fought off reverie and lassitude. After only a few days he set out to investigate the remains of two ancient cities in the neighborhood. Tzak Pokoma perched a thousand feet above the level of the plain. At first he encountered only a few foundations jutting several feet above the ground, but further up the mountain he came upon a palace, an oratory, and walls, and then plazas and buildings; at the top he found a structure 240 feet long and a plaza 400 feet square. He surmised that the place must have housed a population three times that of Guatemala City. "I cannot exaggerate my admiration on seeing so many ruins collected in the same place, so many palaces and temples standing for the most part, and of which no other traveler ever spoke; and I was the more amazed as all assured me that as for Rabinal there was no kind of Indian ruins."[17] A week later, again climbing mountains, he visited Cakyú and found the ruins of a *ciudadela,* a plaza, and a double palace with stairs, but the structures were more ruined than those of Tzak Pokoma. He also visited Mumez, Cawinal, Xécock, and Nimpokam.

Archaeological ruins were of small importance to the abbé compared with what he could learn of the language and customs of the natives for the light they might throw on pre-Columbian culture. In Guatemala City he had acquired two manuscripts. The *Popul Vuh,* with Ximénez's translation, was loaned to him by Padilla, and Gavarette gave him a copy of the *Memorial of Tecpán-Atitlán,* later known as the *Annals of the Cakchiquels.* While studying Quiché at Rabinal, with the aid of dictionaries, grammars, and conversation with the natives, he undertook to translate into French the *Popul Vuh,* the most important historical document of the former Quiché kingdom of Guatemala. He explained how he gained the confidence of the natives by asking about their history and in response heard stories of King Qikab, the Carbuncle of the Black Mountain, the Quiché princes, and the war with the Pokomams.

These conversations led to a discovery he found as exciting as the manuscripts he was working with. Writing from Rabinal in August 1855, he explained the incident: "There is no physician here. Some six weeks ago I gave to one of them [the natives] a remedy that cured him of a pretty severe illness. From gratitude he came afterwards to me and told me that he was the lineal descendant of some great family; that by the orders of his fathers he had learned by memory the whole of one of their *bayles,* or dramatic dances. . . . Knowing that I have vainly asked for that bayle from the other Indians, he proposed to me that I should write it under his dictation. I accepted in spite of the difficulty, for it was to be said in the quiche dialect of Rabinal. But *improbus labor omnia vincit,*[18] after twelve days of the most arduous dictation I ever did, even when I was at school, I got the whole of the *bayle;* with the aid of my grammars and dictionary, I corrected the orthography, and now I can boast of possessing the only aboriginal American drama, that exists in the world. . . . The scene is here in

Rabinal and the personages are the first heroes of the quiche and Rabinal nations, the time being about the beginning, I suppose, of the 12th century. . . ."[19] As usual, he was overcome by the find and made extravagant claims before investigating the subject. Later he published the work as the *Rabinal-Achí*. In the meantime he continued writing his comprehensive history of the ancient tribes of Middle America. The busy months in Rabinal he later considered the most agreeable period he spent in Central America.

When Brasseur returned to Guatemala City, Archbishop Paláez sent him to San Sacatapéquez, a dozen miles northwest of the capital, for a few months to learn Cakchiquel and to translate the Memorial of Tecpán-Atitlán. Then for eight weeks he lived at Escuintla, southwest of the capital, to acquire knowledge of a native language of Nahuatl origin. His health began to suffer, and he left Guatemala for Europe in January 1857.

He was now ready to publish his researches of the past decade. In Paris, he immediately called on Aubin to profit again from the use of his remarkable collection. By June he had completed the introduction to his history; the first volume went to press, and at intervals during the next two years the four volumes appeared with the title *Histoire des nations civilisées du Mexique et de l'Amérique central*. He unfolded the story of the different native civilizations, drawn from Spanish sources and Indian accounts, and presented it in elaborate detail, totaling 2,600 pages. It was the most comprehensive treatment of the subject to date. In addition to the usual political history, he discussed cultural achievements and concluded with the conquest of Mexico. The wealth of information made it the standard reference work for years to come, despite some curious interpretations that were scattered through its pages.

The publication immediately placed Brasseur among the top Americanist scholars. All doors were open to him; in an unusual gesture Spain invited him to make use of its archives, and France gave direct aid to its distinguished citizen. If the history represented the culmination of ten years of devoted, zealous research, ultimately it was only a harbinger of his most productive period.

In the following years he continued research and travel under the auspices of the French Ministry of Public Education. In 1859 and 1860 he toured the southern United States, explored the Isthmus of Tehuantepec and Chiapas, and finally moved over into Guatemala, where he visited the sites of Zacaléu, Iximché, and Utatlán.

Having collected a harvest of documents in Mexico and Guatemala in his earlier travels, he prepared some of those works for publication as fast as his schedule would allow. In 1861 he issued the *Popul Vuh,* the sacred book of the Quichés. Unfortunately, he could not claim priority in making this document known to the world, because Karl Scherzer, a German archaeologist who had arrived in Guatemala City a year before Brasseur, used the manuscript in the library of the University of San Carlos, and published part of the Quiché text and Ximénez's Spanish translation in Vienna in 1857.

Brasseur's publication of the *Popul Vuh* in the original Quiché and in a French translation helped to stimulate additional interest in pre-Columbian America. The collection of fascinating myths, history, customs, and attitudes of the Indian mind is one of the great primitive epics of the world. Brasseur criticized Ximénez's translation for omissions, for literal renditions which sometimes did not make sense, and for a clerical prejudice, though he was fair enough to admit that he found Ximénez's version helpful. In turn, Adrián Recinos, a twentieth century authority on the subject, found the abbé's version not without blemishes. He claimed that Brasseur had attributed to the Indian mind some unrealistically sophisticated concepts, and that he had failed to capture the primitive simplicity of the original in his French translation. In fact, one critic asserts that Ximénez knew Indian psychology better than Brasseur did.

In the following year his Quiché grammar appeared. He

compiled it from various other grammars, presented it in Spanish and French, and for good measure included a vocabulary and the *Rabinal-Achí,* the Indian drama he had taken down verbatim. A striking feature of the book is the fulsome dedication to Archbishop Paláez, which can only be ascribed to Brasseur's deep gratitude for the ecclesiastic's help at a critical time.

In the following year he made the most significant discovery of his career by finding Bishop Landa's *Relación de las cosas de Yucatán* in the Academy of History at Madrid. The manuscript, a copy of the original, had been used by a few early Spanish historians of Yucatán, but then it disappeared for several centuries. From any point of view, its recovery was an outstanding addition to Americanist literature, and it became the single greatest source of information about the ancient Maya culture of Yucatán. Fully aware of its importance, Brasseur immediately published in in Spanish and French. He divided the text into chapters and provided headings, an editorial arrangement so helpful that it was retained in most of the later editions.

These achievements added to Brasseur's stature as an authority on Middle American studies. He taught a course on American archaeology at the Sorbonne in 1864. A more important honor came in September of that year, when he was appointed to the official French commission to study the antiquities of Mexico. This time he went to Yucatán, accompanied by Henri Bourgeois as photographer, to examine and make a photographic record of the ruins. Although Brasseur produced a number of articles during the year, he failed to secure the pictures because of the illness of Bourgeois. Maximilian thought so highly of Brasseur that he offered him the directorship of education and museums in his government, an appointment Brasseur wisely refused. Although the abbé had not yet visited Palenque, his reputation as an Americanist was so well established that he was chosen to write the text to accompany Waldeck's engravings, published by the French government in 1866.

Brasseur made his last significant discovery after returning to Europe. In Madrid he became acquainted with Juan de Tro y Ortolano, a descendant of Fernando Cortés and professor of paleography at the university. He showed the abbé a document that had long been in the family, a Maya book of divination and new year's ceremonies. It was thereafter known as the Troano. Brasseur had Henri Bourgeois, his artist, copy the manuscript, which required two and a half years. In preparing the document for publication, Brasseur added a discourse on the Maya language and a Yucatec grammar and vocabulary. Napoleon III ordered the work printed in two sumptuous volumes. A few years later another document, also discovered in Spain, was given the name of the Codex Cortez; Léon Rosny recognized it as part of the Troano, and the joint work was thereafter called the Codex Tro-Cortesianus.

Brasseur's last assignment was a project which should have utilized his broad knowledge to great advantage. He was commissioned to compile a catalogue of all documents on American antiquities in Spain and South America. Unfortunately, he never made much headway on the task, because unsettled conditions prevented him from working in Spain, and his health continued to decline. He made a trip to Rome in December 1873, perhaps as an unconscious final tribute to the city he loved and to the church which had given him the opportunity to achieve fame. Here Herbert Adams, the American student, met him and succumbed to his kindly and generous personality. Adams failed, however, to realize that the abbé was a sick men. Three weeks after the two men parted, Brasseur went to Nice, where he died.

Brasseur had natural gifts that go far to explain the success he achieved. Until the last decade of his life, he had to carry out research mainly on his own without the aid of patrons or scientific societies. But he had an irresistible personality that aided him far more than grants of money, and he managed to secure easy access to the persons who could help him. In turn he took every opportunity to compliment his friends with graceful flattery that had the ring of sincerity.

His publications contain ample evidence of his charm. His writing is simple and entertaining; the prose flows along effortlessly, and the reader feels the author's enthusiasm in telling his story. In the introduction to the *Histoire* he gives a glowing description of the natural scenery of Nicaragua, El Salvador, and Guatemala, and in the letters to the editor of *El Museo Guatemalteco* he is even more expansive on the beauties of the country. On the other hand, he never mentioned unpleasant things. He never alluded to the inconveniences and hardships of his journey by mule through the steamy, tropical forests of Central America, nor did he complain of traversing the country during a civil war; even in personal letters he avoided controversy by shunning the discussion of politics. Moreover, he wrote about his own activities with no trace of egotism. And when he took up subjects like hieroglyphs and dynastic successions, he explained their most intricate aspects with apparent simplicity.

Happily, he also possessed remarkable natural ability for learning languages, a gift that gave him the advantages of cosmopolitanism in his associations and provided depth for his professional study. Only by mastering Nahuatl, Quiché, and Cakchiquel was he able to exploit the native documents in those languages. No scholar before him had had an opportunity to probe the Middle American past with the linguistic fluency he brought to the task.

His ideas and his interpretations of the facts he uncovered gave a distinctly personal flavor to his work, but unfortunately, as book after book appeared, his ideas grew more strange and his explanations more attenuated, so that serious leaders who had respected him increasingly lost confidence in his utterances. Why his fertile imagination got the better of him is not clear. H. H. Bancroft suggests that he was over-whelmed by the mass of data he had accumulated. It is also possible that he was overcome by the elaborate and complicated mythology. He was a born romantic, and myths appealed to his emotional outlook; consciously or unconsciously, his imaginative mind converted the tales into explanations of history, customs, and folk beliefs.

His most remarkable interpretation centered on belief in the existence of Atlantis. Earlier in his career, he had scorned the theory of that mythical continent, which had been enunciated from time to time since ancient classical days. But later he was suddenly converted to the view, and like many converts he persisted in his faith with dogmatic certainty. Atlantis was an area of land supposedly extending from Central America eastward toward the Canary Islands and Africa in the form of a crescent; there, in the dim past, had lived the first civilized people on earth. It was the cradle of world culture, because all other civilizations sprang from it directly or indirectly. Some 6,000 or 7,000 years ago, a series of terrestrial convulsions submerged Atlantis in the ocean, leaving the geographical outline of Central America as it is today, except for Yucatán, which later rose from the sea. Some of the people of Atlantis saved themselves from destruction on the seven largest islands of the Lesser Antilles, and eventually they came to the mainland, bringing their arts and culture with them.

He cited various reasons for his belief in Atlantis. The Chimalpopoca manuscript, which he had used for the chronological narrative of Anáhuac in his *Histoire,* later appeared to him in an entirely new light. He discovered that the history of the kings and wars was intended only for the mass of unsuspecting readers; the true meaning lay beneath the superficial story and could be interpreted in allegorical terms. When one went back to the period before the last dozen kings, he declared, the account represented a history of nature, giving the story of the great convulsion that submerged Atlantis. Then when he found the Troano Codex, he believed that it too related the Atlantis story, though this account placed the disappearance at 9973 B.C., and he was certain that other codices repeated the legend. He summoned additional evidence from the deluge myths that were widely current among the natives of Mexico and Central America, as well as from the annals of Egypt and from the well-known references in Plato and Plutarch.

The idea of Atlantis provided him with explanations which branched off in various directions. The Toltecs were the descendants of the remnant that survived from the convulsion; thus they had been the only true bearers of civilization, culture, and the art of working metals in Middle America, and they had spread their knowledge to other tribes. The seven islands where the survivors had taken refuge were the seven mystical caves from which the original nations of Middle America emerged. Moreover, the land of Atlantis, shaped like a crescent, was the source of all later native practices and beliefs. His explanation had mystical overtones: "It is the moon, male and female, Luna and Lunus, personified in the land of the Crescent, engulfed in the abyss, that I believe I see at the commencement of the amalgam of rites and symbols of every kind. . . ."[20] On one occasion he went so far as to give a phallic interpretation to the crescent. Likewise, he traced the story of Quetzalcoatl to Atlantis in a long, complicated line of reasoning.

If his interpretations of Atlantis approched the mystical, his views of transoceanic influences were equally vague. Using the legend that the Indians came from the East to Middle America, he assumed that they had come from Denmark or Norway and that Tula had been located somewhere in northern Europe. With etymology as a guide, he traced all nonindigenous words in the Indian languages to Scandinavia or northern Europe, though he sometimes attributed the ultimate source to a common Indo-Germanic origin. In 1857, however, he announced that his earlier assertion of Scandinavian influence had been "only an exclamation and nothing more,"[21] and he added that he could also discern influences from the eastern Mediterranean in Yucatán and the Quiché region and could identify traces of Asiatic beliefs in the religions of Middle America. Nevertheless, he continued to assert that the influence of northern Europe was revealed in the traditions and languages of Central America. Critics believed that in his enthusiasm he stretched the etymology of words to fit his theory. In the 1860s he discussed the mutual influence of ancient Middle America and ancient Egypt. It is difficult to be certain of his conclusions, if any, on the subject of transoceanic contacts, for he constantly changed his ideas, and readers could not always be certain of the theories he had adopted or abandoned at a given time.

Sometimes he took old views and gave them a new twist. From Ordóñez he adopted the story of Votan and identified the followers of that ruler with the Calhuas, who he believed had built Palenque. In Mexican history the Nahuatls had traditionally come from the north, but he insisted that they had originated in Chiapas, had been driven out of that region, and had gone up the Pacific coast to California, where they organized kingdoms. At this point he picked up the traditional story that they had migrated south into Anáhuac. He accepted at face value the legend of Quetzalcoatl and his followers, who spread civilization to other peoples. And generally he ascribed an increased antiquity to the native cultures of Middle America.

When he discovered Bishop Landa's book, with its explanation of Maya hieroglyphs, he was confident that he had found the key to understanding the ancient writings. Triumphantly, he declared that in reading the Troano Codex he had succeeded little by little in deciphering the enigmas: the alphabet and the day sings of the Maya calendar I published five years ago with Landa's *Relation of the Things of Yucatán* have been my Rosetta stone and have served as a point of departure. Today I lack nothing: I am master of all the inscriptions, despite the numerous variations of each character, and the same key that I use to read the Troano Manuscript will allow me to read the Dresden Manuscript, the Mexican Manuscript number 2 of the Imperial Library as well as the inscriptions of Palenque and the monoliths of Copan."[22] He distinguished several kinds of reading on the same page of characters—figurative signs representing the powers of nature personified, phonic letters of the alphabet, and a legendary meaning.

He demonstrated the results of his endeavor with the publication of the Troano Codex. In 136 quarto pages he displayed the Maya characters and their variants, and he presented 57 pages of translation of portions of the document. Unfortunately, his version failed to make sense of the text, and later he had to admit that he had begun at the wrong end of the codex. J. T. Goodman, who later pioneered the correct approach to deciphering the glyphs, showed his appreciation of both Brasseur's contributions and his failure to achieve the ultimate goal when he remarked that Brasseur "supplied all the preliminary stepping stones." "His fevered life just missed its triumph. The foreshadowed discovery that should place him in absolute ascendancy never came. . . ."[23]

There is no doubt that Brasseur had his weaknesses, but they were intimately related to his merits. His farfetched interpretations sprang from the tremendous enthusiasm he brought to his work. When he took myth too much at face value, we must remember, he was investigating a new subject with no guidelines, and a pioneer can take the wrong trail as easily as the right one in exploring new terrain. He could write charmingly, but all told he wrote too much; often he was diffuse, verbose, tedious, digressive, and at times he was vague. H. H. Bancroft pointed out numerous errors in his citation of authorities—a failing that might be attributed to his tremendous output. It is true that he did no significant work on archaeological ruins; the documents were his major concern and the work for which his training fitted him. If he demonstrated the failings of a romantic, it must be granted that he also possessed the merits of that temperament at its best.

Viewed after the passage of a century, his positive contributions still tower over his mistakes. Although he failed to decipher Maya hieroglyphic writing, he brought the subject to the attention of the learned world, and identified day signs, tun signs, and the meanings of bars and dots. His *Histoire des nations civilisées*—now superseded, it is true—was a major contribution in its broad coverage and in its use of primary sources, and it served as an encyclopedia of extensive information for succeeding generations. Even his dubious theory that America was the source of Old World cultures acted as an antidote to the longstanding and overworked ideas of foreign influences on Middle America. Undoubtedly, his greatest service was his preservation and publication of important documents; the discovery and printing of Landa's *Relación* will remain the major accomplishment of his active and productive career.

In the roster of early Maya archaeologists, Brasseur was a pioneer of first rank. If he did little to discover and describe the physical remains of Middle American cultures, he supplemented that approach brilliantly by exploring the documentary field. He opened up more avenues and preserved and utilized more records than any other Americanist of the nineteenth century.

7

Augustus Le Plongeon

There was always an aura of mystery about Augustus Le Plongeon. With his imposing appearance, serious countenance, and grave dignity, he had a way of commanding attention. When he spoke, it was with the authority of a man who knew what he was talking about, whether the subject was medicine, science, photography, or archaeology. In casual fashion he dropped the names of famous people with whom he had associated, and he referred to out-of-the-way places he had visited; he might also mention his discoveries and his books in an offhand manner. The listener quickly concluded that the doctor drew upon an immense reservoir of knowledge; he could cite a host of specific facts with amazing precision and then make a sweeping generalization that demonstrated the tremendous grasp he had of the subject. But the listener also gained the impression that the dignified gentleman held much in reserve, that he revealed only an inkling of what he knew; the toss of the head and the inflection of a word conveyed a mysterious hint of greater things undisclosed. He could heighten the effect by asking questions, for while the listener wondered what he was driving at, the confident doctor appeared to have the answers up his sleeve.

This man was the most curious of the pioneers in Maya archaeology. His personality and his ideas combined to make him a remarkable figure, daring in the eyes of admirers and preposterous to critics. He is sometimes remembered today for his advocacy of the Atlantis theory, but we shall see that that was the mildest of his speculations.

Among other things, he assigned to the Mayas primacy in world history and made this appear to be a fact he had discovered for himself.

We cannot consider him apart from his wife Alice. She shared in his explorations and wrote and spoke much in public on the same topics as he. At first glance it appears that we have here two archaeologists, but actually she did no more than absorb his ideas and tone down the fantastic speculations in order to gain a favorable audience. If she was more practical, he was undoubtedly the source of every idea advanced by either Le Plongeon.

One day in December 1875, a party of visitors from Mérida came to Chichén Itzá to see what Augustus and his young wife were doing. They found him deep in thought. Suddenly he leaped up and raced to a small mound, stamped his foot on the ground, and shouted, "Here it is!"[1] His workers scraped away the rubble, and behold!—there was a carved tiger with a human head.

The figure, found on top of the mound, was a good omen, and in the days that followed after the visitors left, he set Indians to work excavating the mound. Twenty-three feet down they came upon a stone urn and the head of a statue. After they exposed the complete figure, the jubilant discoverer named it Chacmool, or the Tiger King.

The natives stood in awe of Chacmool and hesitated to bring it to the surface. The ingenious doctor, however, was equal to the crisis. He called them to the neighboring Castillo, ascended the steps, and placed his whiskered face in profile against one of the bearded figures carved on a bas-relief. The Indians grasped the message—he was something of a deity, like the fair-skinned god of the ancient Mayas. They returned to do his bidding. Although the anecdote sounds farfetched and has been laughed at as impossible, a half-century later another archaeologist at Chichén listened to the story related by an Indian as he heard it from his grandfather, who believed that Le Plongeon was in communication with supernatural powers.

Augustus considered Chacmool a marvelous work of art, comparable to the sculptures of Egypt and Assyria. Actually, the statue is no esthetic masterpiece. It depicts a man, one and a half times natural size, partially reclining in an impossible anatomical position, legs drawn up, head turned to one side, and the hands holding a flat container over the stomach.[2]

Le Plongeon determined to make the most of his find and achieve fame as an outstanding archaeologist of the New World. Realizing that the centennial exhibition was about to open in Philadelphia, he decided to put Chacmool on display there, where thousands of visitors would see the remarkable sculpture from Yucatán and acclaim him as its discoverer. Of course, there were difficulties to be overcome, but the determined and resourceful explorer made a promising beginning toward accomplishing his aim. With ingenuity he contrived to remove the cumbersome statute from the mound by means of a ramp, capstan, and rope; he employed levers to mount it on a crude cart he fashioned with the aid of a machete; and he built a road four kilometers through the underbrush to Pisté. Triumphantly he moved the statue to that village, where the excited natives welcomed it as a vestige of the former glory of their ancestors.

After the happy reception ended, Le Plongeon proceeded beyond Pisté and met the first problem to try his patience. A messenger arrived to inform him that the governor of Yucatán, acting on an old Mexican law, claimed Chacmool as property of the state. Hurriedly Augustus and Alice hid the figure in the bushes beside the road and rushed to Mérida, the state capital, to clear up the misunderstanding. But the bureaucratic officials were narrow-minded; they could not comprehend the purpose of the doctor's scientific endeavor and would not relent on the confiscation of Chacmool.

So Augustus wrote a long, lesiurely, detailed letter directly to the president of Mexico. Reciting his achievements in archaeology, he gave a general approaisal: "To-day I can assert, without boasting, that the discoveries of my wife and myself place us in advance of the travellers and archaeologists who have occupied themselves with American antiquities." The laws of Mexico, however, prevented him from carrying out his mission, "while autocratic governments, like those of Turkey, Greece, and Persia, do interpose difficulties. . . ." In speaking of the statue he had uncovered, he exclaimed, "I was filled with admiration! Henceforth the American artists could enter into competition with those of Assyria and Egypt!" Momentarily he turned from his accomplishments in order to indulge in flattery: ". . . I have faith in the justice, intelligence, and patriotism of the men who rule the destinies of the Mexican republic." Will the president allow "the greatest discovery ever made in American archaeology, to remain lost and unknown to scientific men, to the artists, to the travellers, to the choicest of the nations that are soon to gather in Philadelphia? No! I do not believe it! I do not wish to, I cannot believe it!"[3] In concluding his appeal, Le Plongeon threw aside even the false modesty he sometimes assumed and made a number of requests. He wanted to take the statute to Philadelphia, he insisted that he should be made a member of the Mexican commission at the exposition because he alone was qualified to speak of the ruins in Yucatán, and he called for armed protection in carrying out his excavations in Mexico.

As he waited for an answer, time passed and it became evident that he could not forward the statue to the centennial on time. So he prepared 125 photographs, including a pictorial record of the excavation, added some artifacts, and dispatched the package to Philadelphia for exhibit in lieu of the statute. Unfortunately the package never reached its destination; instead, for some unexplained reason, it came into the hands of Judge Daly in New York City. Le Plongeon had no exhibit at the centennial.

Nor did he ever retrieve Chacmool from the bushes outside Pisté. It happened that the director of the new museum in Mérida needed objects for display; undoubtedly he had inspired the official order, for he seized the statue and planned to make a prize exhibit of it. After employing gangs of natives to drag the cart to Mérida, the director was about to put Chacmool on display, when the Mexican government stepped in, claimed the find, and sent a warship to Yucatán to carry the sculpture to the capital. And there it remains today, in the National Museum of Anthropology.

Meanwhile, Le Plongeon received no satisfaction for his loss. After a long delay, the president of Mexico flatly turned down his appeal for the return of the statue and for reimbursement of the expense of unearthing it. Then the doctor appealed to John W. Foster, the U. S. minister in Mexico; Foster conferred with the proper Mexican official, and on learning that Le Plongeon had no legal case in his favor, he did not bother to answer the aggrieved explorer. Le Plongeon could never understand why petty laws should interfere with the accomplishments of a great scientist like himself.

Le Plongeon was forty-six years old when he went to Yucatán in 1873 to launch a career in Maya archaeology. The record of his life up to that time is varied and interesting but also difficult to follow with certainty because of exasperating gaps and hazy chronology. For most of the story, a brief memoir by his wife provides the only information.

He came from a family with some claim to distinction. He was born to French parents in 1826 on the island of Jersey in the British Channel; his full name was Augustus Henry Julius. His father was a member of the Legion of Honor and a commodore in the French navy, and his mother was the daughter of the governor of Mont-St.-Michel. Other details of his background include vague connections with nobility and a questionable claim to the title of count of Coqueville, which he never used.

Young Augustus enjoyed the advantages of a good education. At the age of eleven, he was sent to military school in Caen, and four years later he entered the Polytechnic Institute of Paris, from which he graduated at the age of nineteen. During his early manhood he supposedly served in the French navy.

In approximately the mid-1840s, he came to America in search of adventure, and he was not disappointed. The ocean voyage ended with a wreck at sea, leaving him and one companion the only survivors. He landed in Chile, learned Spanish, and taught for a time in Valparaiso. He went to California in 1849, attracted by the gold rush, and survived another shipwreck on the way. The ambitious young man became city and county surveyor of San Francisco and helped to lay out the town of Yuba City.

Restless and venturesome, he continued to travel hither and thither. He went to England and to the West Indies; he claimed some small improvements in photography; then he took off for a visit to Australia, Hawaii, and Tahiti, always entertained by important officials. On his return to San Francisco, he practiced law successfully, but for unknown reasons he shifted to the practice of medicine, in which he accumulated a record of successful cases. No one has ever explained how he trained for these professions; but at some early period he appended "M.D." to his name and insisted on being addressed as "Doctor Le Plongeon."

The eight years he spent in South America, beginning in 1862, provided variety and excitement. Alice later claimed that he had been one of the founders of the California Academy of Natural Science and that that organization commissioned him to study the archaeological ruins of Peru. The records, however, tell a different story. He was not elected a member until three years after the academy had been formed. Furthermore, in 1862 the institution did not have the resources to send out an explorer, though it may have given him its blessing. In Lima, Peru, he set up a private hospital, applied electricity to medicinal baths, and generously treated the poor and those wounded in revolutions. Perhaps he accompanied Ephraim G. Squier, the archaeologist and diplomat, as photographer on one of the expeditions to examine the ruins, as Salisbury reported; but when Squier published his book on Peru he did not mention Le Plongeon. It is clear, however, that Le Plongeon knew Squier, for in 1865, after Squier had returned to the United States, Le Plongeon wrote him several letters asking favors. He wanted Squier to use his influence to get him the post of secretary of legation in Lima and to have him named correspondent in Peru for Frank Leslie's newspaper. Undoubtedly Squier was in a position to pull the proper strings, but Le Plongeon received neither job. In the meantime he wrote a book on the Incas, which failed to get into print.

The years in Peru gave him the opportunity to study earthquakes. His contributions to that subject, however, are not too clear. His wife reported that he invented a seismometer to predict earth tremors and that he published an article on earthquakes. The article appeared in a New York scientific magazine in 1872 in two installments. In it he dealt entirely with premonitory signs of earthquakes, with no mention of a seismometer. Here for the first time we find his disclaiming all reliance on theory: "I have not advanced an opinion, which is not founded on *facts* acknowledged by science, or events recorded in history."[4] This becomes a refrain that recurs in all of his later writings.

He found time to write on other subjects during the sojourn in Peru. One contribution, *Manual de Fotografía*, appeared in 1867 under the imprint of a New York publisher. On the subject of religion, which he viewed from a rationalist approach, he wrote two books at this time. One can only guess at the contents of "the Jesuits and Peru," because it was never published and no manuscript of it has come to light. But the other work, which compared the teachings of Jesus with the doctrines of the Catholic Church, was a rebuttal to an attack on Renan's *Life of Jesus*, supported by what he called an appeal to the "tribunal of reason and science."[5] Although the book, written in Spanish, came from a Boston press in 1867, it is doubtful that it circulated in Peru.

He returned to the United States in 1870, still searching for a career in which he could rise above the general run of professional men. At first he renewed relations with the California Academy of Natural Science by giving to its library a few books, including his own *La Religión de Jesús*. He also managed to secure hearings before the members of the academy at four regular meetings. In September he read a paper on the Incas, supplemented by a display of artifacts and photographs. Two months later he found a convenient opportunity to show the academy that he was an expert on the subject of earthquakes, so he was asked to present a paper on that subject during two sessions in December. Even the bare minutes refer to his "lengthy" paper, which was doubtless the manuscript of the article that appeared in the scientific journal in 1872. One can be sure that Le Plongeon hoped to impress the society so that it would commission him to undertake explorations, but no offer was made. Perhaps he bored his audience; he never learned that, in the company of informed persons, overexposure was his fatal weakness.

Suddenly he appeared in New York in a new role. He announced that he possessed three original renaissance paintings, one by Juan del Castillo and two by Murillo, which he had secured in an out-of-the-way church in Peru. He knew the value of publicity, so he invited a newspaper reporter to his home to see the works. The reporter, or perhaps he was an art critic, had heard this sort of thing before and had little faith in finding masterpieces in private possession. But "The Doctor was irresistible; so we went. . . ." Le Plongeon explained that he had acquired the canvases from a priest who badly needed money to repair his church. The paintings, he said, had come from

Spain in the early eighteenth century. After inspecting the works, the newspaperman was convinced that "They are veritable old masters; of that there is no doubt whatever."[6] On March 2, 1871, the *New York Evening Mail* featured the story in the middle of the front page, with the announcement of "Three Important Paintings from Peru. Their Romantic History," all of which gave Le Plongeon the free advertising he sought. At the end of the account the reporter, perhaps unconsciously, played Le Plongeon's game by suggesting with delicate indirection that the owner would be willing to sell the masterpieces. For some reason, however, American art-lovers made no effort to keep the works in this country, and later on their owner let out the story that the British Museum had acquired them.

He was more successful in finding a faithful partner. Sometime in the early 1870s he married Alice Dixon of Brooklyn. Little is known of her except that she was born in 1851 and came from an old English family. The wedding probably took place early in 1873, just before the couple sailed for Yucatán. Augustus was forty-seven and his wife twenty-two.

By this time he had decided on a career in Maya archaeology, and he sought funds to finance the expedition. He wangled an invitation to speak to the American Geographical Society of New York in January 1873, when the members heard a discourse "On the Coincidences between the Monuments of Ancient America and those of Assyria and Egypt." The topic was an old chestnut which many persons had dealt with over the decades, and it is not surprising that the society responded with starchy formality: he received thanks for the paper, a copy was requested for the archives of the organization, and that was the end of it. His paper was not printed in the annual volume, as was customary on such occasions; no copy has survived in the archives, and Le Plongeon was not elected a member of the society. The only consolation he had for his efforts was the appearance of extracts from the paper in *Tribune Lecture and Letter*

Extras. At the time he did not realize that the advantage he gained from his appearance was the acquaintance of Judge Daly, the president of the organization, a friendship that would prove helpful in the future.

Augustus and Alice launched their joint career in archaeology in July 1873, when they boarded the *Cuba* for Yucatán, apparently relying only on their personal finances and a strong faith in their mission. The sojourn of seven years brought them into the heart of the Maya country and provided the facts and inspiration for future publications. Unfortunately, however, Le Plongeon carried with him a predetermined theory about what he would find. Had he gone with an open mind, he might have received fresh insights and made a more useful contribution.

The couple spent their time so leisurely in Yucatán that they had no results to show by the end of two years. For the first fifteen months they lived in Mérida, observing native customs, making friends, and preparing to examine the ruins. Finally they set out on a trip through the towns to the east of Mérida. On the way Augustus generously administered smallpox vaccine to afflicted natives, explored a passage in one of the mounds at Izamal, and gradually worked his way toward Chichén Itzá.

It was a dangerous area, the borderland between Mexican control and the hostile natives, the *sublevados* who had refused to acknowledge any authority since their revolt of 1847. There was no question of the need for protection, and Augustus resorted to one of his favorite methods; he indirectly hinted to officials how they could help him, and when the aid appeared he characterized it as a spontaneous favor tendered because of high esteem for him. In this way he secured the full cooperation of the Mexican army stationed nearby. Soldiers cleared the way from one town to another, moved on to Chichén, tidied up the hacienda house that belonged to the estate, and fortified it for the benefit of the visiting Americans. Augustus and Alice had just settled down to their work when the military was ordered to move on because of a threatened attack from the *sublevados*. Although Augustus was strongly advised to depart, he had no intention of leaving. Since the guard was gone, he induced a military officer to arm his native laborers for defense; and he and Alice moved their living quarters to the safety of an abandoned church in Pisté, satisfied to walk the three miles to and from their work.

They spent only three months at Chichén, but it was the most productive period of archaeological investigation during their years in Yucatán. He drew up plans of the edifices, made 500 photographs, copied 20 sheets of mural drawings, and examined numerous bas-reliefs. Among the activities of those months, the Chacmool emerged as the greatest of his discoveries.

What did the curious statue signify? For Le Plongeon it was part of a story of love, hate, and murder. Tradition, he said, told of three brothers who ruled all the nations of Central America thousands of years ago. Cay, the eldest, was high priest at Chichén Itzá. His brother Chacmool married a beautiful woman, and as king and queen they presided over a great realm at that city. The youngest brother Aac later established his power at Uxmal.

Chacmool and his queen, Kinich Kakmo, or Móo, were the leaders of a brilliant civilization at Chichén. Fearless in battle, he had conquered the surrounding nations, and he and Queen Móo commanded the devotion and respect of their subjects. Aac became jealous of his brother and murdered him. To escape the queen's wrath, he fled to Uxmal and there set up his own kingdom. The House of the Governor was his official palace and the House of the Turtles his private residence. Over the central entrance of the palace Augustus found the statue of a seated figure, with the head missing, which represented Aac trampling upon the three flayed bodies of Cay, the queen, and Chacmool, all indicative of his triumph over his enemies.

In the meantime Queen Móo expressed her devotion to her departed husband by erecting Memorial Hall, now known as the Temple of the Jaguars, on the edge of the ball court at Chichén Itzá. She had pictures of the jaguar, Chacmool's totem, placed on the exterior walls and had the interior covered with elaborate paintings to tell the story of his life and death. Some distance from the hall was the burial of Chacmool; it was surmounted with the statue of a dying jaguar with a human head, and the wounds made by Aac's lance plainly appeared on the body of the animal.[7] It was inside this mound that Augustus found the statue of Chacmool, which, he asserted, "is not an idol, but a true portrait of a man who has lived an earthly life: I have seen him represented in battle, in councils, and in court receptions." And he added, "I am well acquainted with his life, and the manner of his death."[8]

After the seizure of the statue and the failure of the Mexican president and the U.S. minister to help him, Augustus did not know what to do. If he had been robbed of his greatest achievement, he had not been forbidden to explore; so he and Alice took a boat and visited the islands off the eastern end of Yucatán to search for Maya ruins and artifacts.

At this point, a heaven-sent sponsor stepped onto the scene. He was Stephen Salisbury, Jr., a philanthropist from Worcester, Massachusetts, who was very active in the American Antiquarian Society and also had an interest in the advancement of Maya studies.

Salisbury happened to attend a meeting of the American Geographical Society in New York early in 1877, and there he heard of Le Plongeon for the first time. Judge Daly mentioned the photographs he had received, which never got to the centennial, and summarized a letter the explorer wrote about his discoveries on Isla Mujeres. Salisbury pricked up his ears. Quickly he bought the photographs and began a correspondence with Le Plongeon. For the next four years the Worcester patron shared Le Plongeon's letters with the American Antiquarian Society, printed his reports, and went out of his way to prepare a special article about the discovery of the Chacmool for a geographical magazine.

If Salisbury expected Le Plongeon to discover striking physical remains he was disappointed. In addition to Chacmool and the tiger with a human head, Chichén yielded only the Temple of the Jaguars (Memorial Hall, according to Le Plongeon), the murals, some exterior wall-carvings and a few bas-reliefs. At Uxmal the doctor confined himself to examining the headless statue on the House of the Governor and some phallic ornaments scattered over the site, and at Aké he developed a theory of the age of the Mayas from the standing columns found there. Mayapán and the islands off Yucatán netted few physical remains. Moreover, the sites he visited, except the islands, had received attention from previous explorers.

The officers of the society were concerned with the theories Le Plongeon propounded, for each letter contained more strange ideas than the last. Salisbury and C. E. Haven, the librarian of the society, took a cautious attitude toward the reports from Yucatán. Although the officials welcomed straight scientific description of artifacts, the speculations interspersed with the descriptions were almost beyond credence.

By the early part of 1881, Le Plongeon felt free to resent the imputation that his ideas were mere speculation, and he gracelessly inserted some ill-tempered remarks in a paper addressed to the society. He accused the officers of tampering with his reports, of comparing him with the theorist Brasseur de Bourbourg,[9] and of failing to induce Mexico to act more favorably toward him. His resentment was caused primarily by the refusal of any institution to buy his photographs and tracings of the murals at Chichén. Also, by this time he had secured the patronage of Pierre Lorillard, and he felt freer to express his anger. His outburst closed his relations with the American Antiquarian Society.

The most colorful part of Le Plongeon's story appears in

the startling theories he offered to the public. He was convinced that his announcements advanced the knowledge of Maya studies immeasurably and that he was entitled to a place beside the outstanding archaeologists of the nineteenth century. In fact, it is somewhat unfair to speak of his ideas, for he insisted that he discussed only facts. In answering a correspondent in 1879, he asserted that he never advanced "a single theory of my own. I have simply narrated bare facts" learned from the ruins and the early chroniclers. He added a revealing flourish: "Truth must spring from the shock of ideas, as sparks from the hard bodies."[10]

Atlantis, which played a prominent part in the story of Maya civilization for so many, was little more than a side issue with him. He ascribed the origin and spread of world civilization to the Mayas of Middle America, not to the few survivors who escaped when Atlantis disappeared into the ocean. A reading of the Troano Codex convinced him that the lost continent had actually existed and vanished, and later at Xochicalo he deciphered inscriptions memorializing the catastrophe. As he progressed with his linguistic studies, he professed to find additional evidence of the sudden end of the island.

A theory of human migration supported his major contention. He accepted the common belief of the eighteenth and nineteenth centuries that population moved westward, but he ascribed the cause to the westward motion of the earth. In addition, he held that there had been a less significant movement of human beings eastward; less significant, because those visitors failed to influence the host country, were swallowed up by the dominant population, and left only occasional traces of their presence. This two-way movement provided Augustus with an explanation of the foreign influences that he detected in Middle America. The westward movement operated to carry the ancient Mayas to other lands. He could trace their tracks across the Pacific to the shores of the Indian Ocean and the Persian Gulf, to Babylon and the Syrian desert. Finally the Mayas settled down in the valley of the Nile and from there sent out expeditions to the lands around the eastern coast of the Mediterranean. "Like the English to-day," he wrote, "the Mayas sent colonists all over the earth. They carried with them the language, the traditions, the architecture, astronomy, cosmogony, and other sciences—in a word, the civilization of their mother country. It is this civilization that furnished us with the means of ascertaining the *role* played by them in the universal history of the world. We find vestiges of it, and of their languages, in all historical nations of antiquity in Asia, Africa, and Europe."[11]

This theory required proof of the great age of Maya civilization, and Le Plongeon was happy to supply such proof. Carvings of bearded men at Chichén showed that the Phoenicians had visited that city long ago. The Maya language itself was proof of great antiquity, because the etymology of its words appeared in no other language, whereas many of the oldest known languages contained some Maya words. He was unsuccessful in appealing to the weathering of stones and the accumulation of detritus at the rate of an inch a century, because he neglected to give specific examples of these phenomena. He believed his most convincing argument could be found in the thirty-six stone columns at Aké, which he assumed to be a conscious time-count kept by the Mayas. Each column marked the passage of 180 years, hence all the columns represented a total of 5,760 years; even Egypt, he added, did not date back more than 2,500 years.

Convinced that he had established the antiquity of Maya civilization, he liked to make statements that startled the reader. Thus, the Mayas "laid the foundation of the renowned Egyptian kingdom, some six thousand years before the reign of Menes, the first terrestrial king."[12] In Yucatán he said, Prince Coh reigned five thousand years ago, and the buildings at Chichén and Uxmal dated back twelve thousand years.

From the citation of remote dates, he went on to the interpretation of Maya inscriptions, a subject on which he was always optimistic. In June 1877, he belittled the difficulties of decipherment. "It is said that the deciphering of the American hieroglyphics is a desperate enterprise, because we have no Rosetta stone with a bilingual inscription. I humbly beg to differ from that opinion. . . ." He pointed to other important aids in solving the problem, noting that the language of the builders of the monuments was still used by native Mayas, that Spanish friars had prepared dictionaries and grammars, and that Landa's recently discovered volume discussed signs similar to those carved on the stones. As an afterthought he added, "Their deciphering may give a little more trouble." Unperturbed by any possible difficulty, he went on to discuss the "pictorial writing" of the monuments, that is, pictures telling a story. "These we have already partly deciphered, and now understand,"[13] he announced. The approach could be carried one step further when he discovered that decorative figures could reveal a message. The exterior walls of Memorial Hall, built by Queen Móo, contained no inscriptions, but the architect had cleverly arranged the decorations so as to form a dedication that Le Plongeon interpreted as, "Cay, the high priest, desires to bear witness that Móo has made this offering, earnestly invoking Coh, the warrior of warriors."[14] There is no doubt that he found it easier to divine the message of pictures and decorations than of hieroglyphs. He asserted that he could read the names of certain ancient Maya worthies inscribed on the monuments, "written in characters just as intelligible to my wife and myself, as this paper is to you in latin letters."[15] These personal names, however, were no more than his interpretation of pictorial figures: the turtle was the totem of Aac and the bird eating hearts the totem of Queen Móo.

Six years after he reached Yucatán he admitted that he was still at work on the problem of decipherment, because the Landa alphabet had failed to solve the problem. When Pierre Lorillard partially subsidized his work in the winter of 1880–81, it was for the purpose of deciphering the old Maya characters. At that time Le Plongeon had adopted the approach of reconstructing a Maya alphabet by drawing on the letters of other languages. "On seeing that the Maya is akin to the most ancient languages known," he explained, "and furnishes the etymology of many names of nations, divinities and places . . . ; we naturally inferred that the alphabet of the *Mayas* might also contain letters and characters belonging to the alphabets used by these ancient nations." In summing up his discovery, he noted some trouble: "We found that many of the ancient Chaldaic and Egyptian hieroglyphs . . . had the same meaning and value in Mayapan as in Egypt and Chaldea; while there are other characters, of the precise significance of which, we are yet in doubt, that seem to belong exclusively to the Maya." Thus in typical fashion he announced a discovery only to add as an afterthought that it was incomplete. And incomplete it was, because later in the report he admitted that his theory of an alphabet was surmise until genuine ancient Maya books could be discovered and "someone is found able to translate them into any of our modern languages. . . ."[16]

With Le Plongeon, persistence was a cardinal virtue, and finally in 1885 he published his "Ancient Maya hieratic alphabet," accompanied by an "Egyptian Hieratic alphabet." Using the Maya alphabet he had drawn up, he translated an inscription at Uxmal as "The Cans now fallen are crouching like dogs, without strength; the land of Aac, Oxmul, is securely fettered."[17] He declared that one-third of the ancient Egyptian words that had been deciphered were Maya words and that the grammatical forms of the two languages were similar.

He also found a close relation between the Maya and the ancient Greek languages. In fact the letters of the Greek alphabet could be interpreted in "primitive Maya" with amazing results: they produced a narrative of the destruction of Atlantis. Moreover, two rows of glyphs that he had photographed at one of the ruins he translated as telling the same story.

His knowledge of the ancient Maya language lent itself to strange etymological derivations. Citing the Akkadian language, he found a similarity between its words and some words in Maya. He proceeded to derive the meaning of the ancient name of Babylon from Maya etymology as "the city where reside the priests of the sun," and laughed at the scholars who rendered it as "City of the Sun."[18] A more startling derivation appeared in his rendering of Jesus's words, "My God, my God, why hast thou forsaken me?" The translation is entirely incorrect, said Le Plongeon, for those words ("Eli, Eli, lama sabachthami") are pure Maya, meaning, "Now, now, I am fainting; darkness covers my face."[19]

His "hieratic Maya alphabet" proved fruitless to other persons and was apparently of little value to him. He never found a workable formula to decipher inscriptions nor did he provide more than a few short translations of the glyphs.[20] Even his knowledge of modern Maya was condemned by Daniel G. Brinton, a respected linguist of the day. Aroused by this slur on his character, Le Plongeon challenged Brinton to a public debate—a challenge which the scholar wisely ignored—and then declared Brinton ignorant of the Maya language.

Among his various discoveries Augustus claimed that he found evidences of Masonic rites at Uxmal, which carried the practices of those "sacred mysteries" back to a period of 11,500 years ago. In the Temple of the Pyramid of the Dwarf he identified "symbols known to have belonged to the ancient mysteries of the Egyptians, and to modern Free Masonry."[21] Additional and conclusive proof he found at the foot of the pyramid in the form of the middle portion of a statue of a priest, who "wore an apron with an extended hand . . . that will easily be recognized by members of the masonic fraternity."[22]

Equally striking was his claim that giants and dwarfs had

lived in ancient Yucatán. On visiting Aké, he was astonished at the large columns of unhewn stones, and he concluded that they were "evidently the handiwork of a herculean and uncouth race—the enormous height of each step in the staircase proves it—of that race of giants whose great bones and large skulls are now and then disinterred . . ."[23] A little later he learned of a cemetery near Progreso, where giants had been buried. Excitedly he asked the town council for permission to excavate. Later he explained to the American Antiquarian Society that the reply that all finds would be subject to the order of the state governor "cooled my warmest hopes of being soon able to send for your examination and study, the remains of some of the traditional giants . . ."[24] On one occasion Alice admitted that the bones of giants reported to have been unearthed somehow had not survived, but she and Augustus were convinced of the stories they had heard.

When the Le Plongeons visited the islands of eastern Yucatán, they encountered evidences of dwarfs and pygmies. Some temples were no more than ten feet high, with doors only three feet tall. The whole coast had been inhabited by dwarfs, Augustus concluded. In her popular articles Alice went further and described the people as two and a half to three feet tall, and she repeated traditions among the local natives of a former race of people no more than two feet in height. Later explorers found the minature temples the Le Plongeons had seen; though they were unable to determine the purpose of the structures, they discounted the idea of a race of dwarfs.

The Le Plongeons also reported other wonders in the strange land. Alice claimed that the pre-Columbian Mayas had practiced mesmerism, induced clairvoyance, used magic mirrors to predict the future, and believed in metempsychosis and metamorphosis. Augustus found a recurrence of the mystical numbers three, five, and seven and pointed out that the profile of the Chacmool statue produced an outline of the geographical extent of the ancient Maya empire. The cross, which earlier explorers considered evidence of Christianity, was actually a symbol of the rain god, he explained, because the Southern Cross appeared above the horizon just before the beginning of the rainy season. There was also the matter of the unit of linear measurement used by the Mayas. Augustus decided that they had employed the metric system, because it was the only system that produced even numbers when he measured their buildings; Daniel Brinton was ungenerous enough to point out that Augustus's measurements failed to confirm his contention. Even more remarkable was Le Plongeon's announcement that the ancient Mayas had used the electric telegraph 5,000–10,000 years ago,[25] but in later writings he found it better to omit that amazing revelation.

The antiquity of Maya civilization gained support from the Le Plongeons' claim that the carved masks on buildings at Chichén were the heads of elephants, though they preferred to use the word "mastodon." On the projecting trunks Augustus found inscribed the word "tza," meaning First Great Cause, or Divine Creator. It is not known whether he was familiar with Waldeck's claim of finding elephants in Maya decorations, but the theory supported his belief that the Mayas had existed since the age when the elephant roamed the Americas.

He believed that Copán and Palenque were completely alien to Maya culture. Sculptures at those sites showed deformed heads, and, according to Le Plongeon, the Mayas never followed such practices. Nor could the hideous faces carved there belong to the Maya race. In his opinion, the inhabitants of Copán and Palenque were more probably people from Tahiti or other Pacific islands that the Mayas had visited on their voyages to India. Likewise, he went on, the hieroglyphs at those sites did not represent the writing of the Mayas; hence the attempt of scholars like Rau, Charnay, and Rosny to interpret them was absurd.

Alice and Augustus often hinted at the existence of collections of old Maya books, the writings of the wise men. At first Augustus said that such books *probably* existed, but later the probability became fact. He asserted that he would not disinter those records nor reveal their location until the American government protected him against the arbitrary actions of Mexico. But a reading of the books, he contended, was necessary before the full story of the ancient Mayas could be known. The Le Plongeons always acted as if they held a trump card by claiming that only they knew the hiding places of the ancient libraries. Unfortunately, they were unable to exploit their knowledge of those treasures, and Americanists did not take their pretensions seriously.

Their hope of finding codices in the hands of contemporary Mayas also proved illusory. Like other explorers, they heard numerous rumors of the existence of such volumes, but they were unable to locate them. The conclusion is clear: the Le Plongeons never had the advantage of Maya writings not already known to other Americanists.

After a few more years of work in the field, they gave up exploration and capitalized upon the knowledge they had acquired. By 1883 they made a return trip to Mérida and Chichén, but the scope of their activity and the exact length of their stay are not clear; they reported only on excavations made in the upper room of the Temple of the Jaguars. Sometime in 1885 they returned to the United States and settled permanently in Brooklyn, New York, surrounded by artifacts, tracings of the murals, and some of the casts Augustus had made. In later years Alice bitterly remarked that they had spent $50,000 during the dozen years in Yucatán, though she failed to indicate how much they had received from sponsors.

The publications they issued during this period suggest that they were seeking a wider audience than had been possible when Augustus's reports were addressed only to the American Antiquarian Society. Doubtless they also attempted to gain some income from writing; Alice was able to place numerous short items in newspapers and magazines. Likewise, they clung to the hope of attracting an organization to buy the drawings and casts. Their books and articles varied in emphasis from the announcement of new discoveries to general treatments of the whole scope of their archaeological exploits.

For straight reporting, the most useful account was Alice's article in the *Scientific American* in 1884, detailing the results of their later work at Chichén Itzá. With the aid of photographs and a minimum of speculation, she described an altar, fifteen atlantes, and the carvings on the doorjambs and lintel of the Temple of the Jaguars. Of particular interest is her account of the items found during the excavation of one of the mounds at Chichén. Expecting to uncover an elaborate statue of the high priest Cay, they were disappointed to unearth only the carved figure of a peculiar being which they considered a sacred monkey; it has since been identified as a standard-bearer. They also brought to light 182 pillars and a dozen carved serpents' heads. The Marquis de Nadaillac recognized the potential scientific value of the report and summarized it in detail in *La Nature*.

Alice also turned out popular articles on Yucatán. If most of the short pieces were no more than potboilers, that was probably her aim. She wrote general description as well as articles on history, customs, fables, and superstitions; in fact she exploited every possible subject for these modest essays. She showed good judgment playing down Augustus's fanciful theories or avoiding them altogether.

Her versatility became clear when, in 1886-87, she performed in still another medium, presenting two scientific papers before the New York Academy of Science. Although not brilliant, they were good summaries of the Le Plongeons' archaeological work, and she wisely soft-pedaled her husband's bizarre interpretations. At the end of her first address, she casually mentioned the molds of Maya facades and suggested that a school should be set up in Yucatán for the study of the Maya language and archaeological ruins.

She hinted that she and Augustus had valuable material on hand and would be interested in negotiating for the sale of their collection. Augustus tried another approach to the same goal. In 1882 he sent a collection of artifacts and molds of temple decorations to the Metropolitan Museum of Art for exhibition. If the director, Luigi Palma di Cesnola, had asked for the items, as Le Plongeon believed, he repented of his action and placed the shipment in storage without unpacking it. Augustus complained that his objects were never exhibited for want of space, but it is more likely that di Cesnola had no interest in American objects, as classical archaeology was his exlusive passion. Twelve years later, Le Plongeon requested the return of his items, unaware that the museum officials were more than happy to be relieved of the unopened crates.

By the mid-1890s he was ready to issue his magnum opus. Before it appeared, however, the *Review of Reviews* printed an article intended to create public interest in the forthcoming volume. The anonymous author presented a completely favorable account of Augustus and his theories. But Albert Shaw, the editor of the journal, prefaced the article with a tongue-in-cheek statement noting the extreme claims of the archaeologist—that the Garden of Eden had been in Yucatán, and that Adam, Cain, and Abel (Can, Aac, and Coh) had played out their biblical roles there.[28] This publicity proved to be premature in any case, because the book did not appear until the following year.

Augustus published *Queen Móo and the Egyptian Sphinx* in 1896 as the summary statement of his work and views on Maya archaeology. Although it was his most ambitious production, fortified by 342 pages of text and 73 illustrations, it offered nothing new to anyone who had read his previous writings. All the familiar items were there—the story of Prince Coh and Queen Móo, the claim of having deciphered inscriptions, an account of the Maya colonies, and a tedious array of "coincidences" and "analogies" between Mayas and other people. The volume also displayed the author's characteristic self-confidence, his startling statments and dubious proof, and the suggestion that he was the only authority on the subject.[27]

About this time the writer Elbert Hubbard had the opportunity to meet the Le Plongeons on a ten-day trip across the Atlantic. He described Augustus as "sixty, seventy or ninety years of age. He is becoming bald, has a long snowy, patriarchal beard, a bright blue eye, and a beautiful brick-dust complexion."[28] Augustus was the only passenger not intimidated by a violent storm at sea. But Hubbard had a somewhat higher opinion of Alice, saying that she was of "a little better fibre" than her husband, and had pleased the passengers with an entertaining lecture. However, when Hubbard commented on *Queen Móo and the Egyptian Sphinx,* he carefully steered his way between condemnation and endorsement of thc volume.

A revealing incident, which occurred in 1895, illustrates how Augustus's vanity triumphed over his good sense and led him into error. When Dr. Albert Ashmead investigated the subject of leprosy in pre-Columbian America, he wrote to Augustus for information—a natural choice because Le Plongeon was a physician as well as an Americanist with experience in Peru and Yucatán. Le Plongeon's lengthy reply dealt much more with his achievements than with the subject at hand. Ashmead wrote again, asking him bluntly whether leprosy had been present in early America. Le Plongeon's second letter began with the disclaimer that he had never made a special study of the subject, but he could not stop at that point and proceeded to offer the opinion that leprosy had existed there. Ashmead quoted the letter in his treatise and demolished Augustus's faulty logic. Ashmead concluded in his study that leprosy had never existed in early America.

After the publication of his last book, Augustus lapsed into silence and Alice carried the torch. She addressed the Albany Institute, relating the familiar story but with a tone quite different from that of her husband's writings. No longer did she claim extreme antiquity for the buildings at Chichén Itzá; she judiciously scaled the figure of 12,000 years down to a more modest 2,400 years. She also qualified her statements with such phrases as "it would seem" or "it is reasonable to believe." She did not surrender the ideas her husband had developed but simply presented them without his irritating dogmatism. Her last article, appearing in 1910, emphasized the relations between the Mayas and the Egyptians.

In the meantime, she composed a poetic version of the Queen Móo story. The thousand lines of rhymed couplets, illustrated with photographs and enriched with a musical score of five songs, made a little volume of a hundred pages that appeared in New York and London in 1902 with the title *Queen Móo's Talisman.* The beginning is representative of her style and approach:

> Loved by the Will Supreme to be reborn,—
> In high estate a soul sought earthly mourn;
> Life stirred within a beauteous Maya queen
> Of noble deeds, of gracious word and mien.

The following year Susanna Lawton contributed "Musical Settings," scored for harp, piano or organ, and violin, for the songs. A little later Brooks Betts turned the poem into "a tragic drama of ancient America, in five acts and ten scenes. . . ."[29]

As the years passed, the Le Plongeons suffered increasing disappointment and bitterness over their failure to gain recognition. Augustus complained that publishers would not issue the books he wrote, and no one bought the tableaux of paintings from the Temple of the Jaguars nor the molds of temple facades and inscriptions that he and Alice had laboriously produced in the burning sun of Yucatán. Perhaps the most serious rebuff, never mentioned by them, occurred in the early years of their archaeological activity, when no reputable organization granted them membership in recognition of their work. Augustus had unwisely cut his ties with the American Antiquarian Society in 1881, and relations with the Société des Américanistes in Paris were only nominal. His letter to the International Congress of Americanists in 1877 must surely have disinclined that group toward accepting him.

The financial resources of the couple in their last decades are a mystery. In 1902, Augustus sold a small statue from Uxmal to the American Museum of Natural History; this is the only success he is known to have had in converting his artifacts into cash. It is possible that he and Alice spent their last years in poverty, as their friends later insisted.

Heart trouble confined Augustus to his home from the middle of the 1890s. He busied himself writing books, although there was no prospect of publication, and consoled himself with the belief that his contributions would be valued by a future generation. One product of these years was a manuscript entitled "Pearls in Shells," described in an obituary as "a frank and somewhat daring treatise on religions,"[30] and he worked on another volume designed to explain the common origin of ancient peoples. In December 1908, he died at the age of eighty-three.

What happened to Alice is not known. After she published an obituary of her husband and an article in a London magazine in 1910, she disappeared from public view. She may have gone to England to live with relatives. Even the place and date of her death are unknown.

Opinions of Le Plongeon and his work ranged from denunciation to deep appreciation. In the early years, some people, such as Haven, Salisbury, Frederick Ober and Nadaillac looked upon him cautiously, hoping that he might make worthwhile contributions despite his strange ideas. H. E. D. Pollock and A. M. Tozzer, two twentieth-century archaeologists, believed that useful data could be salvaged from his writings. On the other hand, he was condemned by John T. Short, Désirée Charnay, M. H. Saville, E. H.

Thompson, Justin Winsor, Herbert J. Spinden, and even by Lewis Spence, an ardent advocate of Atlantis.[31]

Not only were Le Plongeon's theories unacceptable to many people, but he was also accused by some of engaging in dubious practices in the field. There is no doubt that he took that small statue from Uxmal and sold it to a museum; he may have taken other artifacts of value as well. He was also charged with deliberately concealing a statue he found in the ruins of Uxmal. Alice explained the incident by saying that he only sealed it up in the niche where he had found it to prevent the Mexican government from seizing it. Moreover, he was accused of using gunpowder to open mounds for exploration, but no substantiation of the claim has appeared. In an interview in 1881 he did mention gunpowder, explaining that he had planted explosives near the location of the statue he had sealed up in order to keep the owner of the hacienda from appropriating the figure.

In the last years, Alice and Augustus had a few friends, none of them archaeologists, who later paid tribute to their accomplishments. In 1923 William F. Johnson defended the value of their work and theories and asserted that time had verified the truth of their revelations, a statement that must be attributed to the blind devotion of a disciple. John Opdycke looked back on the couple as philosophers who clothed every subject they pursued with a rational, artistic interpretation. It is not clear whether Alexander McAllan was a personal friend, but he championed their cause except for a few objections. Perhaps the couple's strongest defender was Col. James Churchward who accepted all of Augustus's views, as is amply evident in *The Lost Continent of Mu*.

Their story ends with a revealing anticlimax. After her husband's death, Alice enjoyed the sympathetic understanding of Mrs. Henry Blackwell, who became a close friend. When Alice realized that death was imminent, she entrusted to Mrs. Blackwell a group of photographs, notes, and floor plans revealing the location of Maya "books" in the ruins of Uxmal and Chichén Itzá, with the injunction to preserve the data until the public showed more interest in ancient Maya culture. That time began to dawn in the 1920s. The Carnegie Institution of Washington inaugurated the restoration of Chichén Itzá under the direction of Sylvanus Morley, and various archaeologists such as Frans Blom and Oliver La Farge made scientific tours of Mexico, all of which received wide public notice.

In 1931 Mrs. Blackwell decided to act. She turned the photographs over to Morley and Blom with the vague directions for interpreting them that she remembered hearing from Alice. The pictures showed the Le Plongeons and some native workers standing before ruined structures, each person holding his arms or an object in a deliberate position so as to suggest the location of the vaults where the "books" were secreted. Apologetically Mrs. Blackwell admitted that Augustus sometimes used strange ways to transmit information. Since 1931 the structures have been thoroughly examined and reexamined by professional archaeologists, but no cache of "books" has appeared.

The pathetic aspect of Augustus appeared in two incidents. For some years before his death, he threatened to destroy all his papers because of his failure to gain recognition. But he lacked the courage to carry out the plan, which would destroy the possibility of posthumous fame. He loaned his writings to Col. James Churchward and entrusted to Alice the data about the hiding places of the Maya "books." On at least one occasion he told his wife that he had actually seen the "books" in a vault, which he hastily resealed. It appears then that he did not intentionally mislead the public, for he believed what he said. Augustus was a victim of self-deception.

As an amateur in Maya archaeology, Le Plongeon occupied an unfortunate position because of the peculiarities of his personality. At his worst, he was opinionated, haphazardly informed, and reckless in the use of data. He did engage in some excavation, however, and helped to call attention to the artifacts that lay buried at the sites. He carried out his work and concocted his ideas near the end of one age and before the opening of a new epoch in Middle American archaeology. Ironically, it is possible that his bizarre speculations did much to discredit broad theorizing among serious thinkers. He unfortunately failed to perceive that excavation would become the productive approach of the next generation in shedding new light upon the pre-Hispanic Mayas.

8

Edward H. Thompson

Edward H. Thompson was the last of the outstanding pioneers in Maya archaeology. A self-trained investigator, he followed no rules but those of common sense; he operated independently of other persons; and, unlike later professionals, he lived permanently in Yucatán. He mastered the language and customs of the natives so thoroughly that the Indians adopted him into one of their organizations, where he gained firsthand knowledge of pagan survivals. Intuition guided him, and imagination clothed the bare ruins with visions of brilliant pageantry of the Maya past. Although he drew up archaeological reports to satisfy patrons for whom he worked, he was happiest wandering about the countryside, poking through debris, and examining the ancient structures at his leisure.

He was a simple, kind person. Six feet tall, he weighed almost two hundred pounds; he had jovial blue eyes and a face roughened from constant exposure. He quickly won the confidence of the natives with his sympathetic disposition and enthusiastic temperament. Because he was naturally generous, extending aid when it was needed, he expected the same when he was in trouble.

The romantic individualism of his nature accounts for some of his virtues and defects as an archaeologist. His reports contained significant observations for his day about the ruins he examined and about the life of the natives, although his prose failed to capitalize on the significance of his finds. The recovery of artifacts from the Sacred Cenote at Chichén Itzá vindicated his individualistic approach. The physical disabilities and economic hardships he suffered in later years were in some ways also the result of his individualism, for trips through the dangerous regions of Yucatán and the descent into the waters of the cenote undermined his health, and his failure to reckon with the rising nationalistic spirit of Mexico blasted his high hopes for achievement near the end of his career.

Unlike many amateurs, he early developed interests that forecast his future work. Born in Worcester, Massachusetts, in 1856, he grew up in a family of modest means, with a lineage that went back to colonial days and included General Israel Putnam among his forebears. His father, a railroad station agent, apparently had little influence on him, but his mother, an amateur artist, took him on walks and perhaps encouraged his inclination to collect Indian arrowheads, which abounded in the neighborhood. He attended public schools in Worcester, and then enrolled in a business college. The local natural history society nurtured his interest in primitive lore, accepted his artifacts, made him a member, and listened to papers he read at its regular meetings. Sometime in these early years Stephens's volumes came his way and left him with a vivid impression of the mysterious ruins of Yucatán.

If personal inclination directed him toward archaeology, chance played a part in making him an Americanist. After completing the course in business, he entered Worchester Polytechnic Institute to study engineering. But that subject did not appeal to him, and he cast about for some other career. For a time he planned to study the Ainus and began to learn Japanese in his spare time. Then he encountered a book by Brasseur de Bourbourg which turned his interest to the legend of the lost Atlantis.

Fired with enthusiasm, he dashed off an article, "Atlantis Not a Myth," for *Popular Science Monthly* in 1879. Although it displayed more eagerness than acumen, it revealed the strong emotional current in the young man.

"Now what are we to believe?" he asked. Either the traditions of Atlantis are "a tissue of fabrications" or "they are truths." If they are correct, then the ancient Americans were the oldest inhabitants of the earth, as Brasseur maintained. "To the imaginative and lovers of the marvelous," he continued, "this theory is particularly fascinating, and the fact that there is plausible evidence of its truth adds to the effect."[1] Easily accepting the theory because he wanted to believe it, he pictured the happy inhabitants of the island and then its tragic destruction, supporting his description with exclamatory prose in lieu of convincing data. The article concluded lamely with the hope that more knowledge of the distant past would appear in the future.

Largely through chance, the article launched Thompson on his career. Because it popularized the story of the lost continent three years before Ignatius Donnelly issued his book-length account, the piece received some notice, but this was of little moment. More significant was the coincidence that Stephen Salisbury, Jr., also lived in Worcester. As vice-president of the American Antiquarian Society, Salisbury had much to say in the direction of that organization, which occasionally sponsored projects to increase human knowledge. Moreover, the wealthy bachelor had influential friends, including George F. Hoar, a senator from Massachusetts, Edward Everett Hale, the influential Unitarian clergyman in Boston, and Charles P. Bowditch, the guiding light of the Peabody Museum of Anthropology in Cambridge. These men, all Harvard alumni, had the influence, the money, and the sense of duty to carry out projects they considered worthy of support.

When Thompson's article appeared in 1879, Salisbury did no more than make a mental note of this fellow citizen who demonstrated so much enthusiasm over Atlantis. At that time, Salisbury was more interested in the progress of Augustus Le Plongeon, who was working under the auspices of the society on archaeological investigations in Yucatán; Salisbury was waiting to see if the Frenchman might make worthwhile discoveries there. Two years later, however, Le Plongeon broke with the society, and Salisbury, always curious about Yucatán, where he had spent six months in the 1860s, began to consider a new project for investigating ruins there. In typical fashion, he kept his ideas to himself until he was ready to consult with his friends Hoar and Hale. The men agreed on a scheme that would increase knowledge of the past and also had the marks of the Yankee character: it emphasized individual initiative, and it was contrived so as to keep the cost at a minimum.

When Salisbury completed his plans, he invited Thompson to his home for dinner. The other guests were Thompson's wife Henrietta, a fromer schoolteacher from West Falmouth, Massachusetts, whom he had married in 1883, Edward Everett Hale, and Senator Hoar. The bachelor host observed the social amenities by going through the entire meal without breathing a word about the purpose of the meeting. After the table was cleared, he broached the proposal to the young man. The American Antiquarian Society and the Peabody Museum, he said, had selected Thompson to carry out archaeological investigation in Yucatán. If Thompson agreed, Senator Hoar would see to it that the president of the United States would appoint Thompson consul for that area, with the understanding that he could devote his spare time to research. Of course Thompson accepted the proposition, and in February 1885, he was appointed consul for the states of Yucatán and Campeche.

A remarkable aspect of the arrangement appears in the complete freedom he was given in pursuing the scientific work. His sponsors asked only that he investigate the ruins and the modern Maya people; within those broad areas he could do what he wanted. Salisbury often moved in mysterious ways, but one can be certain that he learned enough about Thompson to trust his native ability and initiative, or in other words, to rely on the much-vaunted individualism of that day.

With little time to prepare for the assignment, Thompson

hastily set about acquiring essential information. He later explained that he learned something of medicine and surgery, gained some knowledge of psychology for dealing with the natives, and became familiar with the handling of guns and pistols; eventually he also mastered photography. The preparation must have been satisfactory for his needs, for he never encountered trouble because of lack of knowledge in these areas. When he arrived in Yucatán, Dr. Mortimer Tappan, an American physician practicing in Mérida, gave him valuable suggestions for living and working in the tropics. Before Thompson left the United States, he also studied Maya records in the Peabody Museum and the Antiquarian Society, and quickly picked up some Spanish grammar and a little of the Maya language. He was careful, however, to delay intensive training in the native idiom until he could acquire it directly from the Indians themselves, a plan he carried out successfully. From the start, he determined to learn the habits of the natives by living among them as much as possible.

With his wife and infant daughter, he set off for Yucatán in 1885 and found living quarters in Mérida, the urban center of the peninsula. Like every newcomer to that city, he was struck by sights and sounds that soon became commonplace. The songs of mockingbirds, the cries of street vendors, and the clanging of church bells filled the air. Two-wheeled carts lumbered through the streets carrying hogsheads of rainwater for sale to householders. Indian men, short in stature but strong in build, carried on their backs great burdens supported only by a tumpline around the forehead. Dark-complexioned native women in white dresses and rebozos, displaying gold earrings and necklaces, walked barefoot through the streets lined with pastel-colored houses. The venerable cathedral and state and municipal buildings dominated the tree-covered zocalo at the heart of the city, where a seventeenth-century carved portal depicted the Spanish conqueror treading upon the subdued natives. In winter the temperature was delightful; in summer the blazing sun in a clear sky turned the city into an inferno.

Although Thompson's first report was only seven pages long and appeared to be somewhat naive, it indicated alertness, observation, and the ability to generalize. He quickly conquered his initial amazement at the ruins and got down to the business of examining details. As a result of firsthand observation during little more than a year's residence in Yucatán, he was ready to discard several old beliefs. Some of his predecessors had assumed that the accumulation of deteritus indicated the age of a building; Thompson rejected the idea as completely untrustworthy, advancing good reasons for his opinion. He insisted that the massive buildings, often clustered together as in the case of Labná and Uxmal, had not been permanent habitations. He also came out unequivocally for the indigenous nature of the ancient Maya civilization; any coincidence between the Mayas and other cultures he attributed to pure chance or accident. This was a breath of fresh air after the theories of Brasseur and Le Plongeon. We may note as an additional indication of his liberation from the ideas of his predecessors that he adopted a modest estimate of the Maya achievement. "That these ruins indicate a considerable civilization, I cannot doubt," he declared in discounting extravagant claims that the early people had developed the oldest or highest culture in the world. "These ruins tell of a civilization," he added, "of a state far above the nomads of the West and above the communal pueblos of the South-west, but not of that advanced state of progress that sends forth a far-reaching influence."[8]

He devoted major attention to Labná during his first seven years in Yucatán. The site, located seventy-three miles south of Mérida, appealed to him because it had been protected from outside influence more than any other major group of ruins. No inhabitants lived near enough to cart off stones for their houses, and its proximity to the territory of the unconquered *sublevados* had deterred vandals and treasure seekers from ravaging its buildings. He made his first trip with an escort of natives, mules, and packhorses, and in the last stage of the journey the Indians had to hack a path through the tangled, luxuriant vegetation. Several years later a local landlord cleared a road to accommodate a cart, if the vehicle could withstand the uneven, rocky surface of the broad path.

Thompson's discoveries, which appear modest in retrospect, illustrate the achievements as well as the disadvantages of the untrained, independent investigator. Without a knowledge of Maya mythology and religion, he had no basis for interpreting the carved figures on the buildings at Labná. Symbolic forms, statues, and the open jaws grasping a human head expressed more than pure artistry, he was convinced, but beyond that he could say nothing. One decorative figure appeared to be a stylized serpent or the representation of an elephant or tapir, but he spent no time speculating on the puzzle. Nor could he explain the use of small hidden rooms, really alcoves, smoothly plastered but completely empty, which appeared at various places in the buildings. Some of the arched ceilings revealed evidences of green-colored murals, but they were too damaged to indicate what the original figures had been.

In reporting sites he found in the area around Labná, he was no more than an explorer bringing those places to public attention; he lacked the resources to make a thorough investigation or to engage in extensive excavation. As a result, his accounts of the ruins he found are interesting, though they contributed little that was new to the general subject of Maya architecture.

A league north of Labná in a region covered with mounds and piles of carved stones he discovered Chun Cat Dzin, where there was a five-room structure ninety-two feet long. He could only explore the place briefly and take some photographs, because he had to return to Labná to manage the workers. "Besides," he added, "this toiling through a league or more of dense and thorn-covered growth has nearly deprived me of all clothing save my tigerskin leggings. My deerskin shoes had given out under the effect of sharp stones and sharper spines and my feet were bleeding in many places."[3] At Chu-tich-Mool he found a dry chultun with stucco figures of diving frogs and flying ducks in high relief.

The greatest discovery he believed to be the ruins of Xkichmook, or Kich-Moo, which lay just inside the borders of the state of Campeche. The principal edifice was an imposing two-story structure, 220 feet long and 55 feet high, with two wings; a broad stairway, flanked by "elaborately carved and sculptured terraces," swept up to the second story. One of the smaller buildings had "serpent symbols, hieroglyphs, pillars, squares and a peculiar pyramidal arrangement of three balls or globes. . . ."[4] Some years later he made a more thorough study of the Late Classic site.

He first visited Chacmultún in 1899, just in time to photograph the buildings and copy the murals. When he returned two seasons later, treasure-seekers had pillaged the structures for artifacts and had defaced the frescoes. Unfortunately Thompson's excavations at these sites yielded only poorly preserved burials and some commonplace artifacts. He found a diminutive building at Chacmultún that suggested an early race of dwarfs, but unlike the Le Plongeons, he refused to give credence to such an idea. Those miniature buildings, found occasionally in Yucatán, have puzzled even twentieth-century archaeologists.

Thompson led a small party of Mexicans and Americans to the Cave of Loltún, one of the favorite tourist attractions. Although it was only a league and a half from the hacienda house of Antonio Fajardo, who was a member of the party, Fajardo had never seen it. Thompson marveled at "its weird and perfect beauty"[5] and declared that he could spend a month in it looking for archaeological data. Eventually he prepared a full report on the cave.

If he made no spectacular discoveries, he did find and record enough new sites to keep archaeologists busy for years to come. When he was in the region of Cobá, he traced part of the ancient Maya highway and investigated its remarkable construction; later archaeologists made the road the subject of detailed examination and report. More significant in some ways than the ruins he brought to light was his careful examination of prosaic items overlooked by his predecessors. He clarified two important details—the nature and use of chultunes and the character of the habitations of the early Maya farmers.

Curiosity and a desire for adventure took him into the chultunes. Every major site had a number of these bottle-shaped cavities reaching into the earth, with only a narrow opening at the surface. Thompson made careful preparations before descending into the pits. He wore a hat covered with rags to protect himself against falling stones, and he held a machete between his teeth. He had a rope fastened about his waist with one foot in the noose. Holding a candle in one hand, he used the other hand to guide himself down through the narrow opening to the large chamber below. As the natives paid out rope, he was ready for any emergency. At Labná he found and killed a snake at the bottom of one of the chultunes. The exploration of more than a hundred of these cavities in the course of eleven years confirmed his early conclusion that they had been designed for storage, particularly for water and perhaps also for food. Half a century earlier, John L. Stephens had looked into a shallow chultun at Labná and came to the same conclusion, but Thompson went about the task so thoroughly that he was able to establish the fact that they were a typical feature of ceremonial centers.

Likewise, he investigated house mounds of the early Maya farmers—another subject too prosaic to attract the attention of his predecessors, even if they had encountered these simple, unpromising looking remains—and he was able to derive a number of interesting conclusions.

In his first report he casually announced the significance of studying house mounds for the light they might throw on

Maya home life. He returned to the subject six years later after he had examined more than sixty groups of ruins. Extending out from the spectacular remains at Labná, he "found hundreds of sites once covered by the mud-walled, palm-thatched houses of these humbler classes. . . . Excavating these sites," he continued, "I find the ever-present *Koben,* the three-stone fireplace, the broken pottery in the ashes, the fractured *metatl* and roller with which the corn for the early *"uah"* was ground, and children's toys in the shape of polished sea-shells and bits of figured clay, hard burned."[6] He found evidence of oval-shaped huts, and meandering paths that led from dwelling to dwelling; the villages had no streets in the modern sense of the word. The huts were located on the damp soil of the valleys, in contrast to the palaces and temples, which were built on eminences exposed to refreshing breezes.

With this evidence at hand, he moved on to demolish a long-accepted belief. If the common people lived on land surrounding the elaborate ruins, then those ruins were not communal centers, as had been commonly believed; they were sacred structures used for religious purposes. Occasional small stone buildings, with evidence of use as living quarters, must have been occupied by servants connected with the temples and palaces. Cautiously he added, "This is of course but supposition, as no proof is at hand, but the idea is the common-sense one."[7] A simple conclusion, based on elementary logic, came naturally to the Yankee.

His work on house mounds soon suggested that the common Maya farmer of the earlier period lived much like the contemporary Mayas he knew so well from his daily experience. Their oval huts, open through the middle, and the palm-thatched roofs supported by frameworks of timbers, poles, and saplings bound together with lianas, had doubtless come down almost unchanged through many centuries. To clinch his point, he cited murals in the Temple of the Jaguars at Chichén Itzá, which he had painstakingly copied, showing such a hut, the three-stone fireplace, and a basket filled with circular objects suspiciously like tortillas. "The same scene," he observed, "is now met with in every native village . . . every day."[8] This led him to conclude that the present-day natives of Yucatán were descendants of the builders of the remarkable ruins that could be found everywhere.

He concluded, moreoever, that corn had always provided the major part of the native diet. He based his belief on careful observation, noting that he found the same proportion of broken metates and rollers among the ancient sites as he noticed around the villages of contemporary Mayas he visited in his travels. Again making use of personal observation, he estimated that the diet of the natives consisted of 80 percent corn, 12 percent fruits and vegetables, and 8 percent meat. Decades later his statement was overlooked or disregarded by archaeologists, and a team of scientific specialists set about determining the nature of the food used by contemporary Mayas; they came up with substantially the same figures.

He spent considerable time at Labná in order to make molds of some of the structures. The only specific request Salisbury made, some time after Thompson had begun his investigations, called for him to reproduce a section of the palace facade for the American Antiquarian Society. Thompson devised a preparation of paper pulp, native fibers, and plaster, and put the Indians to work at the task. Scarcely had the reconstruction been set up in the society's rooms, when F. W. Putnam, head of the anthropological section of the 1893 World's Fair, asked him to prepare molds of other Maya ruins for the coming exhibition at Chicago. He undertook the commission, which required fourteen months and the work of forty laborers to carry out. The duplication of the portal at Labná, twenty-five feet high and forty feet wide, was relatively easy, because the workers were accustomed to the job and the place was dry and reasonably healthy. But when he moved on to Uxmal to make molds of some of the structures there, he knew that he was tempting fate. Stephens had described the deadly atmosphere of the place half a century earlier, and Thompson found no improvement. Jungle fevers, especially malaria, infested the site, and clouds of mosquitoes pestered everyone. Most of his native workers agreed to accompany him, but eventually up to half of them fell sick. Despite the discouragements, he produced molds of a number of the well-known structures there. The bulky molds had to be packed on mules for transportation to Tabi; there they were repacked in larger cases to go by cart to Ticul; then they were transferred to railroad cars for Progreso, where they were finally loaded on the S.S. *Thornhill* for the United States.[9]

Thompson himself had no magical protection against illness. Near the end of the assignment at Uxmal, Pedro, a native, informed him of a monolith with glyphs at the edge of the site. He and Pedro put the top part in place, and Thompson made two photographs of it. At that moment he succumbed to the fever, and on being led back to camp he temporarily lost his sight.

But the job was carried out on schedule. After he and his wife boarded the *Thornhill,* Thompson collapsed, partly because he knew that the major part of the task was completed. Under his wife's care he recovered, and had the satisfaction of seeing the reproductions on display at Chicago.

The exhibition at the World's Fair provided a striking display that also influenced his future career. The 10,000 square feet of molds reproduced the portal of Labná, the arch at Uxmal, and facades of several sections of the Nunnery. Every effort was made to recreate the original atmosphere of the original works. "The bases of the walls," the *Handbook* explained, "are covered with vegetation as nearly natural as possible, and among it are planted the stones that had toppled off the original ruins."[10] One of the many visitors to the exhibit was Allison V. Armour, a wealthy patron of scientific research, who later subsidized the archaeologist in his explorations of Xkichmook and helped him to acquire Chichén Itzá.

After the success at Chicago, Thompson returned to Mexico to visit Mitla and Palenque in order to make comparisons with the ruins in Yucatán. Traveling with him was William H. Holmes, a splendid scientific companion ten years his senior, who was archaeologist of the U.S. Bureau of American Ethnology and also an artist skilled at sketching ruins and their natural setting. At Mitla they located the quarries that had furnished the stone for the ancient buildings and saw scattered about the place the old instruments —nephrite chisels, quartzite hammers, and flint peckingstones. A practical man, Thompson satisifed himself that these were the tools used by the ancient builders by using a nephrite chisel to incise his name on limestone in letters three-quarters of an inch deep.

He found Palenque very different from Yucatán. Dense tropical forest and perpetual humidity slowed his efforts at exploration. He marveled at the superior sculpture, attributing it to the fine quality of the local limestone. And like many visitors before him, he admired the bas-reliefs, which were executed "with a certain refined freedom of technique," making them "incomparable with any other similar work yet known in the Americas." After examining several tombs, he had to admit that he found little worthy of note. Regardless of his admiration for Palenque, his heart was in Yucatán, as is evident when he concluded his report by declaring that "that gigantic mosaic gem, the House of the Governor" at Uxmal remained the finest pre-Columbian structure.[11]

Before he moved from Mérida to Chichén Itzá, he had the good fortune to capture some living history. A secret society of Mayas, the Sh'Tol Brotherhood, flourished on the edge of the city, and he used his knowledge of the language to ingratiate himself with a few of the members. They appreciated his interest in the old customs and soon trusted him to the point of making him a member and eventually chief of the organization. Every year they performed a symbolic ceremony, which had been preserved unchanged since the twelfth century. The performers wore traditional masks and ceremonial robes, and danced to the music of the tunkel (a drum), sacitan rattle, and flute. Beginning with an invocation to the sun god and the sacred serpent, the dance drama related the story of a war council and the decision to fight, described the battle that followed, and ended with cries of triumph and celebration of victory.

Thompson determined to preserve a record of this vestige of ancient religion. An American had just introduced the phonograph to Mérida, and Thompson secured his cooperation in recording the sound. But for pictures he had to bring a man with a kinetoscope all the way from Veracruz. The brotherhood willingly gave a special performance for the occasion, though Thompson later admitted that the expense was more than he could afford. He had the satisfaction, however, of presenting the reproduction to the International Congress of Americanists in New York in 1902. At the same conference he also exhibited colored reproductions of the murals at Chacmultún that he had copied in 1899 and explained the Maya use of vegetable colors and the way in which they were applied.

On only one occasion did he deal with a theoretical problem in archaeology, and in that instance he believed that theory and fact coincided. Long investigation of contemporary Indian huts and of the remains of stone structures of the earlier period led him to conclude that the roof construction of the huts—he assumed that the native huts remained unchanged through many centuries—furnished the prototype of the corbeled arch, which was found everywhere in the ruins of stone temples and palaces.[12]

After a decade of wandering over Yucatán studying the natives and stumbling upon new groups of ruins, he was able to settle down at Chichén Itzá, one of the richest archaeological sites in Middle America. There he made his home and carried out his best work. Back in 1889 when A.

P. Maudslay had spent some time there, Thompson had acted as his assistant and gained some knowledge of the place. In the 1890s Allison V. Armour met the explorer in person in Chicago, and two years later he visited Yucatán on his yacht, bringing with him W. H. Holmes and members of the Field Columbian Museum expedition. Thompson escorted the party on a wide-ranging exploration of the ruins of the peninsula. In the summer of the previous year Armour had responded to Thompson's dream of setting up a center for scientific research, and he gave him the money to buy the entire estate of Chichén and to put it into good operating condition. The size of the hacienda the explorer acquired is unclear; it was variously estimated at different times to extend anywhere from thirty-six to a hundred square miles.

When Thompson arrived at Chichén Itzá, the ruins, many of them shapless mounds, were covered with heavy vegetation. The hacienda house, originally built in 1681, had been destroyed by the *sublevados* in 1847. And only a bridle path gave access to the outside world. Thompson went to work with native laborers, rebuilt the house and the service quarters, and managed to construct a road to Dzitás wide enough for the passage of a wagon. After completing these improvements in less than a year, he triumphantly brought his wife and children from Mérida to their new home.

He intended the hacienda house as more than a convenient habitation near the ruins. He peopled the place with servants, imported superior cattle, and planned to derive an income from the sale of agricultural products. In later years he hoped that he might clear enough from the sale of corn, cattle, and timber to set aside $15,000 annually to support a scientific center for scholars working in that part of Yucatán.

The archaeological potential of the place was unlimited. The vast estate included several square miles of ruins of ancient Chichén which had never been carefully explored. Although amateurs had visited it ever since the days of Stephens and Catherwood, only Le Plongeon had excavated there, though in a limited and dubious way, and Maudslay's work had been confined to survey, measurement, and photography. Thompson had the advantage of living there for three decades, a period he utilized for leisurely examination and occasional discovery of the secrets of the mysterious structures.

Personal curiosity, rather than a thirst for publication or acclaim by fellow archaeologists, prompted his careful exploration of the ruins. He learned of the pigments and colors the ancient artists had employed in their decorations. Patiently he copied the remains of the murals in the Temple of the Jaguars and studied the drawings for the information they yielded about the daily life of the inhabitants. He penetrated the Monjas and discovered the old inner structure, which had been covered by the present building. Back in the jungle bush some distance from the castillo, he came upon another group of ruins, commonly referred to as "Old Chichén." There at the suggestion of an Indian worker, he made superficial explorations and uncovered a lintel with hieroglyphs, deciphered as A.D. 618, the only date stone he found on the whole site. One of the lesser pyramids near the Caracol intrigued him when he detected a hollow sound on the platform. Raising the paving stones, he discovered a shaft penetrating the structure, and after careful preparations he directed native workers to let him down by rope into the darkness. He found a rock-hewn chamber and a hole in that floor, and he descended once more. All told, he found five successive graves, the last one of an important personage, surrounded by offerings of alabaster, jade, and mother-of-pearl. The pyramid has since been known as the "High Priest's Grave," though it is unlikely that the distinguished person was a priest.

The fate of his report of this discovery provides an example of the way the public failed to learn about his work. F. W. Putnam had commissioned him to explore the pyramid for possible use at the Columbian Exposition. Thompson's formal report and the accompanying artifacts found in the structure were eventually acquired by the Field Museum, but that organization did not publish the document until 1938, three years after the author's death.

Only when it was necessary did he write reports, and there is no evidence that he hungered to inform the public of his archaeological finds. Today a number of his reports and numerous photographs lie unpublished on the shelves of a well-known library of archaeology. He also showed little interest in writing popular accounts of the ruins he found and explored or of his adventures in the bush and forest. Until the last years of his life he published only one popular piece on archaeology, an article on Chichén Itzá in the *National Geographic Magazine* in 1914.

It was not that he disliked writing. But rather than tell about himself, he preferred to explain the picturesque side of contemporary Yucatecan life. Over the years magazines like *The Atlantic Monthly*, *Century*, and *Living Age* carried seven of his popular vignettes of native life and articles on such subjects as henequen, hammock makers, and tropical storms. Two short anecdotal items illuminated minor historical episodes. One described the expedition of 938 Americans who went to Yucatán to fight the *sublevados* in 1847, and the other explained how Augustus Le Plongeon had become a legendary figure among the natives of Chichén Itzá. After his retirement he published a children's book and an autobiography, but these were doubtless desperate attempts to supplement his meager income rather than products of the sheer joy of writing.

For twenty-four years he filled the dual role of U.S. consul and explorer. In the early days the plan operated fairly well. At first he lived in Mérida, where he carried on his official part-time duties; he was able to be absent on exploring jaunts for weeks on end, because his wife doubled as consular clerk and carried on the desk work. Soon after he acquired Chichén, he established his home there and commuted to Mérida. In the early days, before improved methods of transportation, it was a trying trip of eighty miles by pack mule, horse, and rail. By the late 1890s the increased sale of sisal to the United States forced the removal of Thompson's office to Progreso, a port city twenty-four miles north of Mérida. Somehow he retained the official job for twelve more years, probably through the use of clerks. During those years, exploration at Chichén claimed more and more of his time and interest, and finally, in 1909, he gave up the consulship and devoted all his time to archaeology.

Sometime before his resignation he had begun an interesting project at an unattractive water hole at Chichén. He was fascinated by the large natural well, always referred to as the Sacred Cenote, because of the legends that clustered about it. For centuries it had been a place of pilgrimage for natives from far and wide, who cast offerings, sometimes even human beings, into its dark depths to divine the future or to placate the rain god. As early as 1885, Thompson read Bishop Landa's account of the sacred well, and he determined to find the precious objects supposedly lying in its depths.[13]

Despite the legends, the appearance of the cenote and its surroundings is prosaic and uninspiring. The oval-shaped opening in the rock crust measures about 180 feet in diameter, and has perpendicular, craggy sides which support scrawny bushes, small trees, iguanas, and lizards. The water, sixty-five feet below the rim, is calm, muddy after a shower, and generally dark green because of certain algae it harbors; below the water is a forty-foot layer of mud. The only remainder from earlier times is the ruin of a small structure whose original shape or purpose is uncertain, though it was probably the building where the ceremonies were performed and the sacrifices were cast forth.

Thompson studied the cenote carefully. He measured it, sounded its depth, threw objects into the water at the place of sacrifice to determine where they fell and decided that the southern part of the pool contained the offerings. He devised a plan to dredge the mud and then to descend in a diving suit to search the crevices. Of course, he needed money for the project, and he made a trip to the United States to lay the proposal before Salisbury and Bowditch, his patrons. They were fascinated by the idea, but they shuddered at the possibility that he might kill himself and that they would feel responsible for the tragedy. But Thompson, using his gifts of ingratiation and convincing argument, overcame their scruples and gained their moral and financial support. He took deep-sea diving lessons in Boston, bought equipment for the venture, and returned to Chichén.

Although he based his assumptions on flimsy legend, his ingenuity and care led to one of the most spectacular discoveries by an amateur in Middle American archaeology. Late in February 1904, he set up a dredge and a derrick with a thirty-foot boom and a bucket, and assembled thirty natives to help him. By March 5 the machinery began to operate and brought up the first loads of oozy deposit. Although two human bones appeared that day, they left no impression on him. The outlook was bleak; in the five days that followed, "the dredge bucket went up and down interminably it seemed," he later recalled, "bringing up loads of rock, punk and muck, and depositing on the observation platform, rock, punk and muck only. I began to get nervous and sleepless of nights." How could he stand the ridicule of his friends? After all, he had no proof that there were offerings at the bottom of the cenote, and serious archaeologists only laughed at the legend. A few bones and some pottery appeared on March 11, but these objects failed to remove his uneasiness. Finally, on the twelfth, after a full week of dredging, his spirits soared: ". . . I saw in the chocolate covered mud that the dredge brought up an object about the size, color and shape of a baseball. I examined it closely; it looked resinous. I tasted it—*it was resin.* I touched a match to it and at once the odor of incense permeated the atmosphere about me." It was a ball of *pom*, copal incense. "That night I slept long and well."[14]

The whole experiment tested his patience. A few wooden objects appeared during the second week, but almost three months passed before the first metal artifact was brought up, and not until December did objects of gold appear in the muck. Generally, he inspected each bucketful, extracting items that he could see; then the muck was spread over the ground and native workers went over it carefully to retrieve every item of archaeological interest. It is not clear how long and how vigorously he engaged in the dredging operation. From 1907 on, he made annual agreements with Bowditch to continue the work; after 1911, however, it appears that little dredging was done.

From the start, he planned to descend into the water himself to find artifacts missed by the dredge. It seems that he did not resort to that approach until 1909. He brought a Greek diver from the Bahama sponge beds to be his assistant; the diver instructed the natives in the use of the air pumps and devised the signals for going up and down. A pontoon was lowered to the surface of the water, and Thompson and his diver sank into the depths below. This personal examination, though conducted in the dark, revealed a few items as well as some human skulls and bones. In later years Thompson liked to tell the story of his underwater explorations, but it seems that relatively few items were recovered in that manner. In spite of the care he took, he suffered impairment of his eardrums in the diving operations.

His physical disabilities were of small moment—he rarely mentioned them—compared with the scientific and artistic treasure he recovered. Out of the mud came masks, cups, and figurines; there were dart throwers, flint chisels, and ax heads; numerous little copper and bronze bells appeared as well as items of jade, ceremonial daggers, and decorated disks. Unfortunately, many of the items had been "killed"—that is, deliberately broken or mutilated—before they had been sacrificed. But the variety and quantity of the artifacts provided an amazing display of the esthetic achievement of the pre-Columbians of Middle America.

His work on the cenote was an open secret among archaeologists for a long time. In the early years numerous visitors came to Chichén to see the operation. Professor Alfred Tozzer of Harvard witnessed the appearance of a copper disk with repoussé figures. One afternoon in March 1907, Sylvanus Morley, then a young archaeologist, saw Indian workers retrieve a wavy wooden ceremonial dagger with a copper-covered heft. Thompson often asked visiting scientists from the United States to carry small packages of the items back to the Peabody Museum, where the artifacts were stored for future study and kept from public notice.

Among the numerous visitors were two Mexican officials, Justo Sierra, Minister of Public Instruction, and Leopoldo Batres, Inspector of Pre-Hispanic Monuments. They drifted into Chichén like other curious persons, saw what was going on, but uttered no complaint against Thompson. Because both officials were charged with preservation of the nation's antiquities, their failure to take action can be attributed only to the indulgent attitude of the Díaz regime toward foreigners in Mexico.

How complete was Thompson's control over his project? Teobert Maler might have been able to supply interesting data in answer to that question. Maler, an Austrian engineer, draughtsman, and photographer who came to Mexico in the wake of Maximilian's invasion, adopted archaeology as a career in 1865 during Queen Carlotta's visit to Yucatán and spent the following decades tramping over the peninsula, measuring and photographing ruins. For a time the Peabody Museum employed him to report archaeological finds. But by the time Thompson began the project at the cenote, Maler had reached the age of sixty-two and was living in retirement in Mérida, with little apparent income and with the reputation of an eccentric. He spent his leisurely days drinking beer and developing photographs.

Sometime in the past he had become a misanthrope. According to an unconfirmed story, Maler believed that he had some claim to the treasure brought up from the well. So he bribed natives working at the cenote to steal all the objects they could smuggle off the hacienda and sell them to him. When Thompson, who was rather lax in control over his workers, discovered the thefts, he passed off the losses as minimal. It is likely, however, that he lost far more than he realized or wished to admit. On a two-page list of objects known to have come from the cenote, only one of the items could be identified as being in the Peabody Museum. Maler's part in the story will perhaps never be known; at the time of his death in 1917 no artifacts were found among his effects, and it is suspected that he melted them down and converted the metal into cash. This story, we repeat, comes from an unconfirmed account, and may well be aprocryphal.

These thefts, if they actually occurred, were the least of Thompson's troubles over the Sacred Cenote. In 1921 when he attempted to move a 400-pound statue that he had earlier taken from the well and stored in the hacienda house, it accidentally dropped on one foot and crushed the bones. And some years later, as we shall see, the Mexican government struck at him with drastic vengeance for the way he disposed of the objects retrieved from the well.

He did not live to read the scholarly analyses of the artifacts he had sent to the Peabody Museum. Most of the items represented the later Mexican period rather than the Maya regime, and they covered a period of five hundred years. The metal objects came from as far away as Oaxaca, Honduras, and Panama. The striking disclosure, however, concerned the bones of some forty-two human beings brought up from the water. They represented males and females, children and adults. Some of the victims had been diseased or deformed. But only a small number had been girls in their teens, so the romantic legend that the victims were beautiful virgins had to be discarded. Surely Thompson would have been crestfallen at the news.

During his last decade in Mexico, his troubles increased. When the revolution brought the Carranza government into power, the new regime turned upon Americans who had exploited the country under Porfirio Díaz. Thompson boldly rescued some of his friends who wanted to leave the country as fast as possible by crowding them into a fishing boat and heading for Cuba. Although he managed to elude government vessels, he had to struggle with countercurrents in that part of the Caribbean, and the twenty-six men and women spent thirteen days at sea, with rations reduced to a can of beer a day; nevertheless, he landed them safely in Cuba.

He returned to Chichén, ever hopeful of attracting visitors to the ruins and making the hacienda profitable enough to support a scientific center. Perhaps he was too optimistic, and perhaps he was also somewhat careless in his financial affairs, for the hacienda never produced any marked profits. Two other events, however, brought about his undoing.

During the Mexican Revolution the Indians had been encouraged to assert their rights and stand up against the powerful landowners. Thompson had rented patches of ground on his estate to some natives. In 1921, when he ordered several of them to pay their delinquent rent or leave, socialist hotheads led an attack on his property at a time when he was absent in Mérida. They set fire to the buildings and drove off the cattle. On his return he found his library and archaeological collection destroyed, and little more than the walls of the house standing. The economic potential of the estate was severely diminished. With great courage he went to work to rebuild the place, though he surely realized that the plan for a research center would have to be indefinitely postponed. After two years he had repaired the hacienda house so that it was just barely habitable, but he was never able to restore the prosperity of his vast holding. Nevertheless, he remained jovial and ebullient as ever and rarely complained of the misfortune.

A ray of hope appeared. For a decade, the Carnegie Institution of Washington had planned to send Sylvanus Morley to head a vast project of archaeological investigation and reconstruction at Chichén. In 1923, when Carnegie officials received approval of the plan from the Mexican government, they agreed to pay Thomspon $1200 a year for the use of the hacienda house and adjacent buildings. On investigation, they discovered that he owed $400 in delinquent taxes, and reluctantly they paid off that obligation in order to secure unhindered use of the property. The arrangement suited Thompson perfectly, because he was already too deeply in debt to extricate himself. Morley had always liked Thompson from the time of his first visit to Chichén in 1907, but now he found him something of a pitiable nuisance, as he persistently pleaded for loans of money.

Just before the deal had been arranged, Thompson committed an inexplicable blunder that endangered the Carnegie plans and wrecked his own financial future. At the moment the American officials arrived in Yucatán early in 1923 to create good will for their project, he decided to make public the news of his spectacular work at the Sacred Cenote. *The New York Times* carried two articles, quoting his remarks about the valuable objects taken from the well: he referred proudly to turquoise masks, jade carvings, and gold ornaments in the form of shields, pendants, bells, and earrings. The newspaper also explained that most of the artifacts were then in the Peabody Museum at Harvard University, where Thompson had sent them in defiance of Mexico's law against exporting antiquities.

Why he chose that particular moment to break the news is not clear; surely he never dreamed of what might result. Although archaeologists had long known what he was doing, they were careful to make no more than veiled references to it in their publications. Thompson broke the news himself, and he paid dearly for the indiscretion. Moreover, his announcement could have aroused Mexican sentiment against the pending Carnegie project, but Morley had cultivated friends so assiduously in Mexico City that the Carnegie project received approval without trouble. Thompson's newspaper statements, however, gave Mexican officials firsthand evidence of the smuggling in which he had been engaged for almost two decades. At the moment the government did not take action.

Then, in 1926, Theodore A. Willard published *City of the Sacred Well,* a book that had a direct bearing on the case. Willard, inventor of the storage battery, followed archaeology as a hobby for many years. He had made numerous visits to Yucatán, had seen the dredging operation, and had become a close friend of Thompson. In the book Willard told the story of dredging the cenote, and gave vivid descriptions of some of the artifacts, emphasizing those of gold and silver, which had been recovered. The government found another damaging piece of evidence when it pulled from its files a letter written by Maler back in 1909, which denounced Thompson for his work and claimed that valuable artifacts were damaged or broken in the process of dredging.

With this evidence at hand, the Mexican government attached Thompson's estate at Chichén Itzá for 1,036,410 pesos on the charge that he had illegally exported artifacts. The mention of gold and silver objects in the newspaper accounts had touched a raw nerve in the officials, who represented his smuggling as the theft of a great national treasure; curiously, the scientific value of the artifacts scarcely received notice. Years later, reports disclosed that the gold and silver alloy in the objects at the Peabody Museum amounted to only sixteen pounds.

With his Yucatán property attached, Thompson spent the remainder of his days in the United States, a poor man, broken in health, and dependent on little more than the $1,200 a year he received from the Carnegie Institution. He gave some public lectures until the depression wiped out that source of additional income. In 1932 he published an autobiography, which told his adventures in detail and revealed many facets of his personality. Occasionally he did some excavating at Indian sites in Oklahoma and near West Falmouth, Massachusetts, where he lived. His health grew worse. Many years before, one leg had been infected by a poisonous thorn in his rambles through Yucatán; the foot had later been crushed by the falling idol, and now the pain turned to numbness. His wife became an invalid, and eventually he feared that his mind was slipping. Unable to cope with these problems, he moved to the home of a son living in New Jersey. There he died of a heart attack in 1935 at the age of seventy-nine, long forgotten by the public and disregarded by the professional archaeologists who had succeeded him.

The suit over his property dragged on in the Mexican courts until 1944. Although the government gave up the fine of a million pesos, it continued to hold the vast tract containing the ruins of Chichén Itzá and allowed his heirs to retain the hacienda buildings and the immediate grounds. The property remained in the family for several decades and was finally sold to a hotel operator, who converted the hacienda house into a modestly priced hostelry for tourists visiting the ruins.

The adventures of the loot from the cenote provide the final chapter in the story. When Mexico attached Thompson's estate, it also charged the Peabody Museum at Harvard as an accomplice, and demanded the return of the artifacts it had received from him. As far as is known, Mexico made no attempt to press the demands through diplomatic channels, and for years the museum made no move to surrender the holdings.

Harvard proudly displayed the attractive objects in glass-covered cases on the third floor of its large, rambling Peabody Museum. Just before closing time on December 31, 1937, a pale, black-haired man in his late twenties unscrewed the glass cover from one of the cases and scooped up the shiny objects with his hands. At once the burglar alarm sounded, but the man proceeded to open a second case and swept the contents into the pockets of his overcoat. The two museum guards, running about through the cavernous building, were unable to locate the rifled cases before the man left the place. At once the museum issued 4,500 circulars describing the artifacts, offered a reward of $300, and eventually managed to recover the items. According to one version of the story, the thief, an unemployed plumber, had no idea of what he had taken; the objects glistened and he believed they must be valuable.

However stoutly the university refused Mexico's demand for return of the artifacts, it slowly had to modify its position, eventually claiming that it assumed that the items had been received on extended loan until scholars could study them and publish the results. In the 1950s the Peabody Museum issued three volumes about the artifacts; studies of the jades and human bones had already been made by specialists. Finally, in 1958, many items from the collection, particularly the metal objects, were returned to Mexico. Today in the National Museum of Anthropology the tourist sees them among many other artifacts on display, unaware of their checkered history and of Thompson's ingenuity in discovering them.

As the last of the great amateurs, Thompson was in many ways a fitting representative of that breed of archaeological pioneer. He prepared himself for his work according to his best judgment, he learned Maya as a second language, and he associated with the natives on intimate terms. He carried out his explorations as independent ventures, guided solely by a consuming personal curiosity. He measured correctly and photographed effectively, but he gave little attention to excavation and preferred to accumulate miscellaneous knowledge rather than to subject a small sector of ruins to intensive, thorough examination.[15] He wisely shunned the big questions that had wasted the time of his predecessors in debates over the origin of the pre-Hispanic people and the possibility of foreign contacts.

He preferred simply to let his imagination recreate the dramatic splendor of the past. That facet of his temperament was revealed in a popular magazine article in which he told the story of Canuk, ruler of Chichén. After relating the story in detail, Thompson remarked half apologetically: "I confess to have taken this skeleton [the legend] and put a little flesh on here and there, just to round out the form —a little brown and red, just to give a local coloring, and so produce the true general effect; that is all."[16]

On other occasions his romanticism took curious turns. He named one group of ruins Xkichmook, meaning "Buried Beauty" in Maya. In his autobiography he described his first visit to Chichén, which occurred at night: as he made his way through the tangled underbrush toward the dilapidated hacienda house, he conjured up a vision of the sacrifice of maidens at the Sacred Cenote and then stumbled over the bones of the last owner of the hacienda, who had been killed by the *sublevados* in the 1840s. Another incident involved that monolith at the edge of Uxmal. Although he had a photograph to prove that it existed, his failure to locate it in later years struck him as eerie and mysterious. He also related an episode that occurred when he was on the way to find Xkichmook and a native informed him of the strange nocturnal behavior of wild turkeys. One night he and the Indian went to a field, saw the golden turkeys emerge from the bush, and for almost an hour witnessed them dancing with the precision of a highly trained ballet troupe.

He never advanced broad speculations on the origin of the Mayas, although the legend of Atlantis originally attracted him to Americanist studies. In his earliest report from Yucatán he expressed belief in the indigenous nature of the ancient Mayas. And near the end of his life he stated the commonly accepted view that the natives of America had come from Asia by way of the Bering Strait. He explained the end of Maya civilization by saying that their culture had passed through its life cycle and had simply come to its end. But he never completely suppressed the strong romantic vein in his nature. A half-century after he began his archaeological career he still retained a secret fascination for the story of Atlantis; he observed in his autobiography that the widespread legend of the ill-fated continent suggested that a foreign people did come to Central America and leave their influence on the natives.

Thompson was more than a romantic; although he described himself as an enthusiast, he was more than that. He made worthwhile contributions, unostentatious as they appear, in his brief reports. He scoured Yucatán for undiscovered ruins, copied surviving murals, explored the High Priest's Grave, and made occasional observations of considerable importance, like the comments on diet and the significance of house mounds, which went unnoticed at the time. His most fruitful achievement, the dredging of the Sacred Cenote, resulted from a combination of his most notable traits—his constructive imagination and his Yankee practicality. His life and work marked an appropriate conclusion to the age of the amateurs.

Epilogue

Were the first Maya archaeologists a special breed of humanity overly addicted to fanciful theories, as Cass and Haven believed? Did the Maya remains exert a peculiar attraction for enthusiasts or *"exaltés"?*

The claim that amateurs engaged in speculation, sometimes startlingly bizarre, cannot be denied. At first glance, several considerations of time and place might explain this propensity to theorize. It is well known that the early stage of any field of knowledge contains large areas in which the facts have not been established, and people in search of explanation too quickly rush in to fill the vacuum with speculation. Also, it is common procedure to put forth a theory as a temporary hypothesis to provide a framework for asking questions and seeking answers. If this was the amateur's intention when he propounded extreme ideas, he generally failed to distinguish between fact and hypothesis.

But the stories of these pioneers suggest a more obvious explanation. It was not the effect of the ruins on the explorers but the personalities of the explorers themselves that accounted for the nature of their work and thought in Maya archaeology. Far from being cast in the same mold, these men had distinct personalities, no two of which were alike. The biography of each man not only provides clues to his individuality but also indicates how seriously his theories should be considered.

A review of the eight archaeologists demonstrates the connection between these two aspects—the temperament of the individual and the significance to be attached to his speculations.

Antonio del Río, the conscientious army officer, attempted to find answers to the questions that guided his explorations, and admitted that he "conjectured" about data on the origin and history of Palenque; he was warning the reader to treat that part of his report lightly.

Guillermo Dupaix, an older man already acquainted with Mexican antiquities, revealed the expansion of his own esthetic horizon as he moved southward. Cautious and levelheaded, he preferred description to speculation. Only at the end of the report did he reluctantly take up theories, and he disdained most of them as unworthy of notice.

In Juan Galindo we have the political adventurer who temporarily assumed the role of amateur archaeologist; although his brief reports emphasized factual description, his contention that the Mayas were the originators of all civilization amounted to no more than the bombast of a politically ambitious man.

Waldeck was primarily the artist and raconteur, with archaeology trailing a poor second. If we remember that he enjoyed telling "good stories" in his drawings with the same relish that he related intriguing anecdotes of his past, the few speculations that he advanced are reduced to little more than entertainment.

By way of contrast, Stephens displayed ability and good sense and avoided theories until the end of four volumes of description. His comprehensive grasp of the subject, firsthand knowledge of classical ruins of the Near East, and careful reasoning led him to a sound conclusion that commanded respectful attention.

With an instinct for searching in the right directions, Brasseur enriched Maya studies with the discovery of important documents. But unfortunately, especially in his later years, haste and enthusiasm drove him to put his first thoughts into print; thus an active mind and a fertile imagination triumphed over the need for careful and judicious reflection.

The self-deluded Le Plongeon was ill prepared for the

role of archaeologist. If the excavation of Chacmool was an achievement, it was of minor significance; he staked his reputation on bizarre speculations which quickly demonstrated his complete inability to deal with the subject. Even the slightest acquaintance with his life and work reveals an arid pomposity.

In Edward Thompson we see a nineteenth-century romantic attempting to adjust himself to the less spectacular, though more solidly grounded, approaches of the early twentieth century. He lacked pretension, recognized the limits of his knowledge, and made no bid to startle the world with "outstanding discoveries." Instead, he acquired firsthand knowledge of the Mayas, past and present, by long residence in Yucatán. If he enjoyed legends and indulged in visions of pageantry, he also demonstrated that the traditions of the Sacred Cenote were founded on fact. In his work he put all speculation aside, content to search out unknown ruins and report on house mounds, the use of ceremonial centers, and the diet of the Indians.

When the amateurs explored the ruins of the sites they visited, they naturally sought to learn about the creators of the lost civilization. They also wanted to know why and how the Maya had attained a peak of cultural development obviously superior to that of their pre-Hispanic neighbors. With scant information at hand, some pioneers, as we have seen, insisted that only outside influences from civilizations in other parts of the world—in other words, transoceanic contacts—could account for this achievement by American natives. Other pioneers rejected that theory, stoutly maintaining that the Indians had indeed accomplished the results unaided and that indigenous development accounted for the achievements, but this group could not find adequate proof to support the contention.

The archaeologists of the twentieth century managed to provide answers to the questions. In so doing, they placed the Maya in a broader perspective and provided them with a history. Further examination of other areas of Middle America revealed notable developments at Teotihuacán, at Monte Albán, and on the Gulf Coast, where the Olmecs had been active. Those cultures, along with the Maya, originated or developed within a similar matrix from 300 B.C. to A.D. 300. When this knowledge became available, the Maya civilization lost much of its claim as the "mother culture" of Middle America; in fact there was the prospect that the tables might be turned, for devotees of the more recently discovered Olmec culture assigned to that Gulf Coast people the role of disseminators of a "mother culture" throughout the area. In this battle of the cultures, Maya scholars still maintained that the Mayas had been the first to develop the calendar and hieroglyphic dates and to attain sophisticated artistic expression.

If the archaeologists robbed the Maya of some of their exclusive glory, they also constructed a history for them, which, incidentally, supported the theory of indigenous development. In order to establish a time sequence, diverse data were correlated from decipherment of dates, stratigraphy, pottery styles, native chronicles, and carbon 14 dating. The archaeologists set up three major periods, beginning with Late Formative (about 300 B.C. to about A.D. 300), then advancing to Classic (about A.D. 300 to A.D. 900), and ending with Postclassic (from 900 to the Spanish conquest of the sixteenth century). Moreover, the Maya were also divided geographically into the Highland group extending along the Pacific coast from southern Mexico to El Salvador; the Central group, which occupied the inland area from Palenque through the Usumacinta River valley, the Petén, British Honduras, and the western edge of Honduras; and the Lowland Maya of the Yucatán Peninsula.

In the Late Formative period the essential features of Maya civilization appeared in elementary form. Pyramids, temples, corbeled vaulting, and ceremonial centers were evolving; murals, sculpture, pottery, jade, and stucco masks were becoming a part of their culture; and widespread trade stimulated contacts with other people in Middle America. The Maya of this period shared many of their traits with neighboring groups, but there is no evidence of transoceanic contacts. The greatest Maya activity of the period took place in the highland region of Guatemala. Only in the next age did the central and northern areas assume primacy.

In the Classic Period the Maya achieved the triumph of their development, and then suddenly ceased activity. They evolved the Long Count calendar, which reached back to a starting point in 3113 B.C. and thereby enabled archaeologists to correlate it with the Christian calendar. Hand in hand with the calendar went an increased knowledge of astronomy and a mode of hieroglyphic writing. The ceremonial center grew into an elaborate assembly of temples and other structures around a central plaza. Pyramids were built higher—one to over two hundred feet at Tikal—crowned no longer with the perishable pole-and-thatch sanctuary but with a stone temple. And to increase the upward thrust they added a stately roof comb to the temple. So-called palaces, related in some way to the ceremonial centers, increased in number. Often the plaza contained stelae carved in low relief, and at Quiriguá and Copán they burgeoned into carvings in the round. Ball courts and, in some places, sweat baths were constructed. In northern Yucatán Mayas completed a series of roads—one stretch is sixty-two miles long—probably used for ceremonial processions. Their achievements become the more remarkable in view of the lack of the use of metals, wheeled vehicles, and beasts of burden.

At the end of the Classic Period occurred the most enigmatic turn of events in the entire history of the Maya. Rather suddenly the civilization collapsed. After A.D. 800, one ceremonial center after another failed to erect date stelae as was customary in the past. The centers were abandoned. Why? Numerous theories have been put forth to answer the question, but so far no generally acceptable explanation has gained credence.[1]

From A.D. 900 until the sixteenth century, generally called the Postclassic Period, militarism and decline dominated the picture. Invaders from central Mexico, undoubtedly emanating from their capital at Tula, entered Yucatán and established control at Chichén Itzá. This Mexican-Toltec domination made the Maya population a conquered people, though some of their leaders probably acted as junior partners in the new dispensation. The culture of Chichén underwent a visible change, for feathered serpents, Toltec warriors, jaguars, eagles, and chacmools now appeared in the architectural decorations along with the native Maya rain god Chac. The Mexican-Toltec occupation came to an end in 1224.

The Itzá were the last significant group in pre-Hispanic Yucatán. Although they are considered a branch of the great Maya family, their origin is uncertain, and it is clear that the Maya of Yucatán considered them outsiders. The Itzá had absorbed the Mexican-Toltec culture sometime in their past. After wandering over the Petén and Yucatán, they occupied Chichén after the Toltec downfall. At this time the cult of the Sacred Cenote flourished; in fact the name Chichén Itzá means "mouth of the well of the Itzá." Although retaining control of that city, the Itzá built Mayapán as their capital and from there ruled the northern part of the peninsula from the thirteenth to the fifteenth century. Mayapán, in turn, was destroyed by rebels, and the Itzá left for the security of an island in Lake Petén Itzá in the northern part of modern Guatemala. Northern Yucatán disintegrated into petty states until the Spanish appeared and conquered the inhabitants.

Present-day knowledge of the Maya, which archaeologists agree is incomplete, enhances rather than diminishes the stature of the pioneers. They explored a subject obscured by the dense fog of the unknown, lifted only at the few spots where they found and examined ruins. Moreover, they lacked the tools devised by later archeologists to attack the subject systematically. Realizing the handicaps under which the beginners worked, we can even tolerate their errors with some indulgence. On the other hand, if we thoughtlessly accuse them of not discovering more, we should remember that even today some of the problems have not been solved; for example, noncalendrical glyphs still defy decipherment, though some scholars have been making tentative steps in that direction.

After all, the first Maya archaeologists *were* pioneers in the full meaning of the word. If they were ignorant of the content and scope of their search, they were intrepid. If they blundered in their approach, they were also persistent. If the knowledge they gained was limited and faulty, they did not give up their quest to penetrate the unknown. They fulfilled their mission by bringing to the attention of the learned world the existence of the lost civilization of the Maya.

Notes

CHAPTER 1

1. John L. Stephens, *Incidents of Travel in Central America, Chiapas, and Yucatan*, 2 vols. (New York: 1841), 1: 119–20.

2. Lewis Cass, *North American Review* 51 (1840): 432.

3. C. E. Haven, *American Antiquarian Society Proceedings* 70 (1878): 93.

CHAPTER 2

1. Antonio del Río, *Description of the Ruins of an Ancient City* . . . (London: 1822), p. 3.

2. Ibid.

3. See Antonio del Río, "Informe," in Ricardo Castañeda Paganini, *Las Ruinas de Palenque* . . . (Guatemala: 1946), p. 52.

4. *Literary Gazette* (London) 303 (November 9, 1822): 705.

5. John Ranking, "Remarks on the Ruins at Palenque . . . ," *Quarterly Journal of Science, Literature, and Art* (London) (January–June 1828): 323.

6. *Foreign Quarterly Review. American Edition* 18 (October 1836): 18.

7. Alexander von Humboldt, *Researches concerning the Institutions of the Ancient Inhabitants of America* . . . , 2 vols. (London: 1814) 1: 43, 262. Humboldt added that Dupaix "had sketched with great accuracy the reliefs of the pyramid of Papantla, on which he intends to publish a very curious work," and that he made a drawing of the "sacrificial stone," interpreting it as a record of Aztec conquests. Charles Farcy in *Antiquités Mexicaines*, ed. H. Baradère, 2 vols. (Paris: 1834) 1: xiii, gave a brief, favorable estimate of Dupaix, which is still valid.

8. "Nothing is insignificant which points out the origin or

merit of the arts in which they chiefly excelled; viewed in connection with so interesting an inquiry every relic however minute forms a link in the chain of knowledge, and thus acquires value and importance." (Dupaix's report in Kingsborough, *Antiquities of Mexico,* 8 vols. [London: 1830–48] 6: 463.)

9. Ibid., p. 464.

10. Ibid., p. 443.

11. Ibid., pp. 436, 462, 465.

12. Ibid., pp. 447, 454.

13. Ibid., p. 435.

14. Ibid., p. 473.

15. Ibid.

16. Ibid., p. 479.

17. Ibid., p. 477.

18. José Alcina Franch, in "Los viajos de exploración arqueológico por Mexico de Guillermo Dupaix," *Anuario de Estudios Americanos* 12 (Seville: 1965), p. 10, says that a copy in the possession of Latour-Allard formed the basis of the Kingsborough edition.

19. An anonymous writer in the *Foreign Quarterly Review. American Edition* 18 (1836–37): 19, in a survey of publications on Mexican antiquities, considered Dupaix "the chief and best authority." In the twentieth century, H. E. D. Pollock in *The Maya and Their Neighbors,* ed. Alfred M. Tozzer (New York: 1940), pp. 183–84, noted Dupaix's occasional remarks on building materials and methods of construction, and he praised the drawings for their historical record. A Ledyard Smith, ibid., p. 220, took exception to a true arch in one of the sketches of Monte Albán.

CHAPTER 3

1. Juan Galindo, "Ruins of Palenque," *Literary Gazette* (London) 769 (October 15, 1831): 665.

2. Some examples will emphasize this point. In describing a stucco relief, he referred to a group of suppliants as "apparently plebeians"; in another relief a figure was "apparently an old woman." In the subterranean area of the Palace the "number of what are apparently stone couches, lead me to suppose they were used as dormitories," or, he added in another version of

his report, that they might have been prisons. The Temple of the Cross was "apparently used for religious purposes." In describing one of its rooms, he added, "Perhaps I am wrong in supposing this to be a chapel, and that human victims were sacrificed in it"; it might "have been a canopy under which magistrates sat in the administration of justice." In still another structure he found "stone pillars . . . to which victims or culprits may have been tied." He "presumed" that the present Maya language "derived" from that of ancient Palenque. In regard to the downfall of the settlement he was equally tentative: "I would say that this nation was destroyed by an irruption of barbarians from the north-west . . ." He considered it "probable" that the Palenquians never knew the use of iron. (Ibid., pp. 665–66; "Mémoire de M. Galindo . . . ," *Bulletin de la Société de Gé*ographie 18 [1832]: 207, 209.)

3. Ian Graham, in "Juan Galindo, Enthusiast," *Estudios de Cultura Maya* 3 (1963): 11–35 believes that Galindo did not visit Topoxté and probably relied on the report of an employee for the account of those ruins on an island in Lake Yaxhá.

4. "Mémoire de M. Galindo . . . ," p. 198.

5. Galindo, "Ruins of Palenque," p. 665.

6. Galindo, "A Description of the Ruins of Copan," in Sylvanus G. Morley, *Inscriptions of Copán* (Washington: 1920), p. 596.

7. Ibid., p. 601.

8. Ibid., p. 595.

9. Ibid., p. 594.

10. Ibid., p. 602.

11. Ibid., p. 593.

12. John L. Stephens, in *Incidents of Travel in Central, America Chiapas, and Yucatan,* 2 vols. (New York: 1841) 1: 132, wrote, "He is the only man in that country [Central America] who has given any attention *at all* to the subject of antiquities, or who has ever presented Copán to the consideration of Europe and our own country. Not being an artist, his account is necessarily unsatisfactory and imperfect, but it is not exaggerated." E. G. Squier, in his *Collection of Rare and Original Documents* (New York and Albany: 1860), pp. 8, 9, and Morley, in *Inscriptions of Copán,* p. 604, applauded his curiosity, but believed that he suffered from inadequate education, lack of careful observation, and from "crude speculations." The historian Prescott, writing to John L. Stephens, August 2, 1841 (*The Correspondence of William Hickling Pres-*

cott [Cambridge, Mass.: 1925], p. 241) dismissed the report of Copán as "barren description," and A. P. Maudslay, in *Biologia-Centrali-Americana* . . . 4 vols. (London: 1889–1902) 1: 8, claimed that it added little "to our knowledge," which was certainly true at the time Maudslay wrote, a half century after Galindo's day. G. B. Gordon's preliminary report, "Prehistoric Ruins of Copan . . . ," in *Memoirs of the Peabody Museum* 1, no. 1 (1896): 4, 11–12, agreed with Maudslay and added that Galindo's measurements at Copán had several errors. In the present century, H. E. D. Pollock in *The Mayas and Their Neighbors,* ed. Alfred M. Tozzer (N.Y.: 1940), p. 183, paid tribute to the faithfulness of the few drawings which had been published and praised the man for exploration and field work, and Ian Graham, in "Juan Galindo, Enthusiast," p. 32, examined all the drawings and pronounced them good but not up to the sketches by Catherwood.

CHAPTER 4

1. Quoted in Justino Fernández, "El Diario de Waldeck," *Universidad Nacional, Anales de investigaciones estéticas* 22 (Mexico) (1954): 20.
2. Ibid.
3. Ibid., p. 24.
4. Jean Frédéric Waldeck, Diary, November 9, 1829, British Museum, London.
5. Ibid., November 18, December 17, 1830.
6. Ibid., February 6, 1831.
7. Ibid., May 27, 1830.
8. Ibid., January 18, 1830.
9. Ibid., December 20, 21, 1829.
10. Ibid., December 3, 14, 1829.
11. Ibid., February 22, 1830.
12. Waldeck, "Mexico," *Foreign Quarterly Review. American Edition* 35 (October, 1836): 137. The unsigned article was probably written by Waldeck or he provided the facts for the author. It suggests that he prepared 160 watercolor illustrations of items in the museum.
13. Waldeck, Diary, February 26, 1830.
14. Ibid., October 31, 1830.
15. Waldeck was only temporarily successful. William

Brown, whom he described as half English, apparently removed the fragments for the doña after Waldeck departed. Charles Russell, United States consul at Isla del Carmen, shipped the fragments to the United States in 1842. The story is told by Charles Rau in *The Palenque Tablet in the United States National Museum* (1879) which also appeared in the Smithsonian Institution's *Contributions to Knowledge* 22 (1880). In 1908 the stones were returned to the Mexican government; the complete tablet is in the National Museum of Anthropology in Mexico City.

16. Waldeck, "Sur l'Archaéologie Américaine," *Archives de la Société Americaine,* n. s. 1 (1875): 144.

17. Waldeck to Corroy, April 4, 1833, *Bulletin de la Société de Géographie* 4 (1835): 178.

18. Waldeck to Corroy, May 24, 1833, ibid., p. 179.

19. See the elephant head in the second row and another one in the third row of glyphs from Palenque, in Brasseur de Bourbourg, *Recherches sur les Ruines de Palenque* (Paris, 1866) pl. 38.

20. Waldeck, "Mexico," p. 137.

21. Nicté, the maid from the village of Palenque who reputedly made his loneliness in the hut more bearable, naturally receives scant notice in the diary.

22. Waldeck, Diary, February 15, 1833.

23. Ibid., February 26, 1833.

24. Ibid., August 25, 1834.

25. Ibid., January 16, 1836.

26. Ibid., January 21, 1836.

27. Later Waldeck explained that the papers were restored to him through the intervention of Lord Kingsborough. A letter from the British Foreign Office, July 18, 1838, Waldeck Collection, Newberry Library, informed Waldeck of the arrival of his papers and drawings from Mexico.

28. In the 1820s he referred to three children: John Frédéric, born 1807; Caroline, born 1808; and by the marriage with Maria Jarrow, Fritz, born 1821. It is said that he was survived by two sons.

29. Draft of the letter, July 7, 1853, Waldeck Collection, Newberry Library. Of course, we cannot be certain that he actually sent it.

30. The Massachusetts Historical Society, of which he had been a corresponding member, had dropped him from its rolls

on the assumption that he had long since died. In 1869 it hastily restored him to membership.

31. Marqués de Valle Alegre in *La Ilustración Española y Americana,* March 4, 1874, quoted by Mestre Ghigliazzi in the preface to the Italian edition of Waldeck's *Voyage pittoresque et archéologique: Viaje pintoresco . . .* (Merida: 1930), p. xxvii.

32. He described his "Archaeological Encyclopedia" in this advertisement: "Of all the Monuments known but not previously described, as well as many yet unknown to any but the Author, extending from Mexico to Peru, containing more than 2,000 Subjects in 110 Photolithographic Plates from Original Drawings made on the spots, including the early Ceramic[s] of Central America, Mexico, and Peru." "By F. De Waldeck (the oldest Traveller in existence)." Enclosed in Waldeck to Squier, January 9, 1856, E. G. Squier Papers, box 2, Library of Congress, Manuscripts Division, Washington, D.C.

33. In *Voyage pittoresque et archéologique dans . . . Yucatan . . . 1834 et 1836* (Paris: 1838), p. vi, Waldeck maintained that he wrote as a conscientious artist and aimed at rigorous reproduction of the ruins in his drawings. Although his words are open to various shades of interpretation, archaeologists generally did not like the results he produced. John L. Stephens, in *Incidents of Travel in Yucatan,* 2 vols. (1843; reprint ed. New York: 1963) 1: 176, who followed his steps at Uxmal a few years later, could not accept his plans, drawings, or opinions, though he added that Waldeck was "justly entitled to the full credit of being the first stranger who visited these ruins, and brought them to the notice of the public." The historian Prescott (see *The Correspondence of William Hickling Prescott* [Boston: 1925], p. 241) privately considered the man a quack. Daniel G. Brinton had no confidence in the pictures; see *Essays of an Americanist* (Philadelphia: 1890), p. 254. Herbert J. Spinden, in *Maya Art and Civilization* (Indian Hills, Col.: 1957), pp. 13, 258, found the drawings attractive but unreliable, and he condemned those of Uxmal as useless. In the midst of the "elephant" controversy Alfred P. Maudslay understandably discounted the accuracy of the drawings ("The Maya Sculptures," *Times* [London], February 14, 1927, p. 8.). When H. E. D. Pollock in *The Maya and Their Neighbors,* ed. Alfred M. Tozzer (N.Y.: 1940), p. 185, placed Waldeck in the story of the increasing knowledge of Maya architecture, he admitted exaggeration and restoration but credited him with the best pictorial record of the subject to that time. A surprising opinion

came from Manuel Gamio, in Frans Blom and Oliver La Farge, *Tribes and Temples . . .* (New Orleans, 1926–27) 1: 168–69, in regard to Waldeck's rendering of the Beau Relief, a drawing usually considered too French in style and too perfect in execution for Maya art. After studying the fragmentary remains of the plaque still extant in 1923, Gamio concluded that Waldeck's version was generally accurate.

CHAPTER 5

1. John L. Stephens, *Incidents of Travel in Central America, Chiapas, and Yucatan,* 2 vols. (New York: 1841), 1: 102.

2. Ibid., pp. 117–18. Two decades later E. G. Squier, in his *Collection of Rare . . . Documents* (New York and Albany: 1860), 8, remarked that Copán was discovered by Stephens "and admirably illustrated by Catherwood, and for the first Time fairly presented to the World—a Wonder to the Curious, and an Enigma to the Student."

3. Stephens, *Incidents of Travel in Central America,* 2: 291.

4. Ibid., p. 413.

5. Ibid., p. 428.

6. Stephens, *Incidents of Travel in Yucatan,* 2 vols. (1843; reissued in New York: 1963) 2: 264.

7. Stephens, *Central America,* 1: 96, 97.

8. Ibid., pp. 119–20.

9. Ibid., p. 105.

10. Ibid., p. 158.

11. Ibid., 2: 102.

12. Ibid., p. 314.

13. Ibid., p. 422.

14. Ibid., pp. 422, 429.

15. Stephens, *Yucatan,* 1: 156–57.

16. Stephens, *Central America,* 2: 311.

17. Stephens, *Yucatan,* 1: 97.

18. Stephens, *Central America,* 2: 186.

19. Ibid., p. 343.

20. Ibid., p. 356.

21. Ibid., p. 442.

22. Ibid. William H. Prescott to Stephens, August 2, 1841 (*The Correspondence of William Hickling Prescott . . .* [Cambridge, Mass.: 1925], p. 241), agreed on the independent

origin of that civilization. He also approved Stephens's method of describing the ruins and reserving his speculations for the end of the work.

23. In the twentieth century, Harvey E. Mole located Stephens's grave in Marble Cemetery, New York City. In 1947 a plaque with a Maya glyph copied from a Catherwood drawing was placed at the grave with appropriate ceremonies (*New York Times,* October 10, 1947, p. 25).

24. "The Aztecs and the Society," *The International Magazine of Literature, Art, and Science* 5, no. 3 (March 1, 1852): 290.

25. Ibid.

26. Charles Dickens, "A Mysterious City," *Household Words* . . . (April 19, 1851): 94–96.

CHAPTER 6

1. Herbert B. Adams, "The Abbé Brasseur de Bourbourg," *American Antiquarian Society Proceedings* 7 (1891): 283–84.

2. Brasseur de Bourbourg, *Histoire des nations civilisées du Mexique et de l'Amérique-Centrale . . .*, 4 vols. (Paris: 1857–59) 1: iii.

3. Ibid.

4. The Brasseur correspondence in the Squier Papers, Library of Congress, begins in June 1852. Two items might be noted. In July Brasseur asked Squier to address letters to him in Paris without the designation "Abbé." And in December he was sounding out Squier on the possibility of an ecclesiastical appointment in America.

5. Brasseur, *Histoire des nations,* 1: xvi.

6. Ibid., p. xvii.

7. Brasseur to E. G. Squier, August 7, 1855, Squier Papers, Library of Congress, Manuscripts Division, Washington, D.C.

8. Brasseur, *Histoire des nations* 1: xix.

9. Brasseur, "Nociones de un viaje a los estados de San Salvador y Guatemala . . . ," *El Museo Quatemalteco,* September 12, 1857, p. 3.

10. Ibid., p. 1.

11. Brasseur, *Histoire des nations,* 1: xxv.

12. In view of Brasseur's care in mentioning everyone who

aided him, the omission of Gavarette's name from his account in *Histoire des nations* is surprising.

13. According to Nicolaus Trubner, "The New Discoveries in Guatemala," *Athenaeum* (London) 1472 (January 12, 1856): 42.

14. Brasseur to editor of *Gaceta de Guatemala,* July 5, 1855, reprinted in *Sociedad de Geografía y Historia de Guatamala, Anales* 20, no. 12 (1947): 99–100.

15. Ibid.; Brasseur, *Histoire des nations,* 1: xxvii.

16. Brasseur to editor of the *Gaceta,* reprinted in *Anales* 20, no. 12, p. 100.

17. Ibid., p. 102.

18. "Fierce work conquers everything."

19. Brasseur to Squier, August 7, 1855, Squier Papers, Library of Congress.

20. Quoted in H. H. Bancroft, *The Native Races,* 5 vols. (San Francisco, 1883) 5: 112.

21. Brasseur, *Histoire des nations* 1: xcii.

22. Brasseur, *Lettre á M. Léon de Rosny sur la découverte de documents relatifs á la haute antiquité américaine . . .* (Paris: 1869), p. 4.

23. A. P. Maudsley, *Biologia Centrali-Americana . . . ,* 4 vols. (London: 1889–1902) 1: vi.

CHAPTER 7

1. Quoted by Désiré Charnay in "Ancient Cities of the New World," *North American Review* 131 (September, 1880): 196.

2. Almost all the items that excited Le Plongeon at Chichén came from the late period of Mexican-Toltec domination, not from the heyday of the Classic Period of the Maya. The chacmool, a type of statue found in various parts of Mexico, has still not been satisfactorily identified. Some scholars believe that copal incense was burned on the container, while others hold that living hearts from sacrificial victims were placed in the shallow receptacle as an offering to the gods. Certainly Le Plongeon would have rejoiced to learn that by 1926–27 the Carnegie Institution reported a total of twelve chacmools found at Chichén.

3. Letter in Salisbury, "Dr. Le Plongeon in Yucatan," *American Antiquarian Society Proceedings* 69 (1877): 81, 86, 88.

4. Augustus Le Plongeon, "The Causes of Earthquakes," *Van Nostrand's Eclectric Engineering Magazine* 6 (1872): 579.

5. Augustus Le Plongeon, *La religión de Jesús comparada con los enseñanzas de la iglesia . . .* (Boston: 1867).

6. *New York Evening Mail,* March 2, 1871, p. 1.

7. Some persons doubted that the head belonged to the body. See *Landa's Relación de las Cosas de Yucatán,* A. M. Tozzer, ed. (Cambridge, Mass.: 1941), pp. 183–84n.

8. Letter quoted in Salisbury, "Dr. Le Plongeon in Yucatan," p. 77. Once Le Plongeon adopted an idea he rarely surrendered it. Désiré Charney explained as early as 1880 that there were several different statues of the chacmool type in Mexico, found in other parts of the nation, and that scholars held that they represented the god of wine. But Le Plongeon could not afford to heed this warning because he had built up the entire story of Queen Móo and Chacmool from the statue he found.

9. The reader would assume that Le Plongeon disparaged Brasseur. Not so. It was the statement that Brasseur was a theorist that galled him. In order to uphold the originality of his own ideas, Le Plongeon studiously avoided mention of other Americanists except to criticize them. In 1876 he admitted that he had read the "imperfect descriptions" of the ruins by Stephens, Waldeck, Charnay, Brasseur, and others. Then in 1885 he expressed open admiration for Brasseur and respect for Donnelley's *Atlantis.*

10. Augustus Le Plongeon to the Editor, *Nation,* October 2, 1879, p. 224.

11. Augustus Le Plongeon, *Queen Móo and the Egyptian Sphinx* (New York: 1896), p. 3.

12. Ibid., p. 25.

13. Salisbury, "Dr. Le Plongeon in Yucatan," p. 116.

14. Le Plongeon, *Queen Móo,* p. 121.

15. Salisbury, "Dr. Le Plongeon in Yucatan," p. 78.

16. Augustus Le Plongeon, "Mayapan and Maya Inscriptions," *American Antiquarian Society Proceedings,* n. s. 1 (1881): 16, 17, 30.

17. Augustus Le Plongeon, "Maya Alphabet," *Scientific American,* Supplement, January 31, 1885, 7572–73.

18. Le Plongeon, *Queen Móo,* p. 33.

19. Ibid., pp. 37–38.

20. Alice, ever loyal to her husband, continued to uphold his claim of having deciphered the ancient writing. In 1896 she asserted that all translations of the codices were "childish guess-

work" and that her husband was the only one so far to produce a translation so "as to obtain a record with all necessary detail." His fellow workers, she continued, were "tardy" in recognizing the alphabet he published "by which all scholars may learn to read the Maya inscriptions if they apply themselves to it." (*The Monuments of Mayach and Their Historical Teaching* (n.p.: 1896 or 1897), pp. 10–11).

21. Augustus Le Plongeon, *Sacred Mysteries among the Mayas and the Quiches, 11,500 Years Ago . . .* (New York: 1886), p. 46.

22. Ibid., p. 40.

23. Letter to John W. Foster in Salisbury, "Dr. Le Plongeon in Yucatan," p. 100.

24. Le Plongeon, "Mayapan and Maya Inscriptions," p. 36.

25. The claim is typical of the way his mind worked. On April 19, 1876 he wrote that the carving indicating the device was "said to be a prophesy of the electric telegraph. . . ." Ten months later, June 15, 1877, he declared that the same carving revealed that the telegraph had been a reality among the ancient inhabitants. (Salisbury, "Dr. Le Plongeon in Yucatan," pp. 85, 118.)

26. Walter W. Skeat, the distinguished philologist, was moved to comment on the article. "I leave it for others to congratulate the discoverer on having found the tomb of Abel." With classic understatement, Skeat revealed Augustus's colossal ignorance. "It will now appear that Greek scholars have much to learn, and much to unlearn." In regard to Le Plongeon's method of reading the inscriptions, "The decipherer simply has to insert the sense which, in his judgment, best suits the context." (*Athenaeum* [London] [1896]: 453–54).

27. The *Athenaeum,* August 29, 1896, p. 296, carried a notice of the book. The author, it said, "is more often led by his imagination than his knowledge." His philological methods "belong . . . to the antediluvian epoch." The notice concluded that the entire book was full of "crude absurdities."

28. Elbert Hubbard, *The Arena* 17 (January 1897): 342.

29. Alice Le Plongeon, *Maya Melodies of Yucatan, taken from Indian Airs . . .* (Brooklyn: 1903), title page. Brooks Betts, *The Fall of the Maya . . .* (n.p., n.d.), typewritten copy in New York Public Library.

30. *Brooklyn Daily Eagle,* December 14, 1908, p. 16.

31. Adela Breton made a copy of the murals in the Temple of the Jaguars which became the standard reference work on

the subject. In 1906 she generously said that the copies made by Le Plongeon, Thompson, and Maudslay had not received the attention they deserved (*Congrès international des Américanistes; XVe Session . . . , 1906* [Quebec: 1907], p. 166.) At the base of the same structure are numerous figures carved in low relief. Augustus claimed that one of the faces had a beard, and his photograph of it (*Queen Móo,* pl. 20) bore out his contention; but Miss Breton doubted whether it was a beard in the original carving. She added that when she examined the stone in 1900 it was fresher and whiter than the rest. She found, however, a bearded face in the border of the carvings (*Proceedings of the Nineteenth International Congress of Americanists . . . Washington . . . , 1915* [Washington, D.C.: 1917], p. 189n.)

CHAPTER 8

1. Edward H. Thompson, "Atlantis Not a Myth," *Popular Science Monthly* 15 (1879): 759–64.
2. Thompson, "Archaeological Research in Yucatan," *American Antiquarian Society Proceedings,* n.s. 4 (October 1886): 254.
3. Thompson, "Explorations in Yucatan," *American Antiquarian Society Proceedings,* n.s. 4 (April 1887): 385.
4. Thompson, Report in *American Antiquarian Society Proceedings,* n.s. 6 (April 1888): 169.
5. Ibid., p. 163.
6. Thompson, "Ancient Structures of Yucatan Not Communal Dwellings," *American Antiquarian Society Proceedings,* n.s. 8 (1892): 263. For the rediscovery of the significance of house mounds a generation later, see R. L. Brunhouse, *Sylvanus G. Morley and the World of the Ancient Maya* (Norman, Okla.: 1971), p. 154; and Robert Wauchope, "House Mounds of Uaxactún, Guatemala," *Carnegie Institution, Contributions to American Archaeology* 7 (1934): 107–41.
7. Thompson, "Ancient Structures," p. 265.
8. Ibid., p. 267.
9. Two decades later he supervised natives in making molds of the facade of the Temple of the Jaguars at Chichén for the American Museum of Natural History. The Indians had to work in a temperature of 130 degrees, and high winds and vio-

lent rain storms endangered the fifty-foot scaffold and scattered the drying paper molds far and wide. Thompson describes his experience in "Temple of the Jaguars: Report of Work Preliminary to Reproduction of Front Facade," *American Museum Journal* 13 (October 1913): 267–82.

10. *Rand, McNally & Co.'s Handbook of the World's Columbian Exposition* (Chicago: 1893), p. 91.

11. Thompson, "Palenque," *American Antiquarian Society Proceedings,* n.s. 10 (1895): 193, 194.

12. Herbert J. Spinden, in *Maya Art and Civilization* (Indian Hills, Col.: 1957), p. 133n., claimed that Thompson's theory did not apply in southern Yucatán.

13. Alfred M. Tozzer, in his edition of *Landa's Relación de las Cosas de Yucatán, A Translation* (Papers of the Peabody Museum 18 [1941]:182n.), credits Charles P. Bowditch with the idea of investigating the cenote. Thompson worked under Bowditch's auspices and direction.

14. Thompson, "Forty Years of Research and Exploration in Yucatán," *American Antiquarian Society Proceedings* n.s. 39 (April 1929): 45.

15. H. E. D. Pollock in *The Maya and Their Neighbors,* ed. Alfred M. Tozzer (N.Y.: 1940), p. 189, gives a brief, just appraisal of his merits and weaknesses, correctly noting that his work failed to maintain a consistent level of quality.

16. "The Home of the Forgotten Race: Mysterious Chichen Itza, in Yucatan, Mexico," *National Geographic Magazine* 35 (1914): 608.

EPILOGUE

1. *The Classic Maya Collapse,* T. Patrick Culbert, ed., (Albuquerque: 1973), which I have not read (since at the time of this writing it was still in press), promises an answer to the question.

Bibliography

ANTONIO DEL RÍO

The work of Ricardo Castañeda Paganini, *Las Ruinas de Palenque . . .* (see Chapter 2, n. 3), is the best of the subject, giving all of the pertinent documents and illustrations. The English translation, *Description of the Ruins of an Ancient City . . .* (London: 1822), can generally be found in libraries of Middle American archaeology. German translations appeared in Meiningen, 1823, and Berlin, 1832, both with plates. Warden's French version is in *Receuil des Voyages et des Mémoires publié par la Société de Géographie,* 2 vols., (Paris: 1825) 2: 170–93, with the illustrations at the end of the volume. Extracts in French appeared in *Antiquités Mexicaines,* 2 vols., Paris: 1834–35) 1: pt. I, 308. "I. R. G." summarized the report in *El Mosaico Mexicano . . .*, 2 vols. (Mexico: 1837) 2: 330–34. The text of del Río's report, taken from the manuscript copy in the Royal Academy of History, was issued as *Descripción del terreno . . . del Palenque . . .* (Madrid: 1939).

The story of the various copies remains to be investigated. Jean Frédéric Waldeck, in his diary, February 7, 1831 (British Museum), tells of the copy he saw in Mexico. A manuscript copy in Spanish, with sketches, apparently originating in Ciudad Real, is in the Newberry Library. William Bullock, *Six Months' Residence and Travel in Mexico* (London: 1824), p. 331, adds little to the story of the drawings. Clyde Kluckhohn, "A Note on the Source of the Drawings in the del Río Volume on Palenque," *Maya Research* 2 (1935): 287–90, has been superseded by Paganini's treatment, mentioned above.

The assertion that del Río was guided by the questions prepared for Bernasconi is based on a comparison of the questions, given in full in Castañeda Paganini, pp. 30–34, with del Río's "Informe," ibid., pp. 48–69.

The review of 1832 is in the *American Quarterly Review* (March, 1832): 236–42. H. E. D. Pollock in *The Maya and*

Their Neighbors, ed. Alfred H. Tozzer (New York: 1940), p. 183, praises del Río for his factual description and pictorial record of the ruins. Aubin's opinion is in *Anales del Museo Nacional,* 2d ser. 2 (1905): 47.

Of the artifacts collected by del Río and sent to Spain, those that have survived and been identified are discussed and pictured in S. L. Lothrop, "Sculptured Fragments from Palenque," *The Journal of the Royal Anthropological Institute of Great Britain and Ireland* 59 (1929): 53–64.

GUILLERMO DUPAIX

The report and drawings appear in Kingsborough, *Antiquities of Mexico,* Spanish text in 5: 207–343, and English translation in 6: 421–86; and in H. Baradère, ed., *Antiquités Mexicaines* 1, div. I: 13–36; div. III: xi–xlvi; 2: plates. Charles Farcey, ibid., 1: xiv, explained that rectifications had been made in Castañeda's drawings. A manuscript copy of the report of the first and second expeditions and the drawings are in the American Philosophical Society, Philadelphia, a gift of Joel Poinsett. These drawings lack the background and shading of those in the French publication. A selection from the report is in Robert Wauchope, *They Found the Buried Cities* (Chicago: 1965), pp. 71–77.

José Alcina Franch has carried on considerable research on Dupaix. In "Un nuevo manuscrito de los viajos de Dupaix," *XXXV Congreso International de Americanistes, Mexico, 1962. Actes y Memorias, III,* (Mexico: 1964), pp. 415–20, he describes a copy of the report and illustrations found in Seville. In his "Los viajos de exploración arqueológico por Mexico de Guillermo Dupaix," *Anuario de Estudios Americanos* 22 (Seville: 1965), pp. 889–917 (also paged 1–29), appears a lineage of the copies. He brought his findings together in *Guillermo Dupaix. Expediciones acerca de los Antiguos Monumentos de la Nueva España. 1806–1808,* edited by Alcina Franch, 2 vols. (Madrid: 1969); the first volume contains the text and the second volume the plates. This is the best and almost the only biographical memoir of the man.

"El Capitán Dupaix y las ruinas de Ocosingo y Palenque," *Anales del Museo nacional arqueológico,* epoca 2, no. 4 (1907): 1–23, is incorrectly titled; it is a collection of documents detailing the trouble of Dupaix and his party in Ciudad Real in 1808. J. Houdaille, "Los viajos del Capitán Dupaix," *Antropología y historia de Guatemala* 6, no. 1 (1954): 68–69, affords little material. Waldeck's comment appears in his manuscript letter to Jomard, November 17, 1834 [1833?], Newberry Library.

Lewis Cass's discourse in the *North American Review* 51 (1840): 396–433, ostensibly a review of *Antiquités Mexicaines*, in which Dupaix's account is a major item, is disappointing. Cass disclaimed any intention of discussing Dupaix's report, and he almost succeeded in accomplishing his aim. Although he demonstrated a familiarity with the major writings on Mexican antiquities, Cass passed critical remarks only against those theorists who sought a connection between ancient Mexico and other parts of the world.

Charles Farcy, "Discourse preliminaire," *Antiquités Mexicaines*, p. ix, criticized Castañeda's drawings. Carl Nebel, *Voyage pittoresque et archaéologique . . . Mexique* (Paris: 1836), p. 4, complained that the sketches of Xochicalco were so unfaithful that one could scarcely recognize the subjects.

JUAN GALINDO

HIS WRITINGS

The reports on Palenque appeared in (1) "Ruins of Palenque," *The Literary Gazette, and Journal of the Belles Lettres* (London) no. 769 (October 15, 1831): 665–66; reprinted in the *Journal of the Royal Geographical Society* 3 (1832): 60–62. (2) "Guatemala. Visite á Palenque," *Le Courier des Etats-Units* 5 (July 7, 1832), 223–24. (3) "Mémmoire de M. Galindo . . .," *Bulletin de la Société de Géographie de Paris* 18 no. 114 (1832) 198–217; also in J. Baradère, ed., *Antiquités Mexicaines,* 2 vols. (Paris; 1834) 1: Text, Pt. 1, 67–76.

His reports on Copán are in "The Ruins of Copan in Central America," *Archaeologia Americana. Transactions and Collections of the American Antiquarian Society* 2 (1836): 545–50; "Report of Scientific Commission . . . Copán" (1834), in S. G. Morley, *Inscriptions of Copán* (Washington, D.C.: 1920), pp. 593–604, English translation; in Spanish in "Informe de la commissión científica formada para el reconocimiento . . .

Copán," *Anales de Sociedad Histórica de Guatemala* 2, no. 3 (1945): 218–28. Galindo's lengthy unpublished letter is summarized by Walckenaer, Larenaudière, and Jomard, "Rapport," *Bulletin de la Société de Géographie,* 2d ser. 5 (1836): 267–72. The only other report on archaeology describes Topoxté, "A Short Account of Some Antiquities . . . ," *Archaeologica* (London) (1834): 570–71.

On geography he made the following contributions: "Noticias del Petén," *Gaceta Federal* (Guatemala), no. 35 (September 29, 1831): 257–60, reprinted in *Registro Oficial* (Mexico), no. 80 (November 27, 1831). "Central America," *Literary Gazette* (London) no. 965: 456–57; "Notice communiquée par M. le colonel Galindo . . . ," *Bulletin de la Société de Géographie,* 2d ser. 5 (1835): 2d section, 231–33. "Central America," *Journal of the Royal Geographical Society* (London) 6 (1836): 116–36. "Description of River Usumacinta," ibid. 3 (1833): 59–64.

OTHER WORKS

William J. Griffith, "Juan Galindo, Central American Chauvinist," *Hispanic American Historical Review* 40 (1960): 26–52, and Ian Graham, "Juan Galindo, Enthusiast," *Estudios de Cultura Maya* 3 (1963): 11–35, are excellent biographical studies upon which I have drawn generously. William J. Griffith, *Empires in the Wilderness: Foreign Colonization and Development in Guatemala, 1834–1844* (Chapel Hill, N.C.: 1965) gives the larger setting of the Petén concession.

S. G. Morley, *Inscriptions of Copán,* p. 593n., tells of locating the manuscript report. Documents relating to Galindo's diplomatic negotiations in the United States are in W. R. Manning, *Diplomatic Correspondence of the United States, Inter-American Affairs, 1831–1850, III: Central America 1831–1850:* (Washington, D.C.: 1933), pp. 19–21, 89–91, and in U.S. Senate Document no. 37, 32d Congress, 2d Session, 1852–53, pp. 3–13. The reference of Ximénez's manuscript appears in Adrián Recino's preface to Delia Goetz and S. G. Morley, *Popul Vuh* (Norman, Okla.: 1950), p. 33.

JEAN FRÉDÉRIC WALDECK

HIS WRITINGS

Waldeck Manuscripts, Newberry Library, Chicago. The collection includes letters, journals, drafts of several articles, drawings, notes for his encyclopedia, and miscellaneous items. His manuscript diary, 1829–37, is in the British Museum, London. Several Waldeck letters are in the E. G. Squier Papers, box 2, Library of Congress, Manuscripts Division.

"Description du bas-relief de la Croix, dessiné aux ruines de Palenqué en 1832 . . . ," *Mémoires sur l'Archaéologie Américaine et sur l'ethnographie du nouveau-monde* . . . 2 (1865): 69–98.

"Mémoire sur bas-relief provenant de Palenqué (Conferencia)," *Annuaire du Comité d'Archaéologique Américaine* (1863–65): 25–26.

"Mexico," *Foreign Quarterly Review. American Edition* 35 (1836): 137–38. Probably written by Waldeck, though it is unsigned.

"A l'un des amis," *Bulletin de la Société de Géographie* 19 (1833): 113–14. "Extrait d'une lettre de Jean-Frédéric Waldeck . . . à Jomard," ibid., pp. 49–51. "Extrait d'une lettre de Waldeck," ibid., 2d ser. 4 (1835): 2d section, 234–37. "Extrait de quelques lettres de F. Waldeck à Francisco Corroy de Tabasco," ibid., pp. 175–79. "D'une lettre de M. Waldeck à M. Jomard . . . ," ibid. 3 (1835): 207–19.

"Les pyramides de Teotihuacán," *Mémoires sur l'Archaéologie Américaine et sur l'ethnographie du nouveau-monde* 2 (1865): 234–41.

Le sacrifice gladitorial: histoire du Mexique vers le fin de Montezuma (Paris: 1872).

"Sur l'Archéologie Américaine," *Archives de la Société de France,* n.s. 1 (1875): 143–46.

"Sur un portrait de Montezuma (Noticia)," *Annuaire du Comité d'Archaéologie Américaine* 1 (1863–65): 111–12.

. . *Voyage pittoresque et archéologique dans . . . Yucatan . . . 1834 et 1836* (Paris: 1838). Italian translation: (Mérida: 1930).

A brief selection from his writing is in C. W. Ceram, *Hands on the Past* New York: 1966), pp. 327–31.

Bibliography

Antonio del Rio, *Description of Ruins . . .* (London: 1822), contains the plates Waldeck lithographed. His sketches are in *Colección de las antigüedades mexicanas qui existen en el Museo Nacional . . .* (Mexico: 1827), reissued, Mexico, 1927; and in *Recherches sur les Ruines de Palenque . . .* (Paris, 1866).

Documents by and about him are in Andrés Clemente Vásquez, *Bosquejo histórico de la agregación a Mexico de Chiapas y Soconusco* (Mexico: 1932), pp. 453–76; and in Manuel Mestre Ghigliazza, "Algo sobre el Baron de Waldeck," the preface to Waldeck's *Viaje pintoresco . . .* , Carlos L. Menéndez, ed. (Mérida: 1930), pp. vii–xxvii.

OTHER WORKS

Two of his diaries are described in "Baron de Waldeck's Journal," *British Museum Journal* 4 (1929): 15–17, and in Justino Fernández, "El Diario de Waldeck," *Universidad Nacional. Anales del investigaciones estéticas* (Mexico) 22 (1954): 15–32.

Biographical accounts of the man are brief and unsatisfactory. The obituary notice in *L'Illustration* (Paris) 65 (May 22, 1875): 332, is disappointing, though it contains a sketch of his face. Other records appear in S. A. Green, "Notice of Waldeck," *Massachusetts Historical Society Proceedings* (October, 1876): 9–10, also issued as a separate; in Victor W. von Hagen, "Waldeck," *Natural History* 55 (1946): 450–56, and von Hagen, "Vidos sin paralelo; Waldeck, un buscador de ruinas," *Revista de America* (Bogotá), November, 1947, pp. 225–32; also in the same author's *Maya Explorer* (Norman, Okla.: 1948), pp. 152–55. Mary Darby Smith, *Recollections of Two Distinguished Persons . . . Boissey & Waldeck* (Philadelphia: 1878), pp. 57–97, gives a glimpse of the man in his later years. The finest account, excellent as far as it goes, is H. F. Cline, "The Apocryphal Early Career of J. F. Waldeck," *Acta Americana* 5 (1947): 278–300; I have drawn generously upon it.

One of Waldeck's discoveries is discussed in J. Eric S. Thompson, "The Elephant Heads in the Waldeck Manuscripts," *Scientific Monthly* 25 (1927): 392–98; see also G. Elliott Smith, *Elephants and Ethnologists* (London: 1924).

The story of Francis Corroy comes from various sources. The most informative are Waldeck's diary entries for September 28, 1832 and July 30, 1833 and several items in the Waldeck Papers, Newberry Library: Waldeck's Journal No. 26 contains a clipping of Akerley's address from the *New York Evening Post,* October 17, 1833, and Waldeck gives his criticisms, pp. 66 ff.; *Aguila Mejicana,* no. 239, August 27, 1827, announcing the prize, is in MS. 1269. The *Bulletin de la Société de Géographie,* 1st ser. 17, 18: 54–56, prints Corroy's letter of 1831.

H. F. Cline, *J. F. Waldeck Materials I . . . ,* HMAI Project Working Paper 18, July 29, 1962, Hispanic Foundation, Library of Congress, Washington, D.C., 1962 (typewritten), began to list available manuscripts and drawings by Waldeck.

JOHN LLOYD STEPHENS

HIS WRITINGS

Incidents of Travel in Egypt, Arabia Petraea and the Holy Land, 2 vols. (1837; reprint Norman, Okla.: 1970).

Incidents of Travel in Greece, Turkey, Russia, Poland, 2 vols. (New York: 1838).

Incidents of Travel in Central America, Chiapas and Yucatan, 2 vols. (1841; reprints New Brunswick, N.J.: 1949; New York: 1969).

Incidents of Travel in Yucatan, 2 vols. (1843; reprint New York: 1963).

"An Hour with Humboldt," *Living Age* 15 (1847): 151 ff., gives his account of an interview with the great scientist.

Selections from his books on Yucatán and Central America are in Robert Wauchope, *They Found the Buried Cities* (Chicago: 1965), pp. 79–93; C. W. Ceram, *Hands on the Past* (New York: 1966), pp. 332–45; Jacquette Hawkes, ed., *The World of the Past,* 2 vols. (New York 1963) 2: 500–599; Leo Deuel, *Conquistadors without Swords* (London: 1967), pp. 244–65.

Several letters are in the Squier Collection, Library of Congress, Manuscripts Division, Washington, D.C. and in the New York Public Library, Manuscripts Division.

OTHER WORKS

Biographical sketches are in the *Dictionary of American Biography;* in C. W. Ceram, *Gods, Graves and Scholars* (New

York: 1951), pp. 337–56; and in F. L. Hawks, "The Late John S. Stephens," *Putnam's Monthly Magazine* 1 (1863): 64–68. Victor von Hagen has written excellent biographies of the collaborators: *Maya Explorer: John Lloyd Stephens and the Lost Cities of Central America and Yucatan* (Norman, Okla.: 1948) and *Frederick Catherwood Archt* (New York: 1950); they cover their subjects in detail and have full bibliographies.

Other aspects of the story come from diverse sources. The reviews of Stephens's volumes can be traced through *Poole's Index of Periodical Literature*. The wanderings of the Stephens stones have been treated by Herbert J. Spinden in *Natural History* 20 (1920): 379–89, and by Carl Dauterman, ibid. 44 (1939): 288–94. The stones are on display in the Mexican Hall, American Museum of Natural History, New York. The information about Stephens's income from his books is in Samuel A. Allibone, *A Critical Dictionary of English Literature . . .*, 3 vols. (Philadelphia: 1858–71) 2: 2240. A. M. Tozzer, "Stephens and Prescott, Bancroft and Others," in *Los Mayas Antiguos*, César Lizardi Ramos, ed. (Mexico: 1941), pp. 33–60, is worth reading.

The Barnum hoax can be followed in Pedro Velásquez, *Memoirs of an Eventful Expedition . . .*, in various editions and translations (the Library of Congress card labels it "an apocryphal production"); "The Aztecs at the Society Library," *The International Magazine of Literature, Art, and Science* (New York) 5, no. 3 (March 1, 1852): 289–90, contains the quotation by Horace Greeley; "A Mysterious City," *Household Words*, April 1, 1851, 94–96, gives Charles Dickens's reaction. Waldeck to Dickens, July 7, 1853, is in the Waldeck Papers, Newberry Library, Chicago.

An interesting comparison of some of Catherwood's drawings with photographs of the same objects is one of the features of Victor W. von Hagen, "Artist of a Buried Past," *American Heritage* 11 (June 1961): 8–9, 100–103. Catherwood's *Views of Ancient Monuments* (London: 1844) is reproduced in von Hagen's biography of the man, and has also been reprinted (Barre, Mass.: 1963).

BRASSEUR DE BOURBOURG

HIS WRITINGS

Antiquités Mexicaines. A propos d'un mémoire sur le peinture didactique et l'écriture figurative des anciens Mexicains, par J. M. A. Aubin (Paris: 1852). From *Revue Archaéologique.*

"Antigüedades guatemaltecas," *Anales de Sociedad de Geografía e historia de Guatemala* 20, no. 1 (1945): 7–17; 22, no. 1, 2 (1947): 99–104, reprints his letters of 1855–56 to the editor of the *Gaceta de Guatemala.*

Archaéologie Américaine. Cours de M. l'Abbé Brasseur de Bourbourg . . . (n.p., 1864).

Archives de la Commision Scientifique du Mexique, 3 vols., (Paris 1864–67): (1) "Esquisse d'histoire, d'archéologie, d'ethnologie et de linguistique . . . ," 1864, 1: 85–136; (2) letter, November 22, 1864, 1: 454–60; (3) "Essai historique sur le Yucatán . . . ," 1865, 2: 18–63; (4) "Rapport sur . . . Mayapán et d'Uxmal," 1865, 2: 234–88; (5) letters of 1865, 2: 265–311.

Bibliothéque Mexico-Guatémalienne . . . (Paris: 1871).

Collection de documents dans les langues indigenes pour servir à l'étude de l'histoire et de la philologie de l'Amérique ancienne, 4 vols. (Paris: 1861–68). 1: *Popul Vuh,* 1861. 2: *Gramática de la lengua quiché,* 1862; (also, Guatemala; 1961). 3: *Relation des choses de Yucatán de Diego de Landa,* 1864. IV: *Quatre Lettres sur le Mexique* . . . , 1868.

Coup d'Oeil sur la Nation et la Langue des Wabis . . . (Paris: 1861). Also in *Revue Orientale et Américaine* 5 (1861).

De Guatemala à Rabinal . . . dans les années 1854, 1855 (n.p., n.d.). Also in *Revue Européenne,* February 1, 15, 1859.

Dictionnaire, grammaire et chrestomathie de la langue maya . . . (Paris: 1872; also another edition, Paris: 1872).

Essai historique sur les sources de la philologie mexicaine et sur l'ethnographie de l'Amérique centrale (Paris: 1859). Also in *Revue Américaine et Orientale.*

Histoire primitive du Mexique dans les Monuments égyptiens (n.p., 1864).

Histoire de Mgr. de Laval, premier évêque de Quebec (Quebec: 1845).

Histoire du patromoine de St. Pierre (Paris, 1860).

Histoire des Nations Civilisées du Mexique et de l'Améri-

que-Centrale . . . , 4 vols. (Paris: 1857–59).

Histoire du Canada, de son Eglise et de ses Missions . . . , 2 vols., (Paris: 1854; also 2 vols., Paris: 1859).

Histoire du commerce et de l'industrie chez les nations Aztéques . . . (Paris: 1858). From *Nouvelles Annales des Voyages*, June, July, 1959.

"Interesting Discoveries in Quatemala . . . ," *New York Daily Tribune*, November 21, 1855, p. 6.

Lettre à M. Leon Rosny sur la découverte de documents relatifs à la haute antiquité Américaine . . . (Paris: 1869). Also in *Mémoires de la Société d'Ethnologie* no. 1 (1869).

Lettres pour servir d'introduction à l'histoire primitive des nations civilisées de l'Amérique Septentrionale, addressées á Monsieur le duc de Valmy . . . (Mexico: 1851). In French and Spanish.

Manuscrit Troano . . . , 2 vols. (Paris: 1869–70). Part-title: *Mission Scientifique au Mexique et dans l'Amérique centrale*.

Nociones de un viaje a los estados de San Salvador et Guatemala . . . (Guatemala: 1857); also in *El Museo Guatemalteco*, September 12, 1857, and in *Bulletin de Société de Géographie* (Paris), April 17, 1857.

"Notes d'un voyage dans l'Amérique Centrale, lettres à M. Alfred Maury . . . ," *Nouvelles Annales des Voyages* 3 (1855).

Quelques traces d'un émigration de l'Europe Septentrionale en Amérique dans les traditions et les langues de l'Amérique Centrale (Paris: 1858). From *Nouvelles Annales des Voyages* 160: 261–92.

Recherches sur les Ruines de Palenque . . . (Paris: 1866).

"Resumen histórico y cronológico de los Reyes de Guatemala, ante de la conquista . . . ," *El Museo Guatemalteco*, no 29, May 14, 1857.

Sommaire des voyages scientifiques (Saint-Cloud; 1852).

Voyage sur l'isthme de Tehuántepec . . . *dans les années 1859 et 1860* (Paris: 1961). Also in *Nouvelles Annales des Voyages*, November 1861.

OTHER WORKS

Brasseur had a greater flair for autobiography than any of the other amateurs. In most of his publications he described his travels, the people he met, and the manuscripts he found.

The few biographical accounts provide only a beginning on

the subject: Daniel G. Brinton, *Lippincott's Magazine* 1 (1868): 79–86; Herbert B. Adams, *American Antiquarian Society Proceedings* 7 (1891): 274–90; and Henry E. Mole's address, 1945, typescript, Peabody Museum Library. Justin Winsor, *Narrative and Critical History of America,* 8 vols. (1884–89) 1, and H. H. Bancroft, *The Native Races,* 5 vols. (San Francisco: 1883) 5 are the best brief summaries of his activities and ideas. Recent accounts are in Robert Wauchope, *Lost Tribes and Sunken Cities* (Chicago: 1962) and Leo Deuel, *Testaments of Time* (New York: 1965), pp. 511–38.

Various details are explored in the following: Adrián Recinos, "Cien años de la llegada del Abate Brasseur . . . ," *Sociedad de Geografía y Historia de Guatemala. Anales* 29 (1956): 12–17; Recinos's introduction to Delia Goetz and S. G. Morley, *Popul Vuh* (Norman, Okla.: 1952); Nicolaus Trubner, "The New Discoveries in Guatemala," *Athenaeum* (London) no. 1472 (January 12, 1856): 42–43, and in the same author's "Central American Archaeology," ibid., no. 1492 (May 31, 1856): 683–85; *Lettre de M. E. G. Squier à propos de la lettre de M. Brasseur de Bourbourg . . .* (Paris: 1855); M. Larrainzar, *Dictamen . . . sobre la obra del Sr. Abate E. Carlos Brasseur de Bourbourg* (Mexico: 1865); Daniel G. Brinton, "Critical Remarks on the Editions of Landa's Writings," *American Philosophical Society Proceedings* 24 (1887): 1–8, is very unfavorable; Cyrus Thomas, "Study of the Manuscript Troano," with Introduction by Brinton, *Smithsonian Institution. Contributions to North American Ethnology* 5 (1882).

AUGUSTUS AND ALICE LE PLONGEON

WRITINGS OF AUGUSTUS LE PLONGEON

Letters to E. G. Squier, February 12, March 12, 28, 1865, E. G. Squier Papers, box 2, Library of Congress, Manuscripts Division, Washington, D.C.

"The Ancient Palaces of Uxmal, Mexico," *Scientific American,* January 21, 1882, p. 5042.

"Ancient Records," *Nation* 29 (1879): 224–25.

"Archaeological Communication," *American Antiquarian Society Proceedings* no. 71 (1879): 65–75.

"Are the Ruined Monuments of Yucatan Ancient or Modern?" *Scientific American,* October 6, 1883, p. 6468.

"The Causes of Earthquakes," *Van Nostrand's Eclectric Engineering Magazine* 6 (1872): 537–44, 557–84.

"A Chapter from Dr. Le Plongeon's New Book, 'Monuments of Mayas,'" *Scientific American*, Supplement, October 3, 1885, pp. 8130–32.

"The Horse at Kabah," ibid., Supplement, March 14, 1885, pp. 7668–69.

"An Interesting Discovery. A Temple with Masonic Symbols in the Ruined City of Uxmal," *Harper's Weekly*, December 17, 1881, pp. 851–52.

"Letter from Dr. Augustus Le Plongeon," *American Antiquarian Society Proceedings*, no. 72 (1879): 113–17.

Manual de Fotografía . . . (New York: 1867).

"Maya Alphabet," *Scientific American*, Supplement, January 31, 1885, pp. 7572–73.

"Mayapan and Maya Inscriptions," *American Antiquarian Society Proceedings*, n.s. 1 (1881): 246–82.

"An Open Letter from Professor Le Plongeon, of Belize, British Honduras." *The Present Century* 2 (March 27, 1880): 337–39.

Queen Móo and the Egyptian Sphinx . . . (New York: 1896; also London: 1896; 2d ed., New York: 1900).

La religión de Jesús comparada con los ensenñanzas de la Iglesia . . . (Boston: 1867).

Sacred Mysteries among the Mayas and the Quiches, 11,500 Years Ago . . . (New York: 1886; 3d ed., New York: 1909; also Barcelona: 1931, and New York: 1935).

"Vestiges of Antiquity," address to the Geographical Society of New York, 1873; published in part in *The Tribune Lecture and Letter Extras*, no. 8, 1873.

Vestiges of the Mayas . . . (New York: 1881; 4th ed., New York: 1935).

"Yucatan's Buried Cities," *The World* (N.Y.), November 27, 1881, p. 10. An interview with Augustus.

A few of his drawings of ruins in Yucatán are in the files of the Carnegie Institution of Washington at the Peabody Museum, Harvard University.

WRITINGS OF ALICE LE PLONGEON

"Augustus Le Plongeon, M.D., L.L.D.," *Journal de Société des Américanistes* (Paris) 6, no. 2 (1909): 276–79.

"A Carnival at Yucatan," *The World* (N.Y.), March 27, 1881, sec. 3: 3–4.

"Conquest of the Mayas," *Magazine of American History* 19 (1888): 324–30, 449–61.

"Customs and Superstitions of the Mayas," *Popular Science* 44 (1894): 661–70.

"Discovery of Yucatan," *Magazine of American History* 19 (1888): 324–30, 449–61; 20: 115–20.

"Dr. Le Plongeon's Latest and Most Important Discoveries among the Ruined Cities of Yucatan," *Scientific American,* Supplement, August 3, 1884, pp. 7144–47.

"Eastern Yucatan, Its Scenery, People, and Ancient Cities and Monuments (Extract)," *New York Academy of Sciences. Transactions,* November 7, 1887, pp. 45–48.

"The Egyptian Sphinx," *American Antiquarian* 10 (November 1888): 358–63.

Here and There in Yucatan. Miscellanies (Boston: 1886; 2d ed., New York: 1886; also New York: 1889).

Maya Melodies of Yucatan, taken from Indian Airs . . . (Brooklyn: 1903).

"The Mayas: Their Customs, Laws, and Religion," *Magazine of American History* 17 (1887): 233–38.

The Monuments of Mayach and their Historical Teachings (n.p., 1896 or 1897).

"The Mystery of Egypt: Whence Came Her Ancestors?" *London Magazine* 24 (1910); 122–32.

"Notes on Yucatan," *American Antiquarian Society Proceedings,* no. 72 (1897): 77–106.

"Occultism among the Mayas," *The Metaphysical Magazine* 1 (1895): 66–72.

"Occultism among the Tahitians," ibid. 3 (1896): 275–81.

"Old and New in Yucatan," *Harper's Magazine* 70 (1885): 372–86.

"The Potter's Art," *Popular Science* 2 (1896): 646–55.

Queen Móo's Talisman. The Fall of the Maya Empire (New York: 1902; also London: 1902).

"Ruined Uxmal . . . ," *The World* (N.Y.), June 27, 1881, pp. 1, 2. July 18, 1881, p. 2.

"Yucatan, Its Ancient Temples and Palaces (Extract)," *New York Academy of Sciences. Transactions* 5, no. (March 1886): 169–78.

"Yucatan since the Conquest," *Magazine of American History* 30 (1893): 158–80.

BIBLIOGRAPHY

The following items by Stephen Salisbury, Jr., contain numerous selections from the writings of Augustus Le Plongeon: (1) "Dr. Le Plongeon in Yucatan. The Discovery of a Statue Called Chac-Mool, and the Communications of Dr. Augustus le Plongeon concerning Explorations in the Yucatan Peninsula," *American Antiquarian Society Proceedings,* no. 69 (April, 1877): 70–119. The article also appears in Salisbury's *The Mayas* (Worcester, Mass. 1877). (2) "Terra Cotta Figures from Isla Mujeres . . . ," *American Antiquarian Society Proceedings,* no. 71 (1878): 71–89.

OTHER WORKS

A native's recollection of Augustus as told to Edward H. Thompson, "A Maya Legend in the Making," *American Antiquarian Society Proceedings* 61 (1931): 340–43.

For Augustus's early activities in California, see H. H. Bancroft, *History of California,* 7 vols. (San Francisco: 1884–90) 6: 463. The account of his relations with the Academy comes from Robert C. Miller, senior scientist, California Academy of Sciences, to the author, November 13, 1965, and the *Proceedings of the California Academy of Sciences* 1 (1854–57): 95. For his later activity with the same organization, see its *Proceedings* 4 (1870): 138, 143, 148, 149. I. Chaney to the author, March 18, 1966, reported that a thorough search of the archives of the American Geographical Society failed to locate a copy of Le Plongeon's address.

For Stephen Salisbury, Jr., see *New England Historical and Genealogical Register* 40 (1906): 325–39; *Massachusetts Historical Society Proceedings,* 2d ser. 20 (1907): 412–19; and *Salisbury Memorial . . .* (Worcester, Mass.: 1906). Gregory Mason, *South of Yesterday* (New York, 1940), p. 81, describes the miniature temples of eastern Yucatan. The feud with Brinton appears in Le Plongeon, *Queen Móo . . . ,* pp. 202–4, 226–49.

A long and useful obituary of Augustus was published in the *Brooklyn Eagle,* December 14, 1908; a brief, paid notice of his death appeared in *The New York Times,* December 15, 1908, p. 9. Mr. John Buchanan, archivist, Metropolitan Museum of Art, July 7, 1970, provided copy of the correspondence pertaining to Le Plongeon's objects loaned to that institution. The torso and small head originally attached to the belt of the figure are displayed among the Stephens stones in the Mexican Hall of the American Museum of Natural History; Dr. Ekholm kindly provided the data about the acquisition of the pieces.

For Le Plongeon and leprosy, see Albert S. Ashmead, *Pre-Columbian Leprosy* (Chicago: 1895), pp. 30–32, 46–47. Mrs. Blackwell's letters to Blom are in the library of the Middle American Research Institute, Tulane University; Morley to J. C. Merriam, October 10, 1931, Morley File, Carnegie Institution of Washington, summarizes her letter to him and an interview he had with her. Dr. Robert Wauchope kindly directed me to the Blackwell letters at Tulane.

Favorable and unfavorable comment on the Le Plongeons appears in the following: Frederick A. Ober, *Travels in Mexico and Life among the Mexicans* (St. Louis and Houston: 1883), p. 102; Marquis de Nadaillac, "Les découvertes du Dr. Le Plongeon dans le Yukatan," *La Nature* (Paris), no. 593 (October 11, 1884): 294–98; C. Stanisland Wake, "The Mayas of Central America," *American Antiquarian* 26 (1904): 361–63; J. T. Short, quoted in Le Plongeon, "Mayapan . . . ," p. 39n.; Désiré Charnay, "Ancient Cities of the New World," *North American Review* 131 (September, 1880): 196; M. H. Saville, *Bibliographic Notes on Uxmal, Yucatan* (New York: 1921), pp. 56, 94, 111; Edward H. Thompson in Theodore A. Willard, *The City of the Sacred Well* (New York & London: 1926), p. 92; Justin Winsor, *Narrative and Critical History of America*, 8 vols. (Boston & New York: 1884–89) 1: 166n., 186n.–87n.; Herbert J. Spinden, *Maya Art and Civilization* (Indian Hills, Col.: 1957), p. 13; Lewis Spence, *The Problem of Atlantis*, 2d ed. (New York: 1925), pp. 87, 124, 127. Channing Arnold and J. T. Frost, *The American Egypt . . .* (New York: 1908), p. 258, noted Augustus's belief in the priority of the Mayas in world civilization with the comment, "This preposterous proposition was received with the Homeric laughter it so richly deserved." Then with doubtful seriousness the authors praised him for the courage of his convictions, remarking that "he was a Titan among the theorizing minnows . . . ; for he possessed the genius of enthusiasm."

W. W. Skeat's comments are in the London *Athenaeum*, 1895, pp. 453–54. On Le Plongeon's use of gunpowder, see Manuel Cirerol Sansores, *"Chi Cheen Itsa"* (Yucatán; 1948), pp. 60, 67, 209; he apparently based his charges on a claim made by Teobert Maler. Ober, *Travels in Mexico* (cited above), p. 75, noted the accusation that Augustus hid a statue;

Alice's explanation is in her "Dr. Le Plongeon's Latest Discoveries," 1884. H. E. D. Pollock's comments appear in *The Maya and Their Neighbors,* ed. Alfred M. Tozzer (New York: 1940), p. 186. A. M. Tozzer, ed., *Landa's Relación de las Cosas de Yucatán* (Cambridge, Mass.: 1941) gives at least eight references in his notes to the writings of the Le Plongeons.

More favorable appraisals can be found in C. Reginald Enock, *The Secret of the Pacific* (New York: 1912), pp. 41, 133; Willis F. Johnson, "Pioneers of Maya Research," *Outlook,* July 25, 1923, pp. 474–78; J. B. Opdycke in *The New York Times,* February 27, 1927, sec. 8: 14; Alexander McAllan, ibid., February 20, 1927, sec. 7: 18 and April 3; 1927, sec. 8: 18; and James Churchward, *The Lost Continent of Mu* (New York: 1931).

"Central American Antiquities," *Scientific American,* Supplement, July 16, 1881, pp. 4599–4600, reported that Augustus accompanied Charnay's expedition to Yucatán. This is doubtless incorrect; there is no corroboration from other sources. Charnay ridiculed Le Plongeon's ideas in his early archaeological reports of this expedition, and Augustus would not have joined any venture in which he himself was not the chief figure.

Robert Wauchope, *Lost Tribes and Sunken Cities* (Chicago: 1962) gives the best introduction to the story of the Le Plongeons.

EDWARD H. THOMPSON

HIS WRITINGS

A half dozen manuscripts and numerous photographs taken by him are in the Peabody Museum Library, Harvard University.

"Ancient Structures of Yucatan Not Communal Dwellings," *American Antiquarian Society Proceedings,* n.s. 8 (1892): 262–69.

"Ancient Tombs at Palenque," ibid. n.s. 10 (1895): 418–21. Also as a separate.

"Archaeological Research in Yucatan," ibid., n.s. 4 (1886): 248–54.

"Archaeological Researches in Yucatan. Reports of Explorations for the Museum," *Memoirs of the Peabody Museum* 3, no. 1 (1904): 3–20.

"Atlantis Not a Myth," *Popular Science Quarterly* 51 (October 1879): 759–64.

Children of the Cave (Boston; 1929). A children's book, with a brief autobiographical account.

"The Chultunes of Labna," *Peabody Museum Memoirs* 1, no. 3 (1897).

"Explorations in Yucatan," *American Antiquarian Society Proceedings*, n.s. 4 (1887): 379–85.

"Explorations of the Cave of Loltun, Yucatan," *Peabody Museum Memoirs* 1, no. 2 (1897).

"Extract of Letters from Edward H. Thompson, Descriptive of the Ruins at KickMoo and Chun Kot Cin," *American Antiquarian Society Proceedings*, April 25, 1888, pp. 162–70.

"Forty Years of Research and Exploration in Yucatan," ibid. 39 (1929): 38–49.

"The Genesis of the Maya Arch," *American Anthropologist* 13 (1911): 501–6.

"Guitar Maker," *Atlantic* 103 (February 1909): 246–50.

"Hammock Makers of Yucatan," *Living Age* 185 (April 26, 1890): 251–52.

"Hennequin," *National Geographic Magazine* 14 (April 1903): 150–58.

"Hennequin," *Scientific American* 55 (May 9, 1903): 2268–69.

"The High Priest's Grave . . . ," *Field Museum, Anthropological Series* 27, no. 1, Publication 412 (1938). Introduction by J. Eric S. Thompson (Reprint New York: 1968).

"The Home of the Forgotten Race: Mysterious Chichen Itza, in Yucatan, Mexico," *National Geographic Magazine* 25 (June 1914): 585–608.

"Hut in a Village," *Century* 132 (September 1911): 777–81.

"A Kindlier Light on Early Spanish Rule in America," *American Antiquarian Society Proceedings* 21, no. 2 (1911): 277–83.

"Maya Legend in the Making," ibid. 61 (1931): pt. 2, 340–43.

"The Mural Paintings of Yucatan," *Proceedings of the XIII International Congress of Americanists, 1902* (Easton, Pa.: 1905), pp. 189–92.

"A Page of American History," *American Antiquarian Society Proceedings*, n.s. 17 (October 1905): 239–52.

"Palenque," ibid. 10 (1895): 191–94.

People of the Serpent. Life and Adventures among the Mayas (Boston: 1932; reprint New York, 1965).

"Recent Excavations in Northern Yucatan," *Proceedings of the XIX International Congress of Americanists, 1915* (Washington; 1971), pp. 202–5.

"Ruined Cities of Yucatan," *American Naturalist* 21 (1887): 787.

"Ruins of Xchikmook, Yucatan," *Field Museum Publication 28. Anthropological Series* 2, no. 3 (Chicago: 1898), pp. 213–29.

El sisal ó fibra de Yucatán. Informe del Sñor Eduardo H. Thompson, cónsul de Estados Unidos en Progreso, Yucatán (San José, 1903.) This is a translation of "Sisal, the Yucatan Fiber," in *U.S. Consular Reports* 71, no. 271 (April, 1903).

"Some Early American Pioneers," *American Antiquarian Society Proceedings* 28 (1917): 63–66.

"Temple of the Jaguars: Report of Work Preliminary to Reproduction of Front Facade," *American Museum Journal* 13 (October, 1913): 267–82.

"Tropical Tempest," *Century* 76 (May, 1908): 151–53.

"Water Colors of the Mayas," *American Museum of Natural History Journal* 2 (1902): 91–92.

"Yucatan at the Time of its Discovery," *American Antiquarian Society Proceedings*, n.s. 8 (1892): 262–69.

Selections from Thompson's writings are in Samuel Rapport and Helen Wright, eds., *Archaeology* (New York: 1964), pp. 333–48; Robert Wauchope, *They Found the Buried Cities* (Chicago; 1965), pp. 220–29; Leo Deuel, *Conquistadors without Swords* (New York: 1967), pp. 269–83.

OTHER WORKS

The major source is his autobiography, *People of the Serpent,* though it must be supplemented on some topics. A good biographical sketch is in the *Dictionary of American Biography*. Gregory Mason's "Spokesman for the Ancient Mayas," *World's Work* 51 (1926): 412–17, was the only major article published about him during his lifetime, and it appeared after his retirement from Chichén; he did not gain a sketch in *Who's Who* until the same time. Obituary notices appeared in *American Anthropologist* 37 (1935): 711–12; *American Antiquarian*

Society Proceedings 65 (1936): 153–55; *The New York Times,* May 12, 1935, p. 33. Theodore A. Willard wrote two books dealing more or less with Thompson, whom Willard claimed as a close friend: *City of the Sacred Well* (New York & London: 1926), and *Kukulcan The Bearded Conqueror . . .* (Hollywood: 1941). The first volume contains much purported direct discourse by Thompson; both books should be used with care.

The XIII International Congress of Americanists, 1902 (Easton, Pa., 1905), pp. lvii, lix–lx, notes his presentation of the native dance. *The New York Times* provides some helpful articles: for public disclosure of dredging the Sacred Cenote, see March 2, 1923, p. 3, and Alma Reed's two articles in the same year: March 25, sec. 4, p. 14 and April 8, sec. 4, p. 9; the attack on his property appears in May 27, 1921, p. 13; and the attachment of Chichén in July 11, 1926, p. 1 and September 6, p. 2; the theft at the Peabody Museum is reported in January 1, 1938, p. 1, and January 14, p. 14. An account of one of his speeches is in *The New York Times,* March 11, 1932, p. 2. Alfred M. Tozzer, *Chichén Itzá and Its Cenote of Sacrifice . . . , Memoirs of the Peabody Museum* 11, 12 (1957) gives an exhaustive treatment of the Cenote; the account of the dredging, 11: 194–96, should be compared with Thompson's autobiographical versions. Julian Aznar G. Gutiérrez, *La Sucesión de Mr. Edward Herbert Thompson. Las Ruinas de Chichén Itzá y las Antigüedades Mexicanas* (Mexico: 1942), the lawyer's brief presented on behalf of Thompson's heirs, naturally gives major attention to legal arguments exonerating the archaeologist under Mexican laws, but it also discloses interesting sidelights on the story of the dredging. *Enciclopedia Yucatense* (Mexico: 1945): 2: 166–67, adds a few details.

Scholarly reports of the artifacts are in E. A. Hooten, "Skeletons from the Sacred Cenote of Sacrifice at Chichen Itza," *The Mayas and Their Neighbors,* ed. Alfred M. Tozzer (New York: 1940), pp. 272–80; D. Norman and W. W. A. Johnson, "Note on Spectographic Study of Central American and Asiatic Jades," *Journal of Optical Society of America* 31 (1941): 85–86; S. K. Lothrop, *Metals from the Cenote of Sacrifice, Memoirs of the Peabody Museum . . .* 10, no. 2 (1952).

Many decades after his triumph at the Sacred Cenote a succession of persons attempted to retrieve more artifacts from the well. As they came and went, they scarcely noticed Thompson's dredge and winch in a pile of rusty debris by the side of the gatehouse. So far he has had the last laugh on his successors, who hoped to recover far more archaeological loot than he had gathered. See Donald Ediger, *The Well of Sacrifice* (Garden City: 1971) for one of those expeditions and for references to others.

For the relations between Thompson and Morley and for the activities of the Carnegie Institution of Washington, see R. L. Brunhouse, *Sylvanus G. Morley and the World of the Ancient Maya* (Norman, Okla.: 1971).

Index